without a
STITCH IN TIME

A selection of the best humorous short pieces

by peter de vries

little, brown and company—boston—toronto

FIRST EDITION

T 10/72

Most of the material in this book was originally published in *The New Yorker*. "Part of the Family Picture" appeared in *Harper's Magazine;* "The Last of the Bluenoses" in *The London Daily Telegraph;* "Exploring Inner Space" in *Michigan Quarterly Review,* "Mud in Your Eye" in *The New York Times Book Review;* "James Thurber The Comic Prufrock" in *Poetry Magazine;* "The Man Who Read Waugh" in *Saturday Review.*

Library of Congress Cataloging in Publication Data

De Vries, Peter.
  Without a stitch in time

  Short stories.
  I. Title
PZ3.D4998Wi   813' 5'2   72-5163
ISBN 0-316-18186-2

Published simultaneously in Canada by Little, Brown & Company (Canada) Limited

PRINTED IN THE UNITED STATES OF AMERICA

CONTENTS

Contents

WITHOUT A STITCH IN TIME

A HARD DAY AT THE OFFICE

I RECENTLY worked in an office where they had a number of those signs reading "Think," the motto of the International Business Machines Corporation, which so many other business firms seem to be adopting. The signs became almost at once a bone of contention between my employer and me, though not because I was not responsive to them; I have always reacted unqualifiedly to wall injunctions, especially the monosyllabic kind. Confronted, for example, with the exhortation "Smile," my face becomes wreathed in an expression of felicity that some people find unendurable, and as for "Keep On Keepin' On," I mean like one gander at it and it's "Oh, I will, I will!" The "Think" signs, one of which was visible from my desk, so I saw it every time I raised my head, were equally effective As a consequence, by midmorning of my first day on the job I was so immersed in rumination that the boss, a ruddy, heavyset fellow named Harry Bagley, paused on his way past my desk, evidently struck by a remote and glazed look in my eye.

"What's the matter with you?" he asked

"I was just thinking," I said, stirring from my concentration.

"What about?"

"Zeno's paradoxes," I answered. "The eight paradoxes by which he tries to discredit the belief in plurality and motion, and which have come down to us in the writings of Aristotle and Simplicius I was recalling particularly the one about Achilles and the tortoise. You remember it. Achilles can never catch up with the tortoise for, while he traverses the distance between his starting point and that of the tortoise, the tortoise advances a certain distance, and while Achilles traverses this distance, the tortoise makes a further advance, and so on ad infinitum. Consequently, Achilles may run ad infinitum without overtaking the tortoise. *Ergo* there is no motion."

"A fat hell of a lot of good this is doing us," Bagley said.

"Oh, I know Zeno's old hat and, as you say, fruitless from a practical point of view," I said. "But here's the thought I want to leave with you. It's amazing how many of our values are still based on this classic logic, and so maybe the semanticists, under Korzybski and later Hayakawa, have been right in hammering home to us a less absolutistic approach to things."

"Yes, well, get some of this work off your desk," Bagley said, gesturing at a mulch of documents that had been thickening there since nine o'clock

"Right," I said, and he bustled off.

I fell to with a will, and by noon was pretty well caught up. But as I sat down at my desk after lunch, my eye fell on the admonitory legend dominating the opposite wall, and I was soon again deep in a train of reflections, which, while lacking the abstruseness of my morning cogitations, were nevertheless not wholly without scope and erudition. My face must have betrayed the strain of application once more, for Bagley stopped as he had earlier.

"Now what?" he said.

I put down a paper knife I had been abstractedly bending.

"I've been thinking," I said, "that the element of the fantastic in the graphic arts is, historically speaking, so voluminous that it's presumptuous of the Surrealists to pretend that they have any more than given a contemporary label to an established, if not indeed hoary, vein. Take the chimerical detail in much Flemish and Renaissance painting, the dry, horrifying apparitions of Hieronymus Bosch —"

"Get your money," Bagley said.

"But why? What am I doing but what that sign says?" I protested, pointing to it.

"That sign doesn't mean this kind of thinking," Bagley said.

"What kind, then? What do you want me to think about?" I asked.

"Think about your work. Think about the product. Anything."

"All right, I'll try that," I said. "I'll try thinking about the product. But which one?" I added, for the firm was a wholesale-food company that handled many kinds of foods. I was at pains to remind Bagley of this. "So shall I think of food in general, or some particular item?" I asked. "Or some phase of distribution?"

"Oh, good God, I don't know," Bagley said impatiently. "Think of the special we're pushing," he said, and made off.

The special we were pushing just then was packaged mixed nuts, unshelled. The firm had been trying to ascertain what proportions people liked in mixed nuts — what ratio of walnuts, hazelnuts, almonds, and so on — as reflected in relative sales of varying assortments that the company had been simultaneously putting out in different areas. I didn't see how any thinking on my part could help reach any conclusion about that, the more so because my work, which was checking and collating credit memoranda, offered no data along those lines. So I figured the best thing would be for me to dwell on nuts in a general way, which I did.

Shortly after four o'clock, I was aware of Bagley's bulk over me, and of Bagley looking down at me. "Well?" he said.

I turned to him in my swivel chair, crossing my legs.

"Nuts, it seems to me, have a quality that makes them

unique among foods," I said. "I'm not thinking of their more
obvious aspect as an autumnal symbol, their poetic association
with festive periods. They have something else, a *je ne sais
quoi* that has often haunted me while eating them but that I
have never quite been able to pin down, despite that effort
of imaginative physical identification that is the legitimate
province of the senses."

"You're wearing me thin," Bagley warned.

"But now I think I've put my finger on the curious quality
they have," I said. "*Nuts are in effect edible wood.*"

"Get your money," Bagley said.

I rose. "I don't understand what you want," I exclaimed.
"Granted the observation is a trifle on the precious side, is
that any reason for firing a man? Give me a little time."

"You've got an hour till quitting time. Your money'll be
ready then," Bagley said.

My money was ready by quitting time. As I took it, I reflected that my wages from this firm consisted almost exclusively of severance pay. Bagley had beefed about having
to fork over two weeks' compensation, but he forked it over.

I got another job soon afterward. I still have it. It's with an
outfit that doesn't expect you to smile or think or anything
like that. Anyhow, I've learned my lesson as far as the second
is concerned. If I'm ever again confronted with a sign telling
me to think, I'll damn well think twice before I do.

SLICE OF LIFE

WHEN the elevator in which I had been mounting to my
thirtieth-floor office after lunch stopped between the eleventh

and twelfth floors, it stopped cold. The operator shoved his lever back and forth several times, but the car wouldn't go up or down. "Broke," he announced to me and my four fellow-passengers.

There followed fifteen minutes of diagnostic bawling up and down the shaft between the operator and some unseen colleagues, and then certain rumblings and clankings commenced overhead and underneath, which I took to be remedial. The operator folded a stick of Juicy Fruit into his mouth and said, "It looks as if we'll be here for a while."

"How long?" demanded a rectangular woman of forty, in snuff-colored tweeds and a brown corduroy hat of Alpine extraction.

"That's hard to say. They've got to rimify the bandelage that goes around the grims, then marinate the horpels on the rebrifuge," the operator said — or words to that effect.

"*Damn!*" said a thickset man, clearly an executive type, who was clutching a briefcase. I seemed to remember seeing pictures of him in the business sections of the metropolitan dailies. His name was Babcock or Shotwell or something. He and Tweeds were duplicates of impatience; she consulted a wristwatch in an absolute fume. "How long do you *think* it might be?" she inquired of the operator. "Hours?"

He shrugged and smiled.

"Or days," threw in a tall youth, grinning. He leaned, hatless and negligent, against a wall of the car, reading an academic periodical.

"Well, it might as well be days if it's anything more than" — Tweeds shot back a cuff and glared anew at the watch — "than half an hour."

"Me, too," said the executive. "I've got a conference starting in ten minutes that *positively cannot be postponed.*"

"I have a lecture audience gathering two blocks away this

7

very minute," Tweeds said. "Oh, why did I have to pop in here first? Are they doing all they can?"

"Probably," said a handsome woman, brushing from her shoulder a pinch of rust that had sifted down through the ventilation louvers in the ceiling of the car. She was wearing a black suit and what seemed like a series of scarves. The operator had offered her his seat, on which she sat with her legs primly crossed.

Such, then, was our cast of characters: a big shot, a lady lecturer, a casual youth, an enigmatic woman in black, an elevator operator, and myself, an office worker. In other words, what you always get in a group thrown together in a snowbound train or a marooned cabin or a petrified forest — a slice of life.

As the minutes passed into an hour and the hour became two, I marked the rate of attrition on each of my co-victims. I knew that in a slice of life the crisis into which the characters are suddenly thrust affects each according to his inner self, which he thereafter faces with a new, and deeper, understanding. His whole life will be changed by the experience. But first he must be broken open.

Shotwell or Babcock was the first to give. After watching him fidget for some minutes, I went over to him and said, "Why are you in such a stew to get to this meeting?"

"I have to," he said. "When I'm out of the office, everything goes to —"

"That's what you like to *think*." I smiled cannily.

"What do you mean?" he asked, avoiding my eyes.

"In how many years haven't you taken a vacation?"

"Fourteen," he said, momentarily squaring his shoulders.

"Fourteen years you haven't dared to leave town for fear everything would go on running as smooth as —"

"That's a lie!"

"— as silk. It wasn't the other way around, as you've always

8

tried to make everybody believe, *especially yourself*. Oh, everything's going all right up there," I said, following his panicky glance upward.

"It isn't, either! It's not true!" he said. Dropping his briefcase, he seized the bars of the car door in both hands and, rattling it like a caged beast, bellowed to be let out. He was due at a think tank.

I sprang swiftly into action Swinging him around by the coat collar, I slapped him smartly across the chops several times. This brought shocked stares from the rest, but they must instantly have realized my action to be the attested one for staunching hysteria in situations of this kind, for no one spoke. "It is the irony of power that those who wield it become its victims, dependent on it themselves," I told the magnate when I had brought him back to his senses. "If this experience helps you put away false pride, it will have proved a blessing in disguise. Learn that no one is indispensable — and find an enriching sense of the value of others."

I left the executive slumped on the floor, dazedly pondering my counsel, and slipped over to have a word with Tweeds. She was sitting on the floor herself by now. "I wonder how long they'll wait for me," she asked herself aloud.

"Forget it. They've gone home," I said. "It's two hours."

"They can't have gone. It was to be my most important lecture of the year."

"Important to whom?" I said, letting myself down beside her with the expression of stolid yet sensitive understanding of one from whom strength naturally flows. In low, confidential tones, I went on, "What hurts is the thought of their going home, or maybe off to a movie, without feeling they've missed much — idle women who came to hear you because they had nothing better to do. So it's *they* who are important to *you*."

"Of all the unmitigated —"

"That's the discovery you get out of this," I said. "Take that chastening thought home with you and rebuild your life on its hard, firm knowledge — a knowledge without illusions but capable of giving you wider horizons. *Egotism is the pup tent that shuts out the sky.*"

I slid a bit away from Tweeds, who had raised her fist as if to ward off an inclement truth, and now paused in my ministrations to smoke a cigarette. I did not, however, relax my lookout for fissures in the composure of my remaining companions. I puzzled a moment over the aloof air maintained by the slender woman in black. Then I had it. Of course. Every slice of life has a prostitute, or at least a woman of easy virtue, and she, in turn, would not be complete as a character if she did not live this one hour behind a mask of cool propriety. Well, her secret was safe with me. Extinguishing my cigarette on the sole of my shoe, I rose from the floor and drifted unobtrusively to her side.

"Crisis is the great leveler," I observed, in a cordial undertone "You, of all of us, may depart in peace."

"Go boil a banana," she said.

The acidity of her retort only proved to me that my message had gone home, naturally, I did not forget that such a hard shell as hers concealed the more a heart of gold. No, it was the youth I had to worry about — for his insouciance had not fooled me for a second. It was the calm of profound fear. His secret came to me in a flash. He had to prove he wasn't a coward. How could I have missed it until now? In any case, I admired his game — to appear cool as a cucumber while the implacable hammers flattened our brains and the corrosive minutes wore away — but I knew it couldn't last. It was time I gave *him* a bit of myself.

"Would you like to talk about it?" I said, inviting his confidence with a sympathetic smile. "Go back as far as you like

— to your childhood, to how it all got started. For the crust is never so hard that it can't be beaten back into a batter *if we have the will.*"

He gave me a look and, pocketing the quarterly (in which he had all this time affected to remain immersed!), drew out a document typewritten in a language I did not recognize.

"Ah, the intellectual, with his Sanskrit, Phoenician, and the dialects of the Ozarks," I said. "Well, that's all right. Each of us has his defense against the world. Student?"

"I'm writing my doctor's thesis," he said

"Why can't your doctor write his own thesis?" I said, beaming at the others, for it was time for some comedy relief. The uniform grimness of their faces told me how long past due this relief was, and I redoubled my efforts.

"Seems there were these two Swedes," I said, "who went out fishing on this lake in this rowboat. So they pulled in fish like they never had before. Soon the whole boat was full of fish, and the first Swede said to the second, 'Say, Olie, we sure got goot place today. By Yiminy, we ought to remember this spot in the lake, so we can come hair next time, 'cause this yim-dandy —' "

Here the youth cracked. "How much are flesh and blood supposed to stand!" he yelled, rattling the door of the car even more furiously than the executive had. "Are we going to stay in this godforsaken trap forever?"

Wrenching him back from the door, I pinned him against the side of the car and continued rapidly, "And the second Swede said, 'By Yeorge, you right, Sven. We yust got to remember this hair spot. Lucky thing Ay got piece of chalk in my pocket. Ay make mark so we can tell this place next time.' And he reached over and drew a line on the outside of the rowboat."

Clawing free of my grasp, the youth put his hands to my throat in an apparent attempt to throttle me. The situation was more serious than I had thought. Flinging him back against the wall again with all my strength, I planted my knee in his groin and panted, "And the first Swede said, 'Olie, how can you be so dumb? What good it bane do us to make a mark on the rowboat? What if we don't get the same rowboat next time?'"

I released the youth, and we stood a moment straightening our clothes, breathing heavily. There was a cascade of malediction from above, and a large clump of matter struck the ventilation louvers in such a way as to baptize the majority of us with dark silt. Events were moving swiftly to their climax. I gave the youth a grin of new understanding, and then, shaking a cigarette out of a pack, hung it in his mouth. I extended a light to him, striking the match on my thumbnail. "It's no crime to be afraid," I said, for everyone's benefit.

The woman in black dropped her head in her hand and said, "God."

I stepped over and addressed her softly. "I know. The snow of the apple blossoms in the spring, the white rose of winter snows — to think you will never see these again. But you will. We'll get out of this, and everything out there will seem dearer. That's the great value of an experience like this. We come out of it better able — to use the words with which the poet exhorts us — to love that well which we must leave ere long."

The elevator operator was circling the car, swiveling a fist against his palm "Judas priest," he muttered under his breath. Was he going next? I saw him wet his lips and heard him shout rather shrilly up the shaft, "When are you guys ever going to get done?"

"Done now," the answer floated down. "See if she works."

She worked.

And now, the passengers having stirred from their several funks and lethargies, and readied themselves for restoration to the normal world, we resumed our interrupted journey. The woman in black and the youth got off at the same floor, one occupied largely by dentists' offices. The two of them struck up a conversation as the elevator door closed behind them, the woman glancing momentarily back at me. A springing acquaintance? New beginnings . . . ? Tweeds and the tycoon got off at their respective stops And all, on leaving, thanked me (there was no other way of interpreting their parting looks and indistinguishable murmurs as they went past me) for my firm and masterly handling of the situation.

Well, the incident of the stalled car was the talk of the building for some days. Few mentioned it to me directly, but this I laid to their assumption that I might not like to talk about it. However, I did not doubt that some note of my role in the matter would be taken in my office.

I was right. My next salary check was three times its regular size. I had not expected to be rewarded on that scale! There was a brief communication accompanying it, which I unfolded and read: "The recent incident with regard to the broken elevator has come to our attention. The report shows the elevator to have become stalled at 1:07 o'clock, and you were known to have left the building on your lunch hour at a quarter to twelve. This office takes the term 'lunch hour' to mean precisely that — sixty minutes — but you apparently prefer to regard it as any length of time suitable to yourself. Since this has been a continuing offense in your case, we suggest you look for a corporation less interested than we in how you spend the middle of the day. Your services are no longer required, effective today. We are enclosing with your salary two weeks' severance pay."

And that's how *my* whole life was changed by the experience.

FLESH AND THE DEVIL

THE OFFICE where Frisbie worked as vice-president in charge of purchases had its Christmas party a week early, because the head of the corporation was leaving for Miami, but otherwise it was like any other Christmas party. Everyone stood around self-consciously at first, drinking whiskey from paper cups, then bandied intramural jokes as the liquor thawed them, and ended up by slinging arms around one another in general camaraderie. Frisbie found himself dancing (to music from a radio that had been left in the office since the World Series) with a Mrs. Diblanda, hired temporarily for the Christmas rush. He left with Mrs. Diblanda when the party broke up, and they stopped at a neighboring bar for another drink. Frisbie had told his wife not to figure on him for dinner, as there was no way of knowing how long the party would last or how substantial the refreshments would be. There had been loads of canapés, so little edge was left on his appetite, but when, calling a cab, he offered to drop Mrs. Diblanda off at her apartment and she invited him up for a last drink and maybe a bite of supper, he accepted. They had a couple of drinks, and then — quite naturally, it seemed — Frisbie kissed her. Mrs. Diblanda, a divorced woman of about thirty who lived alone, transmitted a clear sense of readiness for anything, but just at that moment the image of Mrs Frisbie interposed itself between him and Mrs. Diblanda, and he rose, got his hat and coat, excused himself, and left.

Now, this forbearance struck Frisbie as a fine thing. How many men he knew — fellows at the office, say — tempted by an isolated pleasure that could have been enjoyed and forgot-

ten with no complications whatever, would have denied themselves? Damn few, probably. The more he thought of it the
more gratifying his conduct seemed, and, presently, the more
his satisfaction struck him as worth sharing with his wife, not
for the light the incident put him in but as a certification of
their bond. Superimposed upon the good spirits in which the
drinks had left him, his moral exhilaration mounted. There
were no cabs outside Mrs. Diblanda's apartment house, and,
hurrying on foot through a cool, needling drizzle that he
found ravishing to his face, Frisbie tried to put himself in a
woman's place, and couldn't imagine a wife not grateful for
the knowledge of her husband's loyalty. By the time he
reached home, he had decided to tell Mrs Frisbie of his.

It was twenty minutes to ten when Frisbie entered the
house. He greeted his wife with a jovial hoot from the hall
when she called from upstairs to ask if it was he. He hung
up his coat and hat and went on up to the bedroom, where
Mrs. Frisbie was sitting in bed, filing her fingernails with an
emery board. He answered a few questions about what the
party had been like, and then took off his coat and vest and
carried them into his closet. "Guess what," he said from there.
"I had a chance to have an affair."

The sound of the emery board, which he could hear behind him, stopped, then resumed more slowly. "I say I had a
chance to sleep with someone. A woman," he said. He reached
for a wire hanger and knocked two or three to the floor in a
tangle. He stooped to retrieve one, slipped his coat and vest
onto it, and hung them up. "But I declined," he said, attempting to strike a humorous note.

The sound of the emery board stopped altogether. "Who's
the woman?" Mrs. Frisbie asked in a tone slightly lower than
normal.

"I don't see what difference that makes," Frisbie said. "All

I'm saying is there was this woman I didn't sleep with. I just have an idea lots of men would have."

"Anyone I know?" she persisted.

"No," he said, looking at her around the edge of the closet door. "It's no matter. As I say, I got on my bike."

Mrs. Frisbie had been looking at the door with her eyes raised but with her head still bent over the emery board. Now she lifted her head. Her gray eyes were flat and opaque. She hitched herself up against her propped pillow and said, "Where?"

Frisbie's elation had worn off, leaving him with a feeling of having stepped out on a high wire on which going ahead might be difficult but turning around impossible

"Where what?" he asked, taking off his tie and hanging it on a rack fastened to the inside of the closet door.

"*Where* didn't you sleep with her?"

Frisbie drew off his pants and overturned them. Clamping the cuffs under his chin, he lined up the creases and let the legs drop over "In her apartment," he said, slipping the doubled trousers on a hanger and hanging them up. He took off his shoes and set them outside the closet door, finished undressing, and got into a pair of pajamas. His wife put the emery board on the nightstand beside her and thoughtfully shook a cigarette out of a pack. Frisbie stayed awhile in the closet, smoothing down the sleeves of hanging coats and making a check of the garments suspended there. "Two of these suits need cleaning," he said, emerging.

His wife struck a match and lit the cigarette. "How did you find out you could sleep with her?" she asked.

A filament of anger began to glow inside Frisbie. "Just a while ago," he said.

"Not when — *how*. How did you find out you could?"

"What's the difference?" he said, kicking his shoes into a corner.

"You were up in a woman's apartment with her," Mrs. Frisbie said. "It was probably somebody from the office. You took her home and went up to her flat." Her hopeless failure to see the gay extemporaneity of all this galled Frisbie, filling him with resentment. The cold résumé continued. "You were drinking. You reached a point where you could have slept with her, which couldn't come out of a clear sky but had things leading up to it What?"

"If you must know, I kissed her!" Frisbie said, well above his ordinary tone.

His wife threw back the covers and got out of bed, punching her cigarette out in an ashtray on her night table. She picked up a dressing gown from a chair, slipped into it, and thrust her feet into a pair of mules. Frisbie stood watching these movements as though mesmerized. "It didn't go any further," he said.

She knotted the cord of her robe and drew it tight. "Come on downstairs," she said. "We'll talk about it there."

Frisbie followed his wife down the stairs, drawing on a warm robe of his own, for the house seemed suddenly chilly. "Don't I get any credit?" he protested. She marched on, her mules making a scuffing thud on the carpeted steps. "I mean there in my mind's eye was your face," he said. "The minute I kissed her, I knew I couldn't go whole hog."

"Fix a drink," his wife said, turning into the living room. "Right."

Frisbie went to the cellarette. He had the illusion that it was the dead of night. The ice cubes clacked idiotically into the glasses. He mixed Scotch-and-sodas for both of them. Behind him, he knew, his wife was sitting erect in the middle of the sofa, her knees together and her hands in her lap, looking across the room. "Isn't there a French proverb 'A stumble may prevent a fall'?" he asked, and a moment later, "Who said, 'Women are not seduced, men are elected'? Somebody."

These remarks were made with no great thought of carrying weight, but were pasted flat on the silence' like decalcomania. Frisbie handed his wife a Scotch-and-soda, and she took several swallows and set the glass down on an end table.

"Now, then," she said, "how did it all get started? What has there been between you?"

"Nothing, really," he said, picking up his drink from the cellarette He had meant the "really" as an emphasis, but he realized that it came out as a kind of qualification, making a total hash of his position. He walked to the mantel and stood there. "You're not looking at this thing right," he said. "Think of it just as the tail end of an office party — and you know what they're like. People kissing one another you'd never dream of" He gave a little reminiscent laugh. "Funny — I mean, to stand off and watch all that, which has *no* connection with their daily lives. Clarke, there, with his arm around his secretary, kissing her. Old H. Denim smacking everybody in sight."

"Smacking everybody is different."

"I kissed others."

It made no sense. They had simply floated off on a cake of ice, Frisbie thought, into a sea of absurdity. That they would at last fetch up on a farther shore he took for granted, though he couldn't at the moment see how, or where.

"How can a woman ever be sure of her husband again?" his wife asked rhetorically, and then talked on.

Frisbie could recall a hundred plays of marital stress in which husbands and wives spatted brightly or tumbled adroitly through colorful arcs of emotion, but he could think of nothing to say now. He frowned into his glass and ran the tip of his finger around the rim. Once, he grinned and looked at his feet. After taking him to task from various points of view, suggesting particularly that he put himself in his wife's place and imagine what *he* might think of *her* in another man's arms, Mrs. Frisbie broke off and looked into her own glass. "How did you feel?" she asked. "When you — did it."

Frisbie spread his free hand in a gesture preparatory to replying, but she interrupted him before he could speak. "No, don't tell me," she said. "I don't want to know about it." She looked at him squarely. "Tell me you'll never do a cheap thing like that again."

With that, Frisbie's resistance, till now smoldering and tentative, flared up. He took a drink, planked his glass on the mantel, faced his wife deliberately, and answered in words that surprised him as much as they did her, "A man can't guarantee his emotions for the rest of his life."

His wife rose and strode to the window. "Well!" she said. "What have we here?"

"Somebody trying to make a mountain out of a molehill," Frisbie said, warming now that he had found his tongue. "It's time we went at these things in a grown-up way. Why shouldn't there be sexual freedom as well as political? Let's look at it from a civilized point of view."

"You must be mad," Mrs. Frisbie said.

"Plenty!" he said. "I was reading an article in a magazine — that one right there on the table — some sex facts about the American male, based on statistics. Well, it seems that before marriage the average man has three point five affairs. *After* marriage — aside from his wife, of course — the average man has point seven affairs."

Mrs. Frisbie dug a package of cigarettes out of the pocket of her robe. "Let's hope you've had yours," she said.

He calculated a moment. "I'd say that's the grossest possible exaggeration of what occurred this evening," he said. "And that so far you've got very little to complain of."

That way lay anything but reconciliation. Mrs Frisbie wheeled around. "Surely you don't mean any of this. You *can't!*" she cried. "Or you wouldn't have brought the whole business up the way you did. You couldn't get it off your chest soon enough." The reflection seemed to give her pause. "I suppose I should have appreciated that more, except that you caught me so by surprise." She assessed this new idea, and Frisbie with it. "You *had* to tell me before you could lay your head on your pillow with any hope of sleep. Wasn't that it?"

Like a man who, trying to trim his sails to contrary winds, finds a breeze springing up from an unexpected quarter, Frisbie prudently tacked for harbor on those lines. He sighed voluminously and flapped his arms at his sides. "I told you what I did because I thought it was something you ought to know," he said.

"You thought you owed it to me."

"Something like that," said Frisbie.

"Don't think I don't appreciate that part of it," Mrs. Frisbie said

"Then let's leave it that way," he said, snapping on a table lighter, and, walking over to her, extended the flame to her unlighted cigarette. He lit one himself.

Still, she seemed to withhold something from the promise of eventual good graces, as though wanting yet a gesture from him to complete the ritual. She prompted him, at length. "You *are* sorry, aren't you?" she said.

Frisbie was reviewing to himself the hour's events, tracing their origins in that misguided impulse he had had when homebound. "I did a damn foolish thing tonight," he reflected, thinking aloud.

"One you'll not do again if the chance arises," Mrs. Frisbie said.

20

"You can say that again!" Frisbie said, walking back to the mantel and reaching for his drink. "You can certainly say that again."

MUD IN YOUR EYE
(P. G Wodehouse joins
the black humorists)

"Cook is most pleased you liked the ragout, sir. You're the finest judge of horseflesh in all of England."

"Thank you, Chives."

I had my mind on more pressing matters, namely a bid to weekend with a girl Chives was convinced had her cap set for me. No cove with all his tiles is going to rush out and enlist in the sex war said to be raging all round, but there's no guarantee he won't be drafted, what? Parthenia had to date uttered only the vaguest of mating cries, but nothing said she mightn't suddenly haul up her slacks and pop the question. And a blister who had just taken a bath in the market, as our American cousins call a drubbing there, might find her property, Stony Stairs, a snug harbor for which to tack.

"You take a murky view of it then, Chives?"

"To accept Miss Coleslaugh's invitation could compromise you irreversibly, sir," said the nonpareil, twisting from my typewriter a necktie I had screwed into the carriage in a fit of improvisation. "If she construed it as a reciprocation of her known interest in you."

I was feeling more tempest-tossed by the minute. I had scraped up an acquaintance on the street that day — at least what was left of him by the omnibus that had narrowly missed myself as well — prior to biffing over to my solicitor's to talk bankruptcy. Chives now shuffled about his chores in a manner all too abysmally in keeping with our decayed lot. His shoes, though buffed to a fare-thee-well, lacked a lace, and one trailed an errant garter. His hair could have done with what birds in the book trade call a little judicious cutting, to say nothing of its being streaked with chutney, and not the best chutney by a long chalk. His tailcoat recalled those getups worn by music-hall comedians who flail one another with animal bladders for the delectation of the low. Yes, there was a distinct whiff of Götterdämmerung about the whole show, and no good blinking it. He set before me a glass of port on which I fairly gagged, but then as a blister down on his uppers must realize, any port in a storm. Chives's thinking powers alone held up to scratch — the ability to help a bloke negotiate to the end the General Mess.

"They are an unstable lot, the Coleslaughs," he went on. "You may remember a sister who did herself in for love of an Hungarian rhapsodist named Nabisco, who had misguidedly encouraged *her* attentions."

I did indeed. Nothing like a spot of the old *Liebestod* to ginger up a godfearing community, and poor Phrensy's tale bade fair to become a legend in ours. Other elements in the bloodlines under review must include dotty old Sir Humphrey, assured of tenure at a local bin, and a brother, Tacky, no slouch as a weekend sponge himself Too, he was a bit of a voyeur, and bore watching. I needed no refresher from Chives on all these dispiriting data I had tossed and turned all morning, revolving them in the old lemon.

"The name itself is hardly a cockle warmer," I mused. "Parthenia Coleslaugh."

"It is not a winning phrase, sir."

"Marriage to me would make her Mrs Teddy Vestige, but there's the far more dismaying factor of her size The throng does not exist into which Parthenia would melt. Throngs, on the contrary, melt into her. Gad, have you seen her lately?"

"As a matter of fact I did run into her recently in the village, sir. She'd just lost fifty pounds, and I must say —"

"Fifty pounds!" I sprang to my feet. "But that would bring her down to where she'd strike a chap about right. To say nothing of being able to get her across the threshold without incident. Chives, why the devil haven't you told me of this before?"

"Sir, I only meant —"

"Say no more. Feed the alligator a few shirts and socks. We're off to Stony Stairs in the morning."

What a blow awaited me there! The grounds were a mess of greens, but they had nothing on Parthenia. She was if anything thicker in the flitch than ever, and I thought her face was beginning to show the ravages of cribbage. "Hullo, dear dear Teddy!" she said, continuing to ogle me even while greeting Chives. She was clutching a book of which I glimpsed the title — *The Single Girl and Gastroenterology*. I found the whole thing really quite *angst*-making. I mean a cove bends every effort to navigate life's stickier situations, but there are those that in their very nature defy all effort bending. A spot of elbow bending is rather what's called for. The instant I decently could, I pelted upstairs and hid in my room till dinner time.

Americans once had something called Prohibition whereby chaps were denied their shellac through a network of meddlers I've never got the straight of. I understood something of their ordeal while waiting for the resident Saint Bernard to fetch the refreshment for which I'd bleated out a request in fleeing. But at last he dribbled into view with a bottle and some glasses. I filed a few away in the old cabinet and, thus fortified, felt ready to face, if not quite yet my hostess, at least the nonesuch in my employ — caught at last, it would seem, with a rift in that famous omniscience.

"Well, Chives," I said, "your intelligence leaves something to be desired this time, it appears. I mean your report, the glad tidings slipped me in all good faith, that the subject in question had lost fifty pounds" I sent home an ironic smile. "You've seen her for yourself in what I may without fear of contradiction call the flesh. Just *where*, pray tell, did she lose them?"

"At the races, sir. I tried to explain at the time, but you overrode me in your ardor to be off. She herself has clearly gained a couple of stone, as we still say here in the British Isles. I'm afraid you've been seeing too much of your American friends. The only thing reduced about her, if I may say so, are her circumstances — which she seems trying to repair with an advantageous marriage, not unlike yourself. You have thus a great deal in common. She too has 'taken a bath' with the little Sir Humphrey settled on her. Speaking of which, I've drawn yours, sir. Will there be anything else?"

"Yes. See that I hold the old bean under water for a count of fifty."

"Certainly, sir."

AFTERNOON OF A FAUN

THIS is only a story about how I became engaged, but the nature and ingredients of that event and of the emotional transactions that immediately preceded it are so of a piece with what went before, and so depend on it for illumination, that a lick of autobiography is indicated.

I think I can say that my childhood was as unhappy as the next braggart's. I was read to sleep with the classics and spanked with obscure quarterlies My father was a man steeped in the heavyweight German philosophers; his small talk ran to the likes of "I believe it was Hegel who defined love as the ideality of the relativity of the reality of an infinitesimal portion of the absolute totality of the Infinite Being." I don't think I need dwell further on the influence which, more than any other single factor in my life, inspired in me my own conversational preference: the light aphorism.

I belonged, in my late adolescence, which I spent in Scranton, Pennsylvania, to a clique of pimpled boulevardiers who met at a place called the Samothrace, a restaurant and ice-cream parlor run by a Greek who let us pull tables out on the sidewalk and talk funny. Andropoulos, which was his name, was a prickly sort who was forever complaining — especially when his trade was slack and the lack of money in the till made him more irritable than usual — that this country was materialistic. Be that as it may, we expatriates-at-home could be seen at the Samothrace almost every evening, loitering over pastry and coffee, or toying with a little of what the Greek called his fruit compost I often wore my topcoat with the sleeves hanging loose, so that the effect was like that of an Inverness cape, when it was not like that of two broken arms. An earnest youth on the high-school debating squad, who got in with our set by mistake one *soir*, tried to interest me in politics by speaking of the alarming layoffs then occurring in the Department of Agriculture. "I had thought," I said, smiling around at my disciples as I tapped a Melachrino on the lid of its box, "that the Department of Agriculture slaughtered its surplus employees."

This attitude grew into a *fin-de-siècle* one of cultivated fatigue and bored aestheticism, marked by amusement with the colloquial main stream. I would lie full-length around the house and with a limp hand wave life away. My mother took this as an indication that I had "no pep," and urged a good tonic to fix me up.

"No, no, no," my father said. "That isn't what the trouble is. It's what they call Decadence. It's an attitude toward life." He looked at the horizontal product of their union, disposed on the living-room sofa with a cigarette. "He'll come to his senses."

"Instead of coming to one's senses," I airily returned, "how much more delightful to let one's senses come to one."

My mother, a slender woman with a nimbus of fluffy gray hair, next tried to get me interested in "healthy" books, like the jumbo three-generation novels she herself "couldn't put down."

"The books Mother cannot put down," I said, "are the ones I cannot pick up."

"He *is* run-down — now, I don't *care!*" my mother said.

My father stamped his foot, for he was becoming as vexed with her as he was with me. "It has nothing to do with his health," he explained again. "This is a literary and aesthetic pose. He's precious."

"Mother has always thought so," I said, and laughed, for there were things that brought out my heartier side.

Such is my memory of seventeen.

I was slightly above medium height, reedy, with clothes either too casual or too studied. I had a pinched-in, pendulous underlip, rather like the lip of a pitcher, which must have conferred on me an air of jocularity somewhat at odds with my intention to be "dry." My best friend was a high-school — and, later, junior-college — classmate named Nickie Sherman. He needed a good tonic, too, being if anything even more *fin-de-siècle* than I. "Thomas Wolfe was a genius without talent," he asserted between sips of hot chocolate at the Greek's one evening, speaking in a drawl suited to the paradox of the statement, which was not meant to be understood by more than three or four of those who heard it. The double dose of nuance entailed by Nickie's visiting my house, as he

26

did sometimes for dinner or even overnight, drove my father to distraction, and he literally took to sending me upstairs to my room for making epigrams and paradoxes. He said that he was thinking not so much of himself as of my mother, to whom he considered these subtleties disrespectful, because they were hopelessly over her head.

One evening just after dinner, for example, my younger sister Lila got to teasing me about a girl named Crystal Chickering, whom I had been dating. My mother remarked that she'd have guessed I'd have preferred Jessie Smithers, because "Jessie laughs at absolutely everything a person says."

"That is because she has no sense of humor," I said.

My father made a truncheon of his *Yale Review*. "I'll ask you to apologize to your mother for that remark," he said.

"Why?" I protested.

"Because we don't engage in repartee with the mother who gave us life," he said in a florid burst of chivalry that in part arose, I think, out of his own sense of guilt at having neglected her, leaving her to what he eruditely called her "needle-pwah" while he sat with his nose in Schopenhauer or went off on vacations by himself. "Apologize!"

"Oh, don't worry about it, Roebuck," my mother put in. "Let him talk over my head the same as I talked over my father's. That's progress."

Feeling perfidy in the form of aphorisms to be uncoiling everywhere about him, my father became angrier still. "Explain to her what that last so-called paradox means," he said, his face red from a lifetime of bad claret and plain damn exasperation. "My father would have given me short shrift if I'd insulted my mother with language fit for nothing but a Mayfair drawing room. All this confounded lint-picking. Upstairs!" he ordered with a flourish of the *Yale Review*. "Go on up to your room, please, until you can learn to talk to your family in considerate English."

"But I've got a date," I objected.

"You should have thought of that sooner," said my father.

Rather than waste precious time arguing, I hurried upstairs to start serving my sentence. It wasn't until nine o'clock, after apologizing for the subtlety of my rejoinder and promising to engage in more normal intercourse, that I was let out. By that time, of course, I was late for my date with Crystal Chickering, toward whose house I legged it, as a consequence, with commendable pep.

Crystal was a girl of my own age who lived about a mile from my house. She was one of the milk-white daughters of the moon, and it goes without saying that I pursued the amorous life with the same easy, half-spectatorial air of inconsequence that I did the intellectual — or tried to. It wasn't easy, for more reasons than one. First, the atmosphere around Crystal's house wasn't right. Her father was a sort of homespun philosopher, who conducted an advice-to-the-troubled column in the local evening paper. He ran readers' letters and his own counsel, which was usually packaged in maxims. He had volumes of these, all (in notebooks of his own) cross-indexed under types of trouble. That he was my favorite character goes without saying, and I was careful not to say it either to him or to his daughter. I felt that one had a lot of work to do on her before she would understand *why* he was one's favorite character; why he was like those Currier and Ives prints which, having outgrown them, one laps the field of Sensibility to approach again from behind and see as "wonderful." Crystal was often, not to make any bones about it, pretty wonderful herself, in those days. The first time I dropped the name Baudelaire to her, I had the queer suspicion that she thought it was the name of a refrigerator or air-conditioner. But I eventually got *The Flowers of Evil* across by reading the bulk of it to her aloud. On the night my confinement made me late, our fare was to be something more conventional. I was taking along a new album of *Boris Godunov.*

Setting the records on the family phonograph, for her parents were upstairs and we had the parlor to ourselves, I asked, "Do you like *Godunov?*"

"Yes," she answered from the sofa, where she was settling herself with a cigarette "Which composition of his is it?"

I heard the great ships baying at the harbor's mouth, and chuckled, already aboard — clean out of this. I had that exhilarating sense of being a misfit that I could taste almost anywhere in Scranton and that was, in a way, my birthright.

Crystal closed her eyes and listened to the music. When the album had been played through and duly enjoyed, we forgot about music and got on a variety of other subjects, among them marriage and families. "I suppose most people want that sort of thing," I said. "You know — the eternal severities."

"Everybody wants children, certainly," Crystal answered. "Don't you think it would be awful to go through life without them?"

"Yes," I said. "There is only one thing worse than not having children, and that is having them."

"Just what do you mean?" she asked.

"I don't want to get married," I said, in clear enough tones. "I just — don't — want to get married."

She looked thoughtfully at the floor. "We're having our first quarrel," she said, as though noting a milestone in our progress.

To kiss into silence the lips from which such bromides fell, and turn them to the laughter and sighs for which they were intended, seemed precisely the formula for tinkling pleasures, for caught felicities, for which we were so sumptuously cued by nature. One evening in midsummer, I was early for a date we were to spend at her house with nobody home at all, even upstairs. Her folks were at a testimonial dinner for the editor of the paper Mr. Chickering worked for. There was no answer when I rang the front doorbell, and, following the strains of the love duet from *Tristan,* which seemed to be coming from somewhere in back, I walked around the house and found Crystal in the back yard with a portable phonograph on a chair. She herself was stretched out in a hammock with her eyes closed and one hand outflung above her head. I had a feeling that she had seen me coming, quickly set the record going, and hurried back to the hammock in time for me to find her lying on it in a trance of appreciation.

She was wearing yellow shorts and a red halter, for the weather was very warm. Her hair was gathered at the back and knotted with a red silk ribbon. On the grass beneath her was an empty Coke bottle with a bent straw in it. She appeared at length to become aware of me standing there, and she rolled her head toward me, her eyes fluttering open.

"Oh, hello," she said.

I snapped a burning cigarette into the grass and walked up to her, my nerves in a trembling knot. She extended a white hand, which I took in both of mine and ate like cake. She rolled her head away with a sigh.

"This music. Lawrence Melchior," she said.

On persuasions from myself, she eased out of the hammock and onto a blanket lying on the ground nearby. She pulled the grass and, as one who knew good music, my hair. "This night." It was darkening, the air wreathed with the musks of summer, as of something crushed from the grape of Dusk. A moon hung like a gong above the grove of birches behind the house.

The night was a success, and I went home ill with fear. I spent the next days scorching myself with one speculation.

The sight of perambulators sent galvanic shocks through me. I was to wheel one through an eternity of ridicule because I had succumbed to a single folly — and that to the music of a composer whose works I had termed mucilaginous. The great ships would bay at the harbor's mouth nevermore for me. I heard, instead, voices, local in origin and of an almost hallucinatory force: "Shotgun wedding, you know." "You mean Charles Swallow? That guy who was always —?" "Yes, the old *flâneur* himself." (*Flâneur:* One who strolls aimlessly; hence, an intellectual trifler.) Think of a boulevardier pushing a baby carriage!

I hid in my room with the door locked most of the time. Once I stood before my dresser mirror and looked at myself. My face was drawn. It was the face of an alien. I contorted it into deliberately gruesome expressions of woe, so as to give everything an exaggerated and theatrical aspect, and, by this means, make what I was worrying about seem to have no basis in fact. My grimaces did create an atmosphere of relative absurdity, and I smiled bravely. Of course all this would blow over! Six months from now I would be laughing at it. I had about convinced myself of that when the idea of tallied months struck me with fresh horror, and I was back where I started.

The voices came again. I tried at first to drown them out with a phonograph I had in my room, but there were no compositions that could not, by deplorable associations, return me swiftly to my *crise*. And the voices continued· "You mean that guy who was always knocking convention?" "The same." "He seemed to be that type they call the carriage trade. Ha! I guess *now* he —" Never. I would go to Lethe first, I would twist wolfsbane. I would slip into the hospitable earth, and among her dumb roots and her unscandalizing boulders make my bed.

I was walking down the street, one afternoon during the cooling-off period, when I saw a sight that gave the winch of agony a fresh turn. Nickie Sherman was approaching. He had our *Zeitgeist* well at heel, for, one hand in his trouser pocket and the other swinging a blackthorn stick he was affecting those days, he drifted up and said "Hı."

Stark, staring mad, I answered "Hı."

"What cooketh?"

Suddenly, instead of dreading the encounter, I saw a way of turning it to advantage. I would remove the sting from having to get married (if such was the pass things came to) by taking the line that that was what I wanted. This would need a little groundwork, and to lay it I suggested we drop in at the Greek's, which was a block from there, for some coffee. We did.

The tables at which it was our wont to dally in the cool of the evening were in their places outside (Andropoulos himself now cultivated the Continental touch we had introduced, and kept a few tables in the open air), but this was the heat of the day and we went inside. Several women gabbled at a table about a movie they had been to.

"Matinee idle," I murmured to Nickie as we took chairs ourselves.

We ordered coffee. Then Nickie, who had laid the blackthorn across an empty chair, asked, *"Was ist los?"*

Glancing around with a matter-of-factness into which some note of furtiveness must also have crept, I drew out cigarettes and answered negligently, "I've been having an affair."

"And?"

I shrugged. "It gets to be rather a nuisance. We pay for security with boredom, for adventure with bother. It's six of one and half a dozen of the other, really." I lit the cigarette and waved the match out. "Shaw makes matrimony sound rather attractive, with that puritanical definition he has of it somewhere. I'm sure you remember it."

Nickie watched Andropoulos shamble over with our coffee.

"Shaw is great, up to a point," he said, "and then one suddenly finds oneself thinking, Oh, pshaw!"

"He describes marriage as combining a maximum of temptation with a maximum of opportunity. He's quite right, of course. It's the most sensual of our institutions," I said. "I've half a notion to get married myself," I added vagrantly, stirring my coffee.

Nickie's problem was to get back into the conversation. I could sense him mulling my gambit as he sipped his own coffee, keeping his dark eyes casually averted. He set his cup down and cleared his throat, appearing at last to have worked something out, and I knew that what he said next would determine whether I would have to blow my brains out or not.

"Yes. The logistics of adultery are awful. Matrimony is a garrison, but one that has its appeal to a man out bivouacking every night," said that probable virgin.

Freeze it there, I told myself. I knew that if a neat way of putting a rebuttal had occurred to him first, instead of a concurrence, he would have rebutted, but it hadn't, and I was to that extent in luck. My object was to get Nickie into as good a frame of mind as possible for my armed nuptials, if any — to give him a viewpoint from which he would see me not as a ridiculous bourgeois casualty going down the aisle but heathen to the end. I had to come out of this making sense as a boulevardier who had said "I do." So I said appreciatively, "That's neat, Nickie. By God, that's neatly put."

33

Next to be prepared were, of course, my parents.

They knew only that I'd been seeing Crystal Chickering for about a year, and talk of wedding bells would fall rather unexpectedly on their ears, aside from sorely disillusioning them about my plans to matriculate at Dartmouth in the fall. Therefore it seemed wise to pave the way a little by giving them to understand that this girl and I were "serious." I let drop this intelligence when they and I were sitting in the living room shortly after dinner on the day of my passage with Nickie at the Greek's.

"I've fallen in love with a girl I rather like," I said. "I suppose I shall marry eventually. One does that. One drifts into stability."

"Upstairs!" said my father.

But my mother clapped her hands. "That's wonderful!" she exclaimed. She was pleased as Punch when I assured her it was the Chickering girl, whom she liked best after Jessie Smithers, and told her that we were informally engaged. The act of betrothal showed pep. It showed downright spunk, she declared, especially considering that I had no prospects whatever and had to finish school first in any case. "Come and sit by me," she said.

I jollied my mother by joining her on the sofa, where she straightway hauled my long legs up across hers, so that I was halfway sitting on her lap, and rummaged in my hair for old times' sake. "I remember when you were a little shaver how you'd crawl across the floor to where I was talking on the phone, and kink the cord," she said. "As though you could stop the conversation coming through it, the way you can the water in a hose. We never knew whether you were joking or serious. Did you really think that cut off the electricity in the wire?"

"Doesn't it?" I inquired with wide eyes. She gave me a

hug that squeezed a groan out of me, like a note out of an accordion.

"We thought for a while you might be feebleminded," my father put in wistfully from the mantel, against which he had backed to scratch a perennially itching spot between his shoulder blades. "Well, all those things come back in a flood at a time like this is what your mother means. I've done my best for you — I believe God will bear me out on that — but you cannot force values on one who will not have them." He fingered an onion wisp of beard, which, together with his harried features and embedded eyes, made him surprisingly resemble the illustrations of depleted sensibility in the very literature with which I outraged him — Baudelaire, Huysmans, and the rest. "I had some standing in the community once, under other spiritual weathers and skies, and cut a fine figure, too, if I do say so myself. Why, the little tots would come out of Sunday school and say, 'There goes Jesus.' " He drew a deep breath, and resumed almost immediately, "And humor — where is *it* today? In my day, we would get up to speak at Thanksgiving banquets, and begin: 'A moment ago you could have said the sage was in the turkey. Now the turkey is in the sage.' *That* was humor, I wish to submit. Well, I've tried to do my best."

"And you have, Popper," I said, looking over at him from my mother's lap "I appreciate everything you've done for me."

"It's a tradition I've tried to give you, not bread alone," he said. "The rest is up to you. You have brains, imagination — but have you the brains and the imagination to apprehend that these in themselves are not enough?" He squared himself a little, and we understood more was coming. "Imagination without discipline," he said, looking the young aphorist steadily in the eye, "is like a pillow without the ticking."

My cries of praise and thumps on his back declared him

to be a success. He pinched his nose and smiled modestly at the floor. "Ah, well, perhaps we can manage a wedding gift of a thousand dollars when the time comes," he said More thumps and outcries attested to the tide of good feeling created by his knack for the right words, and afterward he opened a bottle of Madeira and toasted my eventual departure from his board in lambent words.

So everything, on my end at least, was in readiness; as much in readiness, certainly, as I could make it. There remained now only to await zero hour, as I thought of the time when I was to learn my fate. That was presumably the following Tuesday evening, when I had a date with Crystal. Then I would learn whether it was Heaven or Hell for which I was to leave Purgatory.

Crystal was upstairs dressing when I arrived at the Chickering house that night, so I sat down in the living room to wait. Her father was there, in a Cogswell chair, wearing slippers and reading the evening paper. He was in shirtsleeves, but then, after all, he was the local shirtsleeve philosopher. He put the paper down and regarded me with a deep frown. "I'd like to talk to you," he said

He was a red-haired man of medium size, with green eyes magnified by the heavy-lensed glasses he wore. He had been sunbathing recently, and his was the kind of skin that never tans but only turns the pink of mouthwashes. He removed his glasses and chewed on their bows. I was twiddling my thumbs at a rate not normally associated with that act. "What about, Mr. Chickering?" I asked.

"I think you know."

I met this with a gulp and the word "What?" brought out in a dry treble. The ceiling creaked as under a footstep upstairs. That foolish girl had confessed her condition to her parents, I thought with panic. Even now, she and her mother were up there, hysterically promenading. Paralyzed, I watched Chickering thoughtfully revolve a cockleshell ashtray on a table beside his chair. The cockleshell was — like the resort pillows and the wall thermometers in the shape of keys to cities, which also heavily garnished the living room — a souvenir of some past family holiday. Together, they left me ill with premonition. Now I would never board the great ships. Now I would never bicycle down the Palatinate sampling wines, never sit at the captain's table opposite a woman returning to the States after some years spent in a novel by Henry James. At best, I would see Niagara Falls from the air; it would look like a kitchen sink running over.

"I think we can safely say that now you're a young man with a problem," Chickering said. "And there are some folks who think that's my field."

"There are? I mean, I am? What's my problem?"

"Why, you're about to enter college without any clear idea, I might even say without the *least* idea, what you want to be when you come out of it — butcher, baker or candlestick maker," he said, in the American grain. "Now, wait a minute. I know education is for the mind, and all that. But at the same time a person ought to have *some* notion of where he wants to head. And I just want to leave this thought with you for what it may be worth."

I was spared whatever piece of free wisdom he may have had prepared for me by the arrival of Crystal, who just then slowly descended the stairway. She was wearing a new dress, and she looked singularly radiant.

"Ah, there you are," I said, rising. "Shall we go? We're probably late for the party as it is."

We were going to a housewarming only three blocks away, so we walked. As we strolled toward our destination, Crystal slipped a hand into mine, and from time to time

37

turned to smile at me. "This night," she said, and took a
deep breath. What I died to hear I feared to ask.

At last she said, "I suppose you're anxious to know."

"Know?" I said.

She stopped and turned to face me on the sidewalk. "You
must be out of your mind with worry, the same as I've been,
so I won't keep you on pins and needles any longer. Everything is all right."

I was free—free! The very word went winging and singing through my head, like a bird sprung from a cage. Chains
fell away from me, doors opened in every direction. Flowers
that had withered leaped to life. The hours in Purgatory
were almost worth it, for the joy of this release. I that had
been dead lived again, the master of my fate. I was absolutely and completely Free!

I turned, seized her in my arms, and, in an ecstasy of
gratitude, asked her to marry me.

INTERIOR WITH FIGURES

THE SPREAD of so-called action sculpture poses a new problem for owners of art objects, or, more accurately, adds a
fresh dimension to one already long plaguing them as home-
owners. It's this. When a power-driven assortment of mechanical giblets gleaned from scrapyards goes on the blink,
whom do you get to repair it? It's a headache on which I
can speak with authority, possessing, as I do, a congeries of
available materials entitled *Improvisation No. 18*, which recently stalled on me an hour before a cocktail party at which
I planned to unveil it. The following playlet, already snapped
up by the Yale Drama School for burial in its archives, may

not, when ultimately unearthed by future scholars, bear out the claims for the black comedy in which plain folk are currently said to thrash, but it will, I think, suggest the occasional modest gray *crise* to which we may all reasonably aspire. The action is, as I say, autobiographical, but the names have been changed to protect the sheepish.

The curtain does not rise in the tediously conventional sense, but is rather rent from top to bottom, to reveal Mr. and Mrs. Brent Paternoster, in party fig, anxiously watching an electrician who is lying on his back under an exciting assemblage of pipes, belts, and blades — indeed, the work of an artist of more than promise. Paternoster paces and glances at his wristwatch, his nerves, already a can of worms, declining steadily under the clank of tools and the streams of malediction floating upward through the metalwork. At length, the serviceman crawls out from under.

ELECTRICIAN. Well, your trouble ain't electrical. Connections are all O.K. and so are the switches, transformer, and wall socket. So 'tain't in my jurisdiction. (*Hurls his tools into an open satchel*) That'll be twelve-fifty and a kiss from the Missus — our standard fee for a service call now, as you know. Being as how it's electrical work, I might say our "*current* fee." Oh, that's rich! Our current fee.

MRS. PATERNOSTER. Are you sure you understand this type of collage? It's by the noted Swedish sculptor, Nils Maelstrom.

ELECTRICIAN. Yes, I'm familiar with his work. Why don't you call him in to get her running for you?

PATERNOSTER. He can't be reached. He's in Chicago, delivering a paper at a learned-society meeting.

ELECTRICIAN. You ask me, delivering papers is his what-do-you-call-it. Métier. (*He goes over to collect his buss from the Missus while Paternoster produces the money.*)

PATERNOSTER. (*handing over the twelve-fifty and making no secret of his outrage as a consumer*). And I voted for Roosevelt.

MRS. PATERNOSTER. (*to Electrician, as a woman instinctively concerned over the good repute of her possessions*). What's your opinion of Maelstrom?

ELECTRICIAN. Oh, he served his purpose as an innovator, a sort of catalyst. But as an artist I think he chews out loud. Still, your piece here has its merits. It conveys a fine sense of spatial dilapidation, and the comment in the pipe joints is most caustic. That's not pseudo-junk, lady. That's the real thing. I tell you what. If somebody can give me a hand with it, I'd be glad to load it on my rig and run it down to some garage mechanic for a look-see.

MRS. PATERNOSTER. Oh, you have a truck out there?

ELECTRICIAN. Yes. It's not much of a truck—just a van ordinaire.

PATERNOSTER. (*knowing offenses must needs come in the world, but woe unto them by whom offenses come*). I voted for him four times. I went through the whole thing. The New Deal, the Raw Deal, the Ordeal . . .

ELECTRICIAN. (*to the woman*). It must be a drag for you, with Mr. Nostalgia here casting backward glances like anything. Still, my grandfather always said the Roosevelt era was a great one. Trust-busting, the charge up San Juan Hill —

PATERNOSTER. You may go!

(*Mrs. Paternoster strolls to the door with the Electrician, and as they pass the sculpture she is, again, defensive about her taste.*)

MRS. PATERNOSTER. The whole point of this sort of thing is, of course, to make do with available materials.

ELECTRICIAN . (*with a glance at Paternoster*). Don't we all.
(*Exiting with his bag of tools*) Well, toodle-oo. Don't let
your goat get gotten.
(*Paternoster goes to the improvisation and tries to start it
with a good kick, withdrawing his foot with a howl of
pain. He limps to the telephone, where he paws through
the local directory.*)

MRS. PATERNOSTER. Are you looking up a phone number?

PATERNOSTER. Your powers of divination are uncanny. I'm
going to call a plumber. The trouble may be in the hydraulic assembly.

MRS. PATERNOSTER. That'd be Mr. Vanden Bosch Here, let
me do it. (*From a pop-up book of numbers frequently
used, she instantly has the one she wants and dials it.*)
Hello, Mr. Vanden Bosch? Why, we're having a kind of
emergency here with something I think needs a good
plumber, and I was wondering — Oh, I see. Thank you.
(*She hangs up.*) He no longer makes house calls.

PATERNOSTER. Look, to begin with, you don't handle these
repair people the way you have to these days — with kid
gloves. You made your first boo-boo calling him a plumber.
We don't call them that anymore.

MRS. PATERNOSTER. What do we call them?

PATERNOSTER. House urologists. (*He seats himself resolutely
before the sculpture to study it. Doing so, he props an
elbow on a knee and brings a fist up under his chin, inadvertently striking the pose of Rodin's* Thinker.) What
about the wash-machine repairman? Is that too farfetched?

MRS. PATERNOSTER. No, I wouldn't say anything was too farfetched. Any kind of tinker at all — if you could *get* one.
The wash-machine agency would just take our name and
send us service when they could. It might not be for two
or three days.

PATERNOSTER. Well, with a jam like this, if you can't get a

repairman, in fact don't even know what kind you need, and with guests due to begin arriving any minute, there's only one thing to do that I can think of.

MRS. PATERNOSTER What's that?

PATERNOSTER Hand me my screwdriver.

(*She goes to a nearby table for it.*)

MRS. PATERNOSTER (*taking it to him.*) Here you are. I made it with two jiggers of vodka, the way you like it, and the orange juice is fresh, Brent. Now you just sit there and try to unwind till the others get here.

GOOD BOY

HAVING READ in various periodicals of a recent swing back to a belief in Total Depravity, I am reminded of a slim, bearded sixth-grade teacher whose enthusiasm for this doctrine still casts a shadow over my school-day recollections. The Chicago community into which I was born was composed largely of immigrant Dutch Calvinists, who were of course among the most dour custodians of the idea before it passed out of fashion. Now that it's back, it might be instructive briefly to sketch the man who remains in my mind as synonymous with the tenet.

His name was Van Dongen, his beard was an impeccably trimmed Vandyke, and he enjoyed a reputation for shrewdness which he sustained by habitually looking over the top of his spectacles. He had been a schoolmaster in the Netherlands before he settled, in early middle life, in our Reformed Dutch community. I had heard conflicting reports of his temperament, which was alternately represented as stringent and warm, and it was with mixed feelings that I passed into

42

the sixth grade and came under the scrutiny of his pale-blue eyes.

On the first day of the term, he strode into the classroom, offered a prayer lush with references to man's conception in sin and proneness to all manner of evil, walked to a closet to get out the Bibles that were passed around each morning for the Scripture reading, opened the door, and stepped back as a cat shot out and streaked away through the open window.

It was, unfortunately, a big orange tabby that I had found in the schoolyard earlier and had taken into a broom closet in the basement to see whether or not its eyes glowed in the dark. Van Dongen looked at me over the rims of his glasses and beckoned me with a long, bony finger, and I knew he had seen me toting the cat and was now putting two and two together. Under questioning, I stated the facts, explaining that the animal had got away before the experiment was concluded, adding that I had no idea who had caught it later and put it in the Bible closet Actually, I had a good idea it was an oaf named Red Schaaf, whom I could see snickering behind his fingers.

"So it is not enough that you put cats in the Bible closet," Van Dongen said. "You must lie, too."

"I'm not lying," I said "I don't know who did it."

"Now you lie about your lying. So is your sin already threefold. Does your mother use Kitchen Klenzer?" he asked sharply. I thought at first he was going to send me home for some and wash my mouth out with it, but presently he made it clear what he was getting at. On a can of Kitchen Klenzer, there was a picture of a woman holding up a can of Kitchen Klenzer, which in turn had a picture of a woman holding up a can, and so on, and Van Dongen used these pictures within pictures as a symbol of how evil perpetuates itself into infinity, until, as Saint Paul said, the whole Creation groans and

travails. He told me he'd give me one more chance to check
this sequence and, laying a hand on my shoulder, asked softly,
"Now — did you do it?"

"No," I said.

"Fourfold."

In memory, his voice merges absurdly with that of a radio
announcer on a quiz program saying, "You now have fourfold. Do you want to try for fivefold?" I got up to sixfold
before he sent me back to my seat with orders to stay after
school.

I stayed after school an hour that day. Then Van Dongen,
who had been working quietly at his desk, handed me a crisp
note to my father. It read, "This wicked and stiff-necked boy
put a large, dirty cat in among the copies of Holy Writ. In
addition, he persists in lying about his guilt. I trust you will
labor with him. Try to make him ashamed of his conduct.
And let me know in the morning what happens. Yours in the
Lord, Dirk Van Dongen."

He gathered up his papers and put on his dark felt hat.
"Be ashamed by nine A.M.," he warned me as we parted at
the door.

The note I brought from my father the next morning
attested his belief in my version of the affair and suggested
that it would be useless to labor with me further.

Van Dongen gave me one more chance to confess. "Have
you searched your heart?" he asked me.

"Yes," I said.

"And have you found it black?"

"Not in connection with this," I said.

That brought my blame to sevenfold, which I guess he
figured was a good, round biblical number and as likely a
point as any at which to feature me in the morning prayer
"We bow our heads in meekness and humility," he began,

his beard pointing like a dagger at the class as he raised his face to the Throne of Heaven, "to beseech Thee on behalf of one who has gone astray. It behooves us to remember in judging him that, being human, he is prone to all manner of evil. But though we are *totally*, we are not *absolutely*, depraved," he said, stressing this official distinction and implying that we were at least open to the light.

By now, I saw the light myself. There was to be a ball game that afternoon which I didn't want to miss, and when Van Dongen sent me into the corner to "think it over," with the hint that I'd probably stay after school again if I didn't mend my ways, I thought it over, fast. One thing was clear — there was no telling how long this would go on. I turned from the corner and raised my hand.

"All right, Mr. Van Dongen," I said. "I did it." And I hunched my shoulders, ready for the blow I expected.

Seconds passed, but I got no whack on the head. I opened my eyes and looked up cautiously. I was not prepared for what I saw. Van Dongen's face shone with an almost beatific joy.

"Good boy." He came over and laid a hand tenderly on my shoulder. "And what else do you have to say?"

"That I'm a wretched sinner," I said, "prone to all manner of evil, and not worthy of the least of any blessings."

"Books away, geography lesson aside," he said to the class. "We will have a party."

"A *party*?" I said.

"There is more joy in Heaven over the return of one sheep who has gone astray than over the ninety-and-nine who are safe in the fold. Hymnbooks open. Number thirty-two."

Number thirty-two, into which everybody swung lustily, went like this:

Good Boy

There were ninety-and-nine that safely lay
In the shelter of the fold;
But one was out in the hills away,
Far off from the gates of gold.

I stood before the class blushing modestly. After the hymn, Van Dongen gave one of the kids fifty cents and sent him to the corner store for some maple chews. When the class was dismissed for recess, Van Dongen called me to the front of the room, squeezed my arm happily, and gave me an apple he had on his desk. "Remember we're all miserable sinners," he said. "Full of perversity and deceit. Don't ever forget it."

"I won't," I said, going out the door with my mouth full of apple.

After that, things went along smoothly in sixth grade for some weeks. Then, one afternoon, the history lesson was interrupted by the muffled ringing of an old alarm clock hidden in one of the drawers of Van Dongen's desk. Who had put it there, I didn't know.

"Who did this?" he asked, setting the clock on his desk. "Who did this?"

There was a dead silence.

"Very well, we will *all* stay after school." This was a familiar enough technique, and one with a sound theological underpinning. Van Dongen explained that just as we all have sinned through Adam, who was our "federal head" at the dawn of history, so the entire class had sinned through a single miscreant, and we must all stay until the culprit confessed. *If* he wanted to be that honest, Van Dongen added, looking around the room. I thought his eye, as he went from pupil to pupil, rested hopefully, for just a second, on me. The deep silence continued.

I remembered the fruits of repentance — the apple and the

adulation and the maple chews — and my hand went up. "I did it," I said.

"Good boy!"

He came down the aisle and laid a hand on my shoulder.

"Why do you do these things?" he asked, like one putting a catechism question.

"Because I'm wicked to the core," I said.

"Good stuff."

The hymnbooks were brought out and we had another ninety-and-nine party, as I later came to think of them. The candy I had hoped for didn't materialize this time, but the radiance of Van Dongen's satisfaction almost made up for that. There was no doubt that I was in with him solid.

All through sixth grade I kept confessing things. This may seem to have been a peculiar way of getting into a teacher's graces, but only to someone who hasn't had sufficient experience with Total Depravity to appreciate the relish with which this doctrine can be embraced. I suppose that, as the incarnation of a cherished belief, I afforded Van Dongen his greatest emotional luxury, that of contemplating the corruption of man. He waved cheerily at me on the street, gave me rides in his car, and tossed me an occasional apple or orange.

Red Schaaf, the lout who had been responsible for most of the misdemeanors to which I had confessed, had probably imagined at first that he was pretty clever to be getting away with it, but eventually he caught on to the fact that there was a percentage in being the one who was out in the hills away, and he decided to move in on the racket himself.

Van Dongen entered the classroom one morning and was drenched by a bucket of water rigged up over the transom. Red's hand went up.

"I did it," he said.

Abstract iniquity, mendacity, mischief directed at no one

in particular but only issuing amorphously from the perversity of the human heart — these were one thing; a dignified Dutch schoolmaster standing drenched and ridiculous before a room full of snickering children was quite another. There was no joy in the Kingdom of Heaven this time. Red Schaaf got a belt behind the ear, and instead of having a ninety-and-nine party thrown for him, he was barred from the one scheduled for Lincoln's Birthday the next afternoon, and given a good shellacking with a ruler into the bargain. His slow brain couldn't handle the nuances of the thing at all. He just knew that somehow, somewhere along the line, he'd got cheated out of something, and he laid for me in an alley I passed on my way home from school and beat the daylights out of me.

After that, he felt better, and so, as a matter of fact, did I. I had occasionally been troubled about the lies I was telling, even though I had been forced into them in the first place. So when Red Schaaf beat me up, I felt as though I had got what was coming to me, and that the books Up There were now, so to speak, balanced. Then, one day toward the end of the school year, Van Dongen had occasion to explain to us the meaning of "pseudo," and that night I closed the matter forever. Kneeling beside my bed before going to sleep, I prayed, "Lord, have mercy on me, a pseudo-sinner."

TULIP

RECENT newspaper stories and photographs of the four-year-old ordained minister in Los Angeles take me back to the days of a child prodigy in our old neighborhood. I'm not familiar with what happens generally to children who fall into the hands of the Church rather than into its arms, and my picture of this boy on the Coast is necessarily limited to what I have read in the papers: that he conducts wedding ceremonies and preaches sermons of an interdenominational nature, occasionally over the phone to his contemporaries but usually, under the auspices of something called Oldtime Faith, to mass meetings presumably of adults. The bantling I knew didn't preach and he wasn't four; he was nine. In fact, not to lie about it, he was pushing ten when I knew him What distinguished him was a grasp of comparative religion (Dutch Calvinism as against everything else, it boiled down to) that put many of his elders in the shade and probably would this nipper in California, too.

To begin with, he would not have stood for anything interdenominational. He was a skilled hairsplitter, and that was good in our neighborhood. "One Dutchman, a Christian, two Dutchmen, a congregation, three Dutchmen, heresy" was the charge leveled at us by more Americanized people, who boasted, for instance, of belonging to denominations that hadn't had a schism in a hundred years. To these my father always tersely replied, "Rotten wood you can't split." Expert dialecticians who could put doubters on the right track were highly thought of there, and this boy did a lot of that. Not that he was particularly better grounded in doctrine than many adults, but his youth added a dramatic ingredient that often shamed people into a sense of the shortcomings of their catechism. One day he was sicked on me.

I don't remember exactly how old I was at the time, but I was past adolescence and interested in a girl. That was the rub. She was by secular standards perfectly "nice," but religiously "outside the pale," as the phrase went, and marriage to her might put me forever beyond the means of grace. Her very name, Barbara Gail, rang with a chilling dissonance among the Sadies, Jennies, and Gretas that I knew.

"Why not have a talk with Herman?" my father suggested, referring to the boy. (Straying into alien society was automatically taken as proof of weakened Faith.) I wasn't very agreeable but didn't put up much of a protest, so one Sunday afternoon Herman was invited to drop in and go over some of my doubts. We had coffee (it takes no great precocity to be drinking that among the Dutch at the age of ten), then my father excused himself and left the living room. I knew, however, that he was sitting in the kitchen, just around the corner of the open door, listening.

Herman set his cup aside, crossed his legs, and looked at me. He was a rather fat, overweening boy, dressed in knee pants. I didn't like him.

"How far have you gone with this girl?" he asked.

"If we're here to talk theology, let's talk it," I said. "Leave the girl out of it."

"She's a modern Congregationalist, isn't she? You know where they part company with us," Herman said.

"I know where they keep company with us, too," I said. "At the heart of religion, where all men are one in faith and charity."

There was a sharp scrape of a chair in the kitchen, and Herman shifted in his. "The danger is, you make one compromise, then another, then another, till you're 'unequally yoked together with unbelievers' — Second Corinthians six verse fourteen," he said. He continued to make light of my taste.

We argued in this vein for a while, till, cutting short as fallacious an analysis of mine of the relation between grace and works, Herman questioned my comprehension of the entire meaning of Calvinism. He doubted, next, whether I could enumerate its five basic tenets.

This angered me and I plunged in heatedly. "Total Depravity, Salvation by Grace —" I struck up, then paused, sure only of the first. The second was not an article of creed at all but merely a vague principle. I knew them as well as I did my own name, but I was stopped cold, unable to think of a single other one.

Herman turned his empty cup slowly in the saucer with his fingertips. "I hate to do this to you," he said, "but there's an easy way of remembering." And he cited an acrostic that is still in use among the Dutch Reformed as an aid in teaching the five canons of the Church as officially laid down by the Synod of Dort, in the seventeenth century. "Think of the word 'tulip,' our national flower. It spells out the first letters of the five doctrines· 'T' for Total Depravity — you were right there — 'U' for Unconditional Election, 'L' for Limited Atonement, 'I' for Irresistible Grace, and 'P'?" he put to me pedagogically. " 'P'?" he prompted. " 'P' for — ?"

"Pumpernickel bread," I said, having had enough.

"Perseverance of the Saints," he finished, and looked at me darkly.

Out of resentment, I lit a cigar. which I took from a nearby humidor, and offered Herman a stick of gum. "Thanks," he said, slipping it into his pocket. "I'll chew it later."

Looking at Herman as he sat in the chair, I remembered the last time I'd seen him — at the local department store, buying a new suit and getting a baseball bat with it, free. "You're not so much," I said in a low voice, so my father couldn't hear. "You just memorize all this stuff and reel it off, but you don't understand it. You're just a machine," I went on with growing spite. "None of this has anything to do with general intelligence anyhow. You're nothing but a monstrosity!"

That was in a voice loud enough to rouse my father.

"This will get us nowhere," he said, his face appearing around the edge of the kitchen door.

"Neither will this," I said, pointing at Herman.

I now launched out even more vehemently with my own belief that the meaning of religion lay not in doctrine but in the individual heart, on which basis I regarded myself as just as devout as they were, maybe more. I said that what the Church needed was new elements and fresh points of view, not reactionaries like this kid. "The whole thing will come down around your heads someday, mark my word," I said to the diehard boy.

My father came all the way into the room. He got us back on the original subject — what to do about the girl.

Herman walked the floor, frowning at the rug. "Why not send him off on a trip?" he proposed to my father. "Maybe a new environment, a change of scene, will help him forget her."

The tradition of packing stricken youths off on Atlantic voyages and cruises in the Caribbean was known and accepted by us, except that our destinations were tamer. For diversion, we mostly ran up to Holland, Michigan My father hit on this now. "You'll be just in time for the Tulip Festival!" he said. He was referring to the celebration that was, and still is, held annually in the spring by the residents of Holland, and that attracts numerous tourists in the Middle West. I packed my things and went, to get away from exegesis if not from Barbara Gail.

The weather was beautiful and I had a week in Holland. The Festival opened with a parade of townfolk dressed in Dutch costumes scrubbing the streets, which was our substitute for dancing in them. And the tulips! There were purple, orange, and crimson tulips, tulips in circles, ovals, and squares, tulips on lawns and bordering sidewalks and massed in riotous acres along the outskirts, tulips in hundreds and thousands and tens of thousands, reminding me of the fivefold immutable Truth, and of the depraved dogwood I had savored the year before with Barbara Gail.

The infatuation ran its course and I forgot "the daughter of the Philistines" without any help. Herman made a habit of dropping in at our house Sunday afternoons after church, but just by way of those coffee klatsches that are such an overpowering part of my memory. He would occasionally phone me in the informal way the child parson on the Coast is said to call his friends, ringing me up to see if I had hold of the Free Will–Election distinction, or to ask what I'd thought of some book he'd recommended.

The crisis in our household passed with my feeling for the girl, and the passion with which dogmas were debated dwindled in accordance. I had one last outburst one Sunday after a sermon on the subject of Supralapsarianism versus Infralapsarianism (the question whether, in Election, God did or did not also predestine the Fall of Man). "What is the sense of splitting these everlasting hairs, anyway?" I exclaimed. "Why can't we emphasize instead the central truth on which all Christians can unite?"

"Stop talking like a crackpot," my father said.

Of Herman I lost track many years ago. I have often wondered what became of him — where he is and what he's doing. He must be about thirty now, and in his dotage.

EVERY LEAVE THAT FALLS

THE OTHER NIGHT, leaving a party with a man who was in rather poor condition, I offered to see him home in a cab. It seemed like a simple enough thing to do, but what with all the cajolery, stumbling and scolding it took, and the indistinguishable replies he made to questions about where he lived and how to get there, it was a good hour before I finally delivered him to the doorman of his apartment house. I turned back into the street murmuring "Never again," and the vow struck a familiar chord. I had made the same resolution following an incident with a drunk almost fifteen years ago — an experience that should have taught me more of a lesson than, apparently, it did.

On Saturdays in the fall of 1938, I ran a taffy-apple route between Chicago and Geneva, Illinois, supplying storekeepers in a score or so of the interlying suburbs, and on two of the other days of the week serviced fifty candy-vending machines in the same general region. It was a line of work I had gone into during the depression and, finding it profitable, had continued with afterward, in order to have time for other, less remunerative projects. I had an old Chevrolet that was adequate for carrying the candy but not the taffy apples, since the apples were packed in bulky cartons and I couldn't cram in enough of them to satisfy the demand. My father helped me out, finally, by letting me use his Packard on Saturdays. I could get a third again as many apples into it, because, in addition to being larger than the Chevrolet, it was one of the models from which you could remove the whole rear seat, leaving the space between the back of the front seat and the door of the luggage compartment empty, thus converting the sedan into a kind of small truck. The only stipulation my father made was that I have the Packard home before the stroke of midnight each Saturday, since he had strong religious scruples against the commercial use of the car on Sunday.

I was making my way home one chilly Saturday night around ten o'clock when, at a turn in the road near Wheaton, my headlights picked out a dim shape in the roadside grass. I stopped, got out, and found a small man in a blue serge suit lying on his side, unconscious. Damned hit-and-run drivers! I thought indignantly, heaving him by the armpits to a sitting position. I began to worry him backward through the gravel toward my car, and he emitted a small moan. "There, there," I said. "Easy does it." He was beginning to come to, and with some help from him I finally got him into the car, propped him up on the front seat beside me, and took a closer look at him.

There was an ominous flexibility about his limbs, and I began exploring him gingerly for breaks when my hand encountered a large, round lump the shape and size of a bottle on one flank. Next an odor, imperceptible in the open air, reached my nostrils, and I began revising my inferences. Still, there was a cut over one eye, so I couldn't be sure that he hadn't really been struck by a car. Certainly something had to be done for him — or, anyhow, with him — and I looked around for a place from which to phone. There was a filling station about a hundred feet back, on the other side of the road, and I made for it, trotting carefully since my pockets were sagging with silver from the day's business.

The filling station's sole attendant was a heavy-set man of about forty, who stood with his hands in his coveralls pockets, looking out of the window and inhaling from a panatela that he kept in his mouth. He clipped his sentences rather as if *they* were cigars, dropping the first word of every one.

"Seems to be the trouble?" he asked, not taking his eyes from the window.

"I found a man lying beside the road," I said breathlessly.

"Happened to him?"

"Well, I don't know," I said. "He seems to have been drinking, but I think he was hit by a car."

"Far from the road is he?"

"I didn't leave him lying there," I replied. "I've got him in my car."

The man turned deliberately, taking the cigar out of his mouth, and his sentences became complete. "You should never go to work and move an accident victim," he said. "Say there are broken bones. People have died of being moved by amateurs. Don't ever, ever do that again."

"Well . . " I said, looking at the floor.

He regarded me a moment in silence, to let his words sink in. "Remember that," he said. Then he put the cigar back in his mouth. "Expect you better phone the Wheaton police," he said, nodding toward a phone booth.

I phoned them, and they told me to sit tight, they'd be right over. As I hung up and left the booth, I had a sudden notion that they mightn't be right over at all, and, glancing at an old overstuffed settee against one wall, I said to the attendant, "Look, it happens I'm in quite a hurry to get to the city Could I leave him in here?"

He took the cigar out of his mouth and turned to me slowly. "What, move him again?" he said. He put the cigar back, and I dropped the subject and stepped briskly toward the door. "Sake," he muttered, looking out the window. I buttoned my topcoat and opened the door. I hesitated a moment with my hand on the knob.

"I'm right over there," I said, pointing. "Will you tell the cops when they come?"

"K."

When I got back to the car, the drunk was sitting up inspecting the backs of his hands. "It must be late," he said. "I'm dirty."

I climbed in beside him and pulled the door shut.

"What happened?" I asked.

"Somebody must of hauled me in here," he said, looking around the interior. "This is nice."

I took out a clean handkerchief and began dabbing the cut over his eye, which had begun to trickle again "No, I mean did somebody hit you?" I asked.

He reflected a moment. "You damn right," he said vengefully, speaking in thick, flannelly tones. "And I'd like to get my hands on the son of a bitch."

"So would I," I said. "There, now. Easy."

He settled himself back, evidently reassured. "I'll get him tomorrow. Yellow bastard! No. Monday."

Having brushed away some of the dirt around his cut, which seeemd to be about the extent of his injuries, I made a bandage of my handkerchief, tying it around his head and knotting it firmly behind. "Say, you're all right," he said, looking at me gratefully with what focus he could command. "By God, they don't come any better." He became progressively more sentimental, finally reaching out a hand and starting to pat my face. "Cut it out," I said, drawing back.

We sat there, waiting. Suddenly, something I knew I had heard but hadn't perceived came fully into my consciousness. I looked at him out of the corner of my eye. "Who will you get Monday?" I asked.

"McCaffrey."

I rolled my window down and looked at the cars coming along the road, watching for the police. "That the guy who hit you?"

"Yeah," he said. "I'll get him at work. If he shows up."

From some mumblings that followed, I was able to piece together the events of the evening. He and McCaffrey, both of whom worked at a nearby factory, had drawn their pay and set out to hang one on at a tavern down the road, visible from the car as a streak of indecipherable neon. They had got into an argument, and McCaffrey had taken a poke at him and run — or, anyhow, had gone off and left him.

The drunk stirred, after a silence, and pulled the bottle out of his pocket It was a half pint of Old Oscar Pepper. "Open this," he said, handing it to me. I did and had a drink. Then he took the bottle, slid his palm across the mouth of it, and drank, letting the whiskey gurgle through the neck. "Ah!" he said gratefully, smacking his lips. He passed the bottle back to me, and since it had begun to turn cold, I was far from averse to another. We emptied the half pint, and then he tried to throw it out the window, but the window was closed, and the bottle slammed against the glass and clattered to the floor. "Whoops!" he said equably. "Missed it."

"Hey watch it!" I said, fumbling for the bottle, which I finally retrieved and threw across the road from my window. I glanced at the clock on the dashboard. Ten-twenty-five. I tapped my fingers on the steering wheel and kept watching for the squad car. The next thing I knew, the drunk was at the glove compartment, fumbling around inside it and spilling my taffy-apple records. I yanked his hands out, stuffed the records back in, and slammed the door. "Now, cut it out!" I said. "Or get the hell out of here!"

He turned toward me with a start He shifted in his seat and regarded me for several seconds, narrowly but with a reflective air. "You've changed," he said

The cops didn't come and they didn't come. When the drunk settled, mumbling, into the corner and showed signs of passing out again, I glanced at him and then, speculatively, at the ditch, and the thought of putting him back where I'd found him crossed my mind. I recalled a couple I knew who had tried to return an adopted baby after living with it for several months.

I didn't put the drunk out, however, and presently he began brushing dirt and wisps of grass and foliage from his clothes.

"Every leave that falls shows a Supreme Being," he said, picking a leaf from his sleeve and holding it up contemplatively by the stem. "You," he said, and when I didn't respond, he pulled my sleeve. "You."

"*I* know," I said irritably, watching down the road.

He sighed, and looked around. "Let's go somewhere else. This is no good."

I peeled the cellophane from a fresh pack of cigarettes.

"We're waiting for someone," I said.

"Who?"

I wadded up the cellophane and dropped it out the window. "You'll see," I said.

I had no more than lit my cigarette when the cops arrived, scrunching to a stop behind us. I got out quickly. There were two of them — a tall, rangy, dark one, and a short, roundish towhead with horn-rimmed glasses. Apparently they were both new and were bent on going into the situation with a maximum of conscientious thoroughness.

"Now, where was he when you seen him?" the short one began, after looking briefly in at the drunk, who was muttering about seasonal cycles and design in nature. I pointed out the spot.

Meanwhile, the other cop had poked his head into the rear of the car. "What happened to your back seat?" he called. I explained, and they exchanged skeptical frowns. Openly leery of the idea that anybody would be peddling taffy apples in a Packard, they questioned me further, and I wondered whether they were thinking of the same thing I was — a recent story in the papers about a gangster who had thrown the back seat of his car into the path of a pursuing motorcycle cop, overturning him and nearly doing him in. The fistfuls of money in my pocket, which I offered in evidence, seemed only to make them more suspicious. "Let's see your driver's license," the short one said.

"Sure!" I said. I reached confidently toward the glove compartment, but my movement died in mid-air. "It's in my other car," I said.

The short one nodded sardonically and continued, "Well, then, how about the title to this automobile?"

"That I've got," I said, searching briefly in the disheveled interior of the glove compartment and producing my father's state registration. As they examined it the thought crossed my mind that perhaps, after all, I was lucky to be without my driver's license, since my father's first name wasn't the same as mine. The short cop was studying me through his thick-rimmed glasses.

"How long have you been in this line of work?" he asked. "Taffy apples."

"Seven years," I said. "Now, why don't you take this man and let me go?"

They said that if the drunk was really injured, I'd be detained for questioning in any case, and that therefore I might as well take it easy. So I told them the drunk hadn't been struck by a car at all, that he was just drunk, and they asked me sharply why I was changing the story I'd given over the phone. At that point, the drunk started muttering about what a bastard I'd turned out to be. The cops circled suspiciously around to the front of the car, where they began to examine my fenders and bumper closely, looking, as I gathered from their murmured exchanges, for bloodstains. They came back.

"Did you hit this man?" the tall one asked me abruptly.

I turned and gave the drunk a look. "Not yet," I said.

"Oh, a wise guy," the cop said.

"Now, look," I said, "I want to get the hell out of here and home. I've got to be home by twelve o'clock."

"What for?" the tall one asked.

I threw my cigarette into the ditch. "For religious reasons."

"Let's smell your breath," he said. But what he meant was that he had smelled it already, and presently we were all on our way to the station.

The tall cop drove the police car, taking the drunk with him, and the short one drove mine, ordering me into the back, where, of course, I sat on the floor. "We have to be strict with traffic violations," he called. "We're making a drive on altogether too many accidents." I squatted in the cavernous rear, preparing my defense — not so much for the police as for my father. The cops, since they were certain to phone my home to check on the car ownership, were likely to corroborate my story of the delay, but not in a way that would be found palatable at the other end: driving while under the influence of liquor, suspicion of running down a pedestrian, and operating a vehicle without a license were sure to be mentioned.

Even so, I decided to tell the truth about the car ownership. This involved still *another* shift in my story, but it was with at least a show of open-mindedness that, when we reached the station, the desk sergeant put a call through to my father.

"Do you own a Packard?" the sergeant asked. "Do you have a son driving it around here with taffy apples?" He got what seemed to be a satisfactory answer. "Well, we're having a little trouble with him here," he said, and reeled off the charges I had anticipated. A crackling response, audible all over the room, came through the earpiece.

"Damn it, you're getting him all upset," I said. "Let me talk to him." He handed me the receiver and I explained the complications, as much in my favor as I could, and then hung up and turned back to the cops. They fined me fifteen dollars for operating a motor vehicle without a license and let me go.

61

I sped toward the city in a driving sleet, perfecting my rejoinders all the biblical quotations I could think of that embodied a flexible view of the Sabbath. I got the car into the garage at twenty minutes to one, and found my father sitting in the kitchen waiting for me when I stepped into the house.

"It's Sunday," he said, glancing at the clock.

" 'What man shall there be among you that shall have one sheep, and if it fall into the pit on the Sabbath day, will he not lay hold on it and lift it out?' " I began, wasting no time. " 'How much is a man better than a sheep?' "

" 'Abstain not only from evil, but from the appearance of evil,' " he replied, scrutinizing me.

" 'The Sabbath was made for man, and not man for the Sabbath,' " I said.

" 'Wine is a mocker, strong drink is raging,' " said my father, still examining me narrowly.

I thought for a while. " 'Drink no longer water, but use a little wine for thy stomach's sake and thine often infirmities,' " I said at last. "It was cold out there. That's what you get for trying to play Good Samaritan. I only had a *slokje*," I added, using the Dutch word, which I thought would be less jarring to my father than "snifter."

"I hope you've learned your lesson," my father said.

"I certainly have," I said. And I had. The very next Saturday, a woman flagged me and pointed at a flat tire with which she was stalled beside the road, and I shot past her without a second thought.

COMPULSION

"The things my wife buys at auctions are keeping us ba-roque," I said There was a perceptible movement of cocktail guests away from me, and a round of resentful murmurs varying according to the amount of my talk each person had, in the past hour, been within earshot of. I had in that period stated to a small group discussing modern tonality that not since Debussy had dissonance, in my opinion, lent enchant-ment; asked a woman who was planning to winter in Tijuana, "Tijuana go there for the climate or just to gamble?"; and dilated on music in the heir as potential compositional talent in one's offspring.

The guests were a cross-section (by now, I might add, a *very* cross section) of Westport town life. Psychiatry was represented by a sprucely tweeded man in his fifties named Granberry, who looped an arm through mine, drew me aside, and said, "I think I can help you."

"Help me?" I said, plucking a canapé from a passing tray.

"It's obviously a compulsion with you," Granberry went on. "You know what compulsions are. Hand washing, crack avoiding, counting —"

"I know what compulsions are," I said, and went on to note that an acquaintance of mine at this very party couldn't eat salmon caviar because of a need to tally the roe as they ex-ploded against the roof of his mouth.

"All right," Granberry said. "Your trouble is, you can't pass a word up. You're a compulsive punner. Your mutilating conversation springs from whatever subterranean conflict hinders you from participating in it maturely."

"Don't you fellows ever have a fear you're not being followed?" I said.

Granberry's manner became arch. "Mind telling me your earliest recollection?" he asked, with a small, pursed smile that gave him rather the look of a winsome weasel.

"Not in the least," I said. "It's about an alarm clock I had in my bedroom when I was a kid. A clock I always think of as the potato clock."

"Potato clock?" Granberry repeated, with a puzzled frown. "Why potato clock?"

"Because I had to get up potato clock every morning."

"You're a sick man," Granberry said, "or you're pulling my leg with an old vaudeville joke." He pursued the more succulent of the alternatives. "There is something we call *Klang* associations It's a sort of chain punning, and is characteristic of certain encysted types. Your pattern is a complex and refined variation of these word salads."

"It is also," I answered coolly, "if I am not mistaken, the method by which James Joyce constructed *Finnegans Wake*."

I turned and walked off.

For some days, however, I was unable to get Granberry's impromptu observations out of my mind. I sedulously derided his phrase "mutilating conversation" in talking the encounter over with my wife, aware that I was doing so because that quill had gone home. One aspect, in particular, of my habit tended to bear Granberry out — the fact that these rejoinders of mine did not arise principally out of a wish to play the wag, and not infrequently fell as drearily on my own ears as on those of my hearers. Perhaps I was indeed driven by some subcutaneous need to sabotage dialogue. Since Granberry had put his finger on that much, why not, I thought, let him try to uncover the cause of my compulsion, which was really so much sand in the gears of my social relations and repeatedly cost me my wife's good graces? So I took up the genial challenge, "Come see me sometime," which Granberry had flung over his shoulder — or, rather, over mine — as I walked away from him, and made an appointment for the first of what was to be a series of interviews, in his midtown office.

Granberry's headway with me may be inferred from the way matters stood at the end of one month. As my fourth weekly consultation drew to its close, he leaned across his desk and asked, "Do you feel, now, that you're acquiring a better grasp of your symptoms?"

"Symptoms I do," I answered, "and then again, symptoms I don't."

"*Don't be discouraged,*" Granberry said, with a smile that tendered me every good wish "*I'm* not."

Granberry remained, throughout the proceedings, the soul of patient industry, never doubting that we were burrowing steadily toward the root of my *volonté.* His confidence buoyed me. Then, suddenly, my responses became completely phonetic. When, in some illustrative reference of Granberry's to his own formative years, he mentioned that he was born in Oklahoma, I threw out "Oklahoma tell your mother she wants you."

I wet my lips nervously and slid up in my chair. "Good God," I said, "I was never *that* bad before. What's happened? Now I even dream in puns. Like last night I dreamed of a female deer chasing a male deer in the mating season."

"?"

"A doe trying to make a fast buck."

"!"

I was vexed to see Granberry, while I was visualizing ostracism from all but the most undiscriminating circles, rise and rub his hands.

"We're muddling the disease, so to speak — the way medication sometimes stirs up an infection before it can get to correcting it," he said. "Your white count, as it were, is way up."

"Well, let's get it down," I said.

But up it stayed. I now not only refrained from mingling in society — I didn't dare leave the house (except, of course, to visit Granberry). During this period, only my wife knew that I was "worse." I wouldn't care to give any detailed evidence of my white count other than the above ramshackle instances. Granberry, on the other hand, had never been so optimistic, he said that nothing proved so much as the intensification of my condition how close we were to uncovering the traumatic incident that undoubtedly lay at the heart of it. But weeks went by and still no traumatic incident.

So finally, resentful of Granberry and the pass to which he had brought me, I made up a traumatic incident that I felt would, preparatory to my bailing out on the whole business, caricature both him and the calling he professed.

I sprang it on him midway of an interview.

"Say," I said, pausing in a train of reflections on my early school days, "I just remembered something. Something that comes back to me now, after all these years."

"What's that?" Granberry said alertly

"I was in fifth or sixth grade," I said. "We were being asked to use words in a sentence. When it came my turn, the teacher gave me the word 'ominous' 'Let's hear you use "ominous" in a sentence,' she said. I got up and stood in the aisle." I hesitated in my narrative, as though the strain of resurrection were a taxing one.

"Go on," Granberry said.

"I groped desperately for a way to use the word assigned me," I resumed. "As I did so, I heard the kid in the seat behind me — a kid who was always razzing me in the schoolyard — I heard him whisper something to somebody and snicker. Burning with anger, I turned and said, 'If he doesn't shut his mouth, ominous sock him one!' "

Granberry set down a letter knife he had been bending back and forth in his hands. He coughed into his fist and rose.

"It's impossible, you see, to cheat," he said. "I mean a hoax is just as significant as a bona fide memory. More so, in what it reveals of you, because it's an act of *conscious* selection, whereas memory is an *un*conscious one."

Embarrassed for me, he walked to the window and tugged at the cord of a Venetian blind. "I can never seem to adjust this thing," he said. "Why, I have no choice but to take your little charade at face value. And I think that what it constitutes is nothing less than an X-ray of your personality."

The thought seemed to steep him momentarily in a gloom as great as my own; Granberry, that is, had the same sense as I of being stuck with this very corny case history.

"Couldn't it be part of the white count?" I asked, trying to renege.

Granberry shook his head. "It would still be just as revelatory," he said.

Returning to the chair behind his desk, he plunged into an interpretation of the data I had given him.

"It confirms and crystallizes what I have felt about you all along," he said "You are fundamentally afraid of people. I said from the start, this habit of yours was a way of mutilating conversation, and now we know why you mutilate it. You do so in order to escape the risks of engaging in it on an adult level, because you're afraid you won't stand up to the test of social comparisons it constitutes. Everybody you meet is that boy in the schoolyard — oh, I don't doubt that there *was* one, or many — and you ought to recognize that, in trying to grasp why you deflate people." He paused, then went astringently but sympathetically on. "Freud has explained that humor is a denial of anxiety, so you must understand that these puns of yours arise from one of the most intense forms of belligerence — the belligerence of the insecure."

He let this sink in a moment. "Let that do for today," he concluded. "Think over what I've said, and we'll talk about it some more next time."

There weren't many more next times. At first I was piqued, but soon I came to feel that Granberry was probably right. With this new insight into myself, I determined to control my tendency, and, slowly, I succeeded. Success came somewhat faster once Granberry had stressed this important point. "Always bear in mind that the other fellow is just as afraid of you as you are of him."

At length, my habit cleared up. When, for example, some friends of my wife's and mine named Pritchett phoned to invite us to come listen to a record they had just acquired, adding that it was "the new long-playing *Godunov*," I did not reply, as once I might have, "That's Godunov for me." Nor, when a dinner companion exclaimed that she had glimpsed three wedges of southbound geese over her rooftop in one day, did I succumb to the temptation to murmur, "Migratious!"

Granberry dismissed me as arrested. "I think it'll stick," he said. "Your adjustment should last indefinitely. Unless, of course, you have some experience sufficiently unsettling to jar loose your old resentment and antagonism. But I think that unlikely. I can't imagine what it could be."

Nor could I. Matters seemed to have been resolved.

Then, one Saturday morning a month or so after Granberry and I had shaken hands and bade one another farewell, I was drinking midmorning coffee at home with my wife when I saw the mailman drive up.

"I'll get it," I said, and rose and went out to the mailbox.

There were three pieces of mail — one, I saw by the return

address on the envelope, from Granberry's office. I had not opened it by the time I rejoined my wife.

"This is from Granberry," I said, giving her the two others, which were addressed to her. "Probably his bill."

"Well, whatever it is, it's worth it," she said, abstractedly perusing the other things. "There's nothing whatever left of that awful habit of yours. Not one iota."

I opened the envelope and peered inside. I uttered a cry of genuine shock.

"How do you like that!" I exclaimed. "Fifteen calls and iota bandit seven hundred and fifty dollars!"

SCENE

SHE OPENED the closet door to hang up her coat. "That was a good picture," she said, and it struck her that that was the first thing either of them had said since they left the theatre. She heard no answer and, looking into the living room, saw that he had sat down there and lit a cigarette. "Didn't you think?"

He murmured agreement, dropping his ashes into the ashtray from a height, with an abstracted air.

She yawned. "Well, what do you say we hit the hay?"

He took a puff of his cigarette and blew the smoke thoughtfully at the glowing end. "Have you ever noticed anything funny about our marriage?"

She came to the doorway. "What do you mean, funny?"

"Well, we never seem to talk about it, or go into the thing," he said. "We never analyze it. I don't know."

"Analyze what? Because I'm tired."

"Why, what we mean to each other," he said, crossing his

69

legs. "You know very well what I mean. The way Tracy and Hepburn did in that bar tonight. The way Powell and Loretta Young did in the resort cottage last week. The way everybody does." He reached for the bourbon which she now saw he had poured himself and took a swallow. "Going into the whole thing, to work things out and see what they've got and what they want from each other. But we go along from day to day — twenty-two years now — and never once try to figure out what we've got, how it's working out, and what we're heading for."

"But what is there to head for?"

"We've never, from the very beginning, analyzed ours. As though," he concluded, looking at his glass as he held it out at arm's length, "there's nothing *to* analyze."

She came in. "Well, if you want," she said, and glanced at her wristwatch. "We can analyze it a while." She sat down. "What would you like to go into?"

"Oh, well, you know what I mean," he said, uncrossing his legs and putting his feet on the ottoman. He punched out his cigarette and immediately lit another.

"They analyze it because they run into complications," she said.

"And why do they run into complications? Because the thing is alive It's a *love affair*. You get trouble when there's two people vibrating on each other, is when you get trouble. You can't have a crisis where nothing's going on. All right. They have a misunderstanding. Then they separate, and finally come together again with a richer, deeper understanding. Right?"

"Yes." She nodded slowly. "That seems to be the way it usually goes."

"But we never argue about any part of it, or even have a quarrel, let alone a misunderstanding you could get anything

70

out of. Maybe," he said, looking through the doorway into the dark vestibule, "we were never meant for each other."

They were silent, and she stared soberly at her lap for some time. Then she looked up hopefully. "Maybe we're analyzing it now."

He shook his head. "I doubt it," he said, getting up, "but we might start any minute."

She watched him walk around the room a few moments, then asked, "How long have you been thinking along this line?"

"It started when Spencer Tracy took the swizzle stick out of Hepburn's hand and said, 'Just what is it you want of me, how do I fit into your life?' and she answered, 'Why, I don't know.'" He looked at her sharply. "Supposing I was to ask you that — what would you say?"

"Why, I don't know," she said. "I never gave it any thought."

"That," he said ominously, "is what Hepburn said, sending Tracy back to the Pacific Northwest to think things through."

She thought about this "Well, what do you want me to say?"

He walked to the window, and as he stood there with his back turned, there was something familiar in his stance, something she had seen a thousand times, though not precisely on the premises. "I don't know," he said, looking out. "I don't know what we know or what we want to know. I don't know whether you've ever been married to the real me, or whether I've been married to the real you, and neither do you. Twenty-two years and nobody knows who's been married to who." He gave a soft, bitter laugh.

"Are we doing it now? Is this what you mean?" she asked hopefully.

"Twenty-two years of taking everything for granted."

"How else is there to take it?"

He turned around abruptly. "Just what do you want out of marriage?"

"Want? Well, I never gave it a thought. What is there to want? I want a home, I guess, a husband —"

"What do you want a husband *for?* What do I mean to you? *What* am I? *Who* am I? Have you got the slightest idea?"

"Can't we talk about this in the morning? I'm perfectly willing to analyze our —"

"You think of me as a pretty simple person, don't you? But after twenty-two years of taking everything for granted, have you ever asked yourself whether I'm finding myself in this whole thing?"

"How do you mean, finding yourself?"

He looked down at her. "That," he said, "is what Joan Bennett said in the small hotel, and by evening Raft was on the train on his way back to the other woman." He regarded her a moment. "How do you know," he said, his eyes narrowing, "I'm not complicated?"

"Well, I never gave it a thought. I just go on from one day to the next trying to make a home, be a decent wife, cooking your meals, ironing your —"

"Tchah!" He emptied the glass, and then turned it slowly in his fingers. "Never wondering, never questioning, never asking what is this thing all about and where will it lead." He walked to the table, and, pouring out some more bourbon, turned to glance at her. "Have you got any idea what I'm talking about?"

"Well, sure, I guess so. But I keep thinking maybe we're not the type who —"

"Maybe what we've got is perfect — in everybody's opinion — smooth and even, because it's dead." He ran his eyes skeptically over the furniture. "Maybe what we've got," he said, "is a glass grape." He fired a jet of soda into his tumbler from the Seltzer bottle he had recently bought.

"How can we find out?"

He sat down again. "I'm glad we started this. It'll prove to have been a good thing. Brings it all out in the open, clears the air." He studied his glass a moment. "The whole thing will, of course, be straightened out when I come back."

"Are you going away?"

"What else is there to do? I've got to go away and think things through."

"Where would you go?"

"I think Albuquerque. It's all desert around there."

"Why Albuquerque? It's way in New Mexico and would be pretty expensive. I don't know whether we can afford to do it on that scale."

"Albuquerque is far away and nobody knows me there."

"There's plenty places closer by where nobody knows you," she said. "Look, why don't you run up to Poughkeepsie for a few days? You could stay at the Nelson House, where we stopped on our way to Hank and Betty's and that you liked so much. Remember? I'd like to go along, but I suppose that would throw the whole thing off."

He got out of the chair. "Poughkeepsie! Sometimes I don't know whether you're trying to make a fool of yourself or me, or whether you know what I'm talking about half the time. Who would ever go to Poughkeepsie to think things through? It would be ridiculous. People would laugh in your face if it ever got around. It would all fall down in a heap."

"Why?"

"Because there's nothing *to* going to Poughkeepsie. It has no body."

"Well, when would you leave?"

"Couple days. I've got three weeks' vacation piled up that I can take whenever I want now."

73

They were both silent, thinking it over. Then she said, "I read somewhere that separate vacations sometimes can be a very good thing." Before he could speak, or the exasperation even appear on his face, she went on, "How long will it take you, do you figure — the whole three weeks?"

He shrugged. "You can see things in a new perspective, sometimes, in no time at all. But I'll probably stay the whole three weeks"

She got up, tugging her skirt into place. "That's settled, then. I'll run down to my sister's and stay with her She needs some help now with the new baby and all, so it works out fine. Of course, I'll say you're going for your sinus. We've never had anybody go away to think things through in our family, that I know of, and I wouldn't want it to get around. You hear?"

"O.K., O.K."

She yawned. "So I think I'll hit the hay. You coming?"

"I'm going to sit here awhile."

"Well, don't stay up too long. It's late."

He listened to her footsteps go along the hall and the bedroom door close. He settled down in the chair, holding the drink between his hands and swirling it slowly as he gazed into the glass.

A CRYING NEED

SOME YEARS AGO, in Chicago, I worked on a community newspaper for which, among other things, I reviewed movies. The editor, a mass of muscle named Braunschweiger, told me to be casual — relaxed about the whole thing — but I was young then and brought to my task an armament of intellectual and aesthetic principles that brooked no compromise. I gave no quarter to the second-rate, the obvious, or the mawkish. It was the last-mentioned that oftenest drew my fire, because the six or seven months of my tenure on the semiweekly *Clarion* coincided with a period when a series of particularly sentimental entertainments were issuing from Hollywood. The first one I inspected in the line of duty concerned an orphan girl who was both overworked and maltreated by her foster parents, and it overlooked none of the time-honored devices for putting audiences through the wringer. "The briniest bit of fiddle-faddle to come along in years," I wrote, my eyes still moist from the experience.

I had taken a girl to see it with me, and when she read my review, she said, "But Marvin, I thought you liked it."

"Liked it," I said. "That piece of tear gas?"

"It seemed to me I heard you sniffle a time or two."

"That's what I mean. It was mawkish."

The next important release was a version of *Little Women* starring Katharine Hepburn, to an afternoon performance of which my friend, a spirited brunette named Thelma, also accompanied me. (I covered pictures only in their neighborhood runs, so gala Chicago Loop premieres were not among the perquisites of my job, which paid thirty-five bucks a week.) One knew what to expect here, all right, and it was early in the film that the handkerchiefs began to come out and the hysteriasts to tune up. The death of Beth came along in due order. Gazing from her pillow at the sunlit window sill, she smiled wistfully and murmured, "My bluebird came again."

A sob racked my frame as tears welled to my eyes and down my cheeks. I was aware that Thelma was watching me more closely than she did the action. The movie ended in keeping with the book, with Jo becoming engaged to Professor Bhaer under the umbrella. He had nothing to give, he cried, "but a full heart and these empty hands," and Jo, slipping her own into his, answered, "Not empty now."

As we stumbled up the aisle toward the street, I told Thelma that I had to write my review immediately, because the printer was waiting for the copy, and I suggested that if she came with me to the office, I would make it snappy, and then we could go out for a bite of dinner. She agreed, and we climbed into a cab.

At the office, she sat in a club chair, paging through magazines and smoking cigarettes while I hammered out my notice. When I had finished and was about to stuff it into an envelope for the office boy to take to the printer's, she said, "Could I see that, I wonder?"

I said, "Certainly," and handed it to her.

It ran in part: "Well, the old chromo is back again, and it can be imagined that Hollywood has missed few of the plenteous opportunities it offers for bringing in the gusher. Katharine Hepburn makes a fetching Jo, and the rest of the cast are properly charming, but it remains, for the most part, the maudlin affair it always was, and the wary are hereby warned that, rather than plunk down their six bits at the neighborhood wicket, they can get the same effect by staying home and peeling an onion."

Thelma rose and dropped the copy on my desk.

"But you sat there and *bawled*," she said.

"So? I said it was maudlin, didn't I? What's that got to do with it? I sometimes wonder what ails you."

"But —" she spluttered, and then gave up. "I just don't understand you, Marvin."

I hung a cigarette in my mouth and thoughtfully set fire to it. "If you mean my intellectual approach to things and all, I can't help that," I said. "It's the way I am. I suppose we might as well face up to the fact that we're not very compatible, if that's what you're hinting at."

76

I was giving her the air before she could give it to me, as I had clearly sensed she was about to do, or was debating doing. I never dated her again. Instead, I took up with a pink-skinned blond girl I had recently met in the office — the boss's niece.

With Beverly Braunschweiger it was just the other way around from what it had been with Thelma. She had read my criticisms *first*, and been dying to meet me, though at the same time afraid to, because I was such a brain. I analyzed everything with such glacial detachment that she hardly dared to open her mouth for fear of saying something that I would secretly laugh at. "You've got such a keen mind a person never knows where they're at," she told me early in the course of our first dinner together. "You could be too clever for your own good, you know. Your stuff is brilliant — Do you mind my criticizing you this way, Marvin?"

"No, not at all," I said, buttering a roll "Go right ahead."

"It's terrific, sure, but I wonder if life can always be lived on that plane." She shook back her gold hair with a slim hand, and gazed thoughtfully into her plate. "I mean I just wonder."

Our first diversion together was a hillbilly musical so horrible as to be incapable of breeding divergent opinions between any two people above the level of those it depicted. We walked out when it was half over. Our next date was a garden party, in the process of which some romantic progress was made. Then, two weeks later, I took her to a film entitled *Broken Melody*. This concerned a violinist-composer whom a tragic experience had crushed both creatively and personally. He went to the dogs. The obligatory scene showed him slumped over a table in a waterfront bar, into which walked the woman who had never lost faith in him, carrying his instrument, which she had salvaged from a hock shop. "I dare you to look at this," she said as he dazedly raised his head. She got him cleaned up and back to work at an interrupted concerto, at the premiere of which, acknowledging a thunderous ovation in Carnegie Hall, the artist said, "Ladies and gentlemen, I want you to meet the real composer of my concerto," and drew from the wings his tremulous girl, who stood hand in hand with him as the audience rose to their feet against a burst of climactic background music. Beverly and I sat shoulder to shoulder, sharing a handkerchief, our tears pattering like rain into a common bag of popcorn.

"Sentimental slop," "pure hokum," and "more treacle than Hollywood has ever extruded from this tired old theme" were among the strictures composing my savage review.

Two afternoons later, Beverly called me on the phone. "I'm absolutely flabbergasted, Marvin," she said. "I've just read your review. I thought you enjoyed the movie as much as I did. That you thought it was good, and had heart."

"Please," I said, wincing. "At least spare me that."

"But I simply don't understand you. A person sits there blubbering, and then —"

"Oh, good God!" I groaned. "Must we go through that again?"

"What do you mean, 'again'?"

"Nothing. I was just talking to myself. Look, I'll call you next week."

I was in no mood to be patient, or even civil, having just been called on the carpet by Braunschweiger himself over the very same subject.

It seemed there had been a flood of letters from readers protesting the austerity of my notices, and he was taking them seriously. "Cerebral block of ice," "sophisticated snob," and "If he doesn't like movies, why does he go to them?" were among the snatches I caught in the samples Braunschweiger showed me. I put up a brisk defense, knowing damn well my job was at stake. "There's a crying need for critical standards," I said, "in the movies as well as in other art forms. If we can't maintain some kind of criteria, and do so honestly and vigorously, then what's the good of noticing anything at all?"

He said he saw my point of view but that my smart-aleck tone of knocking everything had crept into all my coverage — whether of church suppers, political rallies, or exhibitions of water colors by the wives of advertisers real or potential — and that while he liked me personally and appreciated my integrity, it was increasingly apparent that I was unsuited to a newspaper serving a community of homes. He must, regrettably, let me go.

It turned out to be a good thing, actually. I got a job in the office of a textbook publisher, where, for the first time in my life, I earned enough to get married on — a wish very much inspired by the next girl I met. Before I knew what had happened, I was marching down the aisle to faintly throbbing organ music, in a small chapel, by candlelight.

I held myself in rigidly as the reading of the form began. Presently, there was a rustle in one of the pews behind us, and the sound of a sob stifled in a handkerchief. I set my teeth. Visual details — the chancel banked with flowers, the stained-glass window, the clergyman's powdered jowls — all swam in a Post-Impressionist blur. "I now pronounce you man and wife," the minister said, and as my hand groped to my breast pocket, I was dimly aware of my bride appraising me with some surprise.

Our first dispute occurred a few months after we had settled down in our tiny apartment, over the subject of the marriage bond itself. I had analyzed sex as a biochemical urge on which a tribal curb is required. I had pointed out that

Romantic Love is a more or less semantic concoction guaranteeing woman's deification through a period of delay known as courtship — an exquisite frustration to resolve which a man commits himself to an institution vital to the security of her young.

My wife slammed down some knitting on which she was engaged, and stalked out of the room.

"Now what?" I asked, following her into the bedroom. "Must you fly off the handle just because I say marriages aren't made in Heaven? Are we to live forever on honey?"

"Oh, you intellectuals!" she exclaimed, tweaking her nose with a handkerchief plucked from a bureau drawer, which she now banged shut with an elbow. "Must everything be analyzed and dissected to a fare-thee-well? I'm sorry, but must it always be anthropology or psychology or whatever, for everything? It's all very well to have a mind like a steel trap, but is nothing safe from it? Not even — motherhood?"

"Darling, you mean —?" I said, stumbling toward her with eyes that saw not, a catch in my throat. "You mean this flat won't be big enough for all of us soon?" She nodded, and we melted into one another's arms, my shoulders heaving as I took her head to my breast.

We had a fine, bouncing boy. That was some years ago, and though it seems only yesterday that he was laughing in his shoofly and sticking cucumbers in the car exhaust, he is now a high-school student telling the old folks how much they are worth chemically.

"I will not have that kind of talk around this house," I told him one evening, following a remark of that nature inspired by the science homework over which he was bent at a living-room table. "Telling your mother she is worth ninety-eight cents in physical elements! You ought to be ashamed."

"I didn't tell her," he said. "I told you. I said —"

"It's the same thing. She probably overheard it in the kitchen, and by extension it includes her anyway. For myself I don't care, but I'll not have you speaking disrespectfully of the mother who bore you. She carried you under her heart once, do you know that? How much in chemical elements was she worth then — a dollar ninety-six, all told? Because she was metabolizing for two." I was tired and irritable after a long session with my insurance agent, with whom I had been hammering out a whole new life-insurance-and-annuity program, and I was trying to refresh myself with a glass of the dietetic soda pop the doctor had advised my switching to from after-dinner beer and highballs. "I don't hold with this detestable materialistic viewpoint. We're human beings with a soul, not animals reducible to elements you can put in a test tube, or a mass of reflexes that can be pinned down by psychological analysis. And next year let's don't start dishing out that anthropological malarkey about symbolically Killing the Old Man every time we get the car for tonight, Pop. Let's just taboo that one in advance, shall we? *Shall we?*"

"Why, yes, sir," he said, looking at me in surprise, and some alarm. "Of course. Please don't get upset like this, Popper. You know it isn't good for your —"

"All right, then." I took a swig of the soda and opened my evening paper. When I was breathing normally again, a few moments later, I said, "Besides, this intellectualizing everything, it finally leaves a person bored. Did you know that, young fellow-my-lad? Bored — to — tears."

IN DEFENSE OF SELF-PITY;
OR, PRELUDE TO LOWENBRÄU

IT SEEMS TO ME that we encounter increasing references
these days to self-pity. The term crops up everywhere — in
articles, editorials, books — and always with the same underlying assumption; namely, that it is something to be deplored.
That is taken for granted. Why? What's wrong with self-pity? I would like to say a few words in its defense, if I may.

Had it not been for a bit of self-commiseration now and
again, I would not be here to defend it, and neither, I suspect,
would some of its detractors be here to belittle it. A style of
tight-lipped endurance would long ago have split me down
the middle and sent me to the cleaner's, whereas an occasional
well-timed bout of sheer maudlin wallowing in melancholy
enables me to pull myself together, get back on my feet, and,
as the grand old wall motto has it, "Keep on keepin' on!"

I learned early that mystic solitude in which we all walk
(you, too, out there, you yacking extrovert) — can remember,
in fact, the exact moment when the truth broke upon me
like an apocalypse. It was the luminous hour of dusk, in the
dead of winter. I had gone as a boy of six to play with a new
neighborhood kid, at his house. He proved so obnoxious that
his mother, determined to punish him for his rudeness to a
guest by depriving him of something he valued, said, "You
don't *deserve* such a nice playmate as him," and sent me out
again into the cold. As I stood there on the blue snow,
looking in at the brat playing with his toys and munching
cookies in the warm, well-lighted parlor, what was there to
do in all God's world but feel sorry for myself? What other

emotion was there available to me — then, or some years later, when the following incident occurred?

The time was the great depression when, freshly armed with a college degree, I got a job in a Chicago lumberyard. Sometimes I worked outside stacking lumber, sometimes in the office at clerical tasks. There was another youth in the office, who prided himself on the facility with which he could "dig up a couple of quail." Once, he fixed me up with a blind date and then at the last minute backed out, leaving me to fend for myself with a girl I had never seen before, who lived on a street I had never heard of, in a quarter of town where I had never been. In view of all this, and because it was pouring rain, I decided to set out early, directly from the lumberyard. Having neither hat nor umbrella, I made a dash to the second-hand Hupmobile I then owned, wearing a typewriter hood As I stood with my head in the hood, unlocking the car door, I sensed that I was launched on one of those strings of mishaps that must simply run their course.

I was glad to see the rain stop, presently, for, after blundering about looking for the girl's street, which was called Emerald Avenue, I had to get out to ask directions of a group of men gathered beside the curb. When I approached them, I saw that they were gazing down sadly at a dog that had evidently been done in by a hit-and-run motorist. I couldn't very well ask them where Emerald Avenue was — it would have seemed too frivolous — so after standing in the circle with them for a while, looking down at the dog also, I got back in my car and drove off.

I found the girl's place at last, and soon was sorry that I had. She was a butterball in yellow wool, as round and about as high as the hassock on which she remained seated while she read aloud to me a poem she had just written. She was one of the many social-conscience poets spawned by the depression, and she expressed her scorn for tradition and her

love for the working classes by rhyming "duet" with "suet."
For a poem intended to be inflammatory, this one had re-
markable sedative properties, especially for a man who had
been stacking two-by-fours all day. However, I managed to
murmur a few words of praise, and then, in the manner of
more hedonistic types of that era, I patted the couch on
which I had contrived to dispose myself and said, "Lie down.
I want to talk to you"

Instead, we had to run out to Clearing, a remote western
section of the city, and pick up some petitions. They were
mimeographed manifestoes addressed to the Secretary of
Labor, demanding action of some sort or other on a current
industrial dispute. It was now raining cats and dogs again,
in addition to which we ran out of gas halfway to our destination. A quick investigation in the rain revealed a filling station a quarter of a mile ahead, at the foot of a long slope
fifty feet from the top of which we were stalled If we could
just push the car those fifty feet, we could coast the rest of
the way — or, rather, if *I* could, for someone had to steer.

So I got behind the Hupmobile in the pouring rain and
shoved, again wearing the typewriter hood for foul-weather
gear. Once or twice I lifted the front of it off my face to look
through the back window and make faces at the girl, sitting
there nice and dry behind the wheel. I was, of course, feeling
sorry for myself. Why not? What had any self-respecting
man recourse to under those circumstances but some solid,
honest solicitude for himself? It was precisely the self-pity
that enabled me to get through the evening at all. "You poor
boy," I said aloud, soaked to the skin and grunting sterto-
rously behind the inching Hupmobile as the rain fell in torrents on my cowl. "If she really loved the working classes,
she'd give you better proof of it on a night like this than
reading aloud that half-baked Auden and then making you
chase clear out to Clearing to get petitions from some sod

who probably hasn't done a lick of work in his life either."
And so on.

This line of thinking got me through not only that night
but that week. Because that was the week I lost my job, had
the Hupmobile repossessed, and flunked a medical examina-
tion for an insurance policy I was trying to take out for the
benefit of my mother, who had no one in the world but me.
What was then indicated was a real wallow in the nearest
bar, where I drank bottle after bottle of my favorite beer,
Löwenbrau, followed by several hours of Tchaikovsky on
the phonograph at home. I played the last movement of the
Sixth, the *adagio lamentoso*, over and over, accompanying
the New York Philharmonic on my own clarinet, walking
around the room as I did so in long woollen underwear,
which was how I had heard Yehudi Menuhin practiced the
violin. The music is sheer mush but I managed, in its pauses,
to interpolate some even treaclier arpeggios of my own,
sometimes augmenting my contribution by howling like a
dog, sometimes standing before a pier glass as I played, and
giving myself in the mirror a bittersweet smile of understanding and sympathy.

I will cite one more example of the use and value of self-
pity as a way of coping with reality, not selected at random,
as were the foregoing, but chosen specifically to show that
the emotion under review is not always unilateral, or "nar-
cissistic," but can and does often involve a sense of other
people.

In the town where I now live there is a woman, middle-
aged and recently widowed, whom I knew fairly well at the
time I ran into her at a political clambake last summer. The
discussion at our table got around to the stock market, and
I remembered a hot new security I had just learned about
from some friends of mine, men high up in Wall Street. It

was one of those low-priced issues selling in the category reminiscent of hat sizes — 6⅞, 7¼, and the like — so-called "growth stocks," which, because of some electronic break-through or a fat government contract, are bound to soar within a few months to many times their original value. Should I recommend the stock to this widow? I thought fast. Quick thinking has got me into more than one jam, and before I knew it I was urging her to sell everything her husband had left her and put it into Astro-Nucleonics, Inc. It was essential, I told her when she took me aside later to ask for further particulars, that anybody interested move quickly, as news of the government contract the firm was getting would be public knowledge in a few days, after which the stock would begin its skyrocketing.

The woman did as I suggested, but she need not have hurried. The government contract fell through and the stock sank within a month to 2½, where it is now, paying no dividends.

I have spent most of my time since then avoiding this woman. I saw her recently on the main street of town, wearing a shawl and pulling along two little girls, equally shabbily dressed. They are evidently in classic penury. I ducked into an alley till they were gone. The following Saturday morning, as I was padding through town in sneakers and smoked glasses, trying to get some weekend shopping done, I saw them again, and again ducked for cover. I waited till I thought the coast was clear, but it wasn't. When I stepped out onto Main Street once more, there they were, coming out of the five-and-dime, the mother clutching a brown sack that had an air of containing materials for all of them to twist into paper flowers, for sale to kind neighbors and people hurrying to the theatre. They were heading straight toward me.

If there was anything for me to do but flatten myself into
the nearest doorway, gritting my teeth and cursing my luck,
I would like to know what it was Here I was, established at
last in a fine community in which I had spent years putting
down roots, with my own house, where I could sit, after a
day's work, in a spacious glassed-in living room high on a
hill, overlooking my defects — and now this. What a rotten
break! I might have to leave town.

The woman had seen me, and stopped on the sidewalk in
front of the doorway. She faced me squarely. "Any more
bright ideas, *Mister* Financial Expert?"

"I'll buy it back at what you paid for it," I offered, stepping out.

"No, thanks. We don't take charity."

"Then won't you join me in some lunch?" I said, for the
place before which we stood happened to be the Chinese
Gardens, newly opened. "I hear the food is very good here."

"Thank you again. The answer is still the same."

Now, the woman had no one to blame but herself for the
difficulty she was in. Anyone who listens to every damn fool
with a tip on the stock market deserves what he gets — and
that includes me for listening to the hot shots no less than
her for listening to me. Nevertheless, I felt wretched. We
were in this together — no man is an island, her misfortunes
were mine, and so on and so on, till there was nothing for it
but to go into the Chinese Gardens alone and head for the
booth nearest the bar, there to drown my miseries in Löwenbräu. I ordered glass after glass of my beloved brew, which
they had on draft there, and also an egg roll and a plate of
pressed duck. I had more beers than I can remember. Later,
the waiter brought a few fortune cookies, one of which I
picked up and began abstractedly to eat without first removing the prognostication. It was not until I had been chewing

it for some moments that I detected an alien sensation, and, turning to look into the small wall mirror in the booth, stuck my tongue out and found adhering to it, sure enough, a small strip of paper on which appeared the assertion that I must be careful in money matters. Still gazing into the mirror, I shook my head, as though to say to myself, "How do you stand it?"

The whole point I am trying to make, of course, is that that *is* how I stand it. I bend in order that I do not break. I see it through by frankly and freely embracing the total human outrage of which I form a modest part, a minuscule fragment in a hostile, or at any rate incomprehensible, Whole. Contemplating myself in the glass with a fragment of tissue hanging out of my mouth, or clarinetting away in woollen drawers, I know that there is nothing else quite like me in the universe at the moment, and this is a kind of comfort. Doing these things is a way of affirming myself, of upholding the dignity of man, if you will, or at least a little of my end of it. I will never understand the theory of relativity, but I have an excellent picture of Einstein with his tongue hanging out a mile. He apparently stuck it out for the photographers — a request few would rate in this world, and fewer still feel secure enough to comply with. Anyone doing it in private is operating at the other end of the status spectrum. Anyhow, the photograph is a newspaper clipping, which I keep in a drawer and take out occasionally to look at, though not often, and not for very long at a time, since it is a little rich for my blood.

Self-pity, in conclusion, hurts nobody else, offering, indeed, an interior mood all the more conducive to giving others their external due. I never beat my wife, except at double Canfield, or even ever speak a harsh word to the woman. I am not boasting about this, either, because the explanation for it is obvious. A man busy nursing his own wounds has no time to inflict them on others

THE HIGH GROUND; OR, LOOK, MA, I'M EXPLICATING

WHEN the helpmate pointed out how I tended to mumble and grunt in confrontation with paintings and other works of art, and suggested I might try framing my reactions in more articulate English, or at least sentences that parsed, I was at first resentful. I remembered T. S. Eliot's remark about how he hated being pressed for his opinions when strolling through galleries and museums, preferring to accumulate and discharge them at his leisure, if at all. Yet that position is hardly tenable under circumstances such as formed the occasion for my wife's whispered stricture — the black-tie opening of a one-man retrospective that we attended with some newly acquired friends, Bill and Jessie Gmelch. Such an event is in its nature half social — something one cannot in all conscience negotiate with a mouthful of teeth. So I made an effort to hitch up my responses onto a plane more nearly approximating that of ordered evaluation — with results that surprised and, I must say, delighted me.

"What we have here seems to me an organic fusion of form and content," I said, of an oil before which we four collectively stood, shortly after the murmured complaint for which the helpmate had momentarily drawn me out of the Gmelches' hearing, "one in which linear and compositional values are also happily resolved. I like especially the juxtaposition of contrasts, which are at once subtle and intrepid, forthright without being obtrusive."

Bill Gmelch nodded, tapping against pursed lips a catalogue which he had rolled into a tube. "Hmm," Jessie said, gazing at the picture I continued.

"The amalgamation of subject and object, which was but tentatively realized in the artist's earlier period — in such efforts as the *Blue Configuration* over there, where an ostensibly abstract intention is still somewhat qualified by representational elements — seems to me consummately achieved in this more recent *City Modality*, where the object qua object, the *Ding an sich*, if you will, disappears in the chromatic boil."

"Oh, there are the McConkeys," Jessie said, and made for the new arrivals, hastily followed by Bill. The helpmate again waited till they were out of earshot. Then she said, "Go back to the way you were."

This was more easily said than done. When a man has found his tongue on the level I had, the cat is not likely to get it again very soon. I could hardly wait for the next chance to practice my newly discovered gift, which was like a heady wine. It came the very next week when we attended an all-Chopin concert by a Brazilian pianist, again with the Gmelches.

"Like him?" Bill said in the lobby during the intermission, eying me warily as he shook a cigarette from a pack. "I think he's good. His reading of the sonata struck me as especially fine."

"Except in the slow movement," I said, "where I detected a certain viscosity in the phrasing. Also his tempi were at times heretical, to say the least, notably in the more reflective passages, where the lyrical intent of the original was distorted by an overinflation of its rhythmic values, I thought. I find the performance in general somewhat marred by a willful pyrotechnicality, which repeatedly sacrifices the composer's avowed melodic line to a heedless personal panache. Where is everyone going?"

Bill gesticulated through the doorway to a bar across the street, sucking back a large mouthful of smoke. "Time for a quick one before the buzzer."

I chased them through a light drizzle, shouting explications lost in the noise of the traffic and then that of the bar, which discouraged all but the small talk into which my three companions seemed, for some reason, eagerly to plunge. I listened with abstracted smiles to their gossip as I mentally drafted amplifications of the points I had raised. I was now beginning to wonder about Eliot. The pleasures of pontification were none he had ever passed up in his prose writings!

Something or other was causing a steady decline in the Gmelches' state of mind. They were in quite a foul humor when we got up to our place for a nightcap after the concert. I noticed them whispering angrily together in a corner of the living room, glancing in my direction and breaking off as I approached with brandies. Evidently a little domestic spat of some sort. It showed me how urgent the need for a bit of stimulating talk. A new novel, lying on a coffee table, offered just the opportunity.

"I felt it a distinct advance over the author's previous work," I said, "particularly compelling in its portrayal of the slob as counter-culture. Here the grubby romanticism of asphalt vagabondage, long familiar to us in a rash of 'road' fiction from those still into words, is elevated into an outright arraignment of the work ethos as more puritanic dregs. Especially notable are the scenes in which the protagonist takes to the streets and asks nonentities for their autographs, as Whitmanesque gestures of democracy. Would, alas, the style were more Whitmanesque."

They all watched in hangdog silence as I packed and lit a pipe.

The High Ground; or, Look, Ma, I'm Explicating

"My quarrel is not that it's recycled Faulkner — what isn't these days — but that rhetoric is, *en principe*, incongruous with so putatively skeptical a vision. Let me just get the book and read a passage illustrating —"

"No." Both Gmelches spoke as they rose simultaneously and stood with clenched fists, as though prepared to bar my passage to the book with physical force if necessary. "We have to toddle along," Bill said, levelly. "We have to get up tomorrow," Jessie explained. The helpmate now climbed to her feet, like a third guest I must see to the door. Until we actually reached it, there was the eeriest sense that she might indeed sail through it and out into the night, remembering only at the last moment that she lived here.

"Well, you've driven them away," she said when we were alone. "Probably for good. In God's name, can't you stop it? Talking like that?"

"It would be dishonest to guarantee anything. Once you've got the hang of something —"

"Then I'll guarantee something. That I can't take much more of this phase. Look. We're all going to the Bilkingtons' cocktail party Saturday, and you'd damn well better talk United States there, is all I can say, Buster."

The helpmate's misgivings were not without foundation. Bo Bilkington is a tired businessman who encourages canards such as that he carries a hip flask to the opera. When he shakes hands, he will fold his fingers back two joints, so that you think you are grasping stumps, and say, with a laugh, "Lost 'em on a minesweeper." Saturday evening saw me being greeted again in that vein, and smilin' through in my own, as I rolled an eye around the apartment to see who was on deck. A large mixture of friends and strangers. Plucking a drink from a passing tray, I made for a group at the far end of the living room who were listening to an L.P. of some

92

new poet reading his stuff — an album entitled "Vibes," of which I caught the last ten minutes.

"Like it?" Jenny Bilkington said, when the stereo had clicked off.

There were murmurs of approval, a few polite shrugs and exclamations. I could feel the helpmate's eye on me, though from behind. I made an effort to get a grip on myself. The brief, foredoomed struggle of a man hooked on exegesis. I cleared my throat as Jenny moved to play the flip side.

"I find it on the whole creditable of its kind, allowing for the element of naiveté in colloquial art generally," I said. "The style is basically folk collage rather than formalized song, of course. The use of slang, clichés, and the like, wedged arbitrarily into what systematic verse there is, offers a literary counterpart of the 'found objects' incorporated into contemporary junk sculpture — yet another example of the fragmentation that has marked our art for half a century, reflecting a dilapidated Western psyche Each generation espouses its argot with more bravado than the last (the hippie lexicon is almost all cult verbiage), a development hardly surprising, for in the beginning may have been the word but the end is always jargon."

"How about that?" said Bo. He glanced wretchedly over at another group as he reached for his highball. "Let's —"

"I liked especially the passage beginning, 'What availeth it a lawn mower?,' as a wry commentary on certain pernickety homeowning elements comprising in fact a culture in midslide. Also effective was the symbolism of the carpenter's apprentice who throws down his tools and leaves Scarsdale, as allusion to the current Jesus bag."

The plan to hear a little of the flip side was abandoned as the group dispersed, to re-form into smaller knots of muttering guests. One especially exercised little cluster, incidentally including Bill Gmelch, were shaking their heads and even their fists. A mob can be an ugly thing. I caught the words "be allowed out" and other such inflamed scraps. In this way the party now began to take more discernible shape. The helpmate grasped my hand at one point and towed me across the long living room to a group clear at the other end. "They're discussing movies," she said with a smile intended for public consumption, adding, through gritted teeth, "*thank God.*"

That lot were talking about a picture I happened to have seen, and so was fortunately able to join in the conversation. A groan went up from some woman as I approached, probably someone bored with Al Herndon's two cents about the film, for he was holding forth in typical style on its merits. One thing is, he's loaded with inherited money, which always sets people's backs up. I stood with the flat of a hand against the wall, hearing him out like the rest.

"The art that conceals art," I said the instant Plentykins paused for breath, "is nowhere more important than in the cinema, where we have such a variety of techniques to keep scrupulously in line. I found both the photography and the direction in *Bus to Scranton* obtrusive. The long coal-pit and slag-heap shots were beautifully realized as anti-scenery, but the close-ups became much too studied, as did the raffishness of the male principal, whose exposition of the role was an uneasy hash of Bogart and Mastroianni, which any director worth his salt could have disciplined. . . ."

Among the last to arrive, we were the first to leave. The helpmate seemed anxious to get me alone in a taxicab.

"Well, that tears it," she said as we sped for home. "Did you notice the Herndons and the Gmelches and the Busta- mentes talking about getting theatre tickets to something and breaking it off when we came up? We'll never be invited anywhere again, except to a dogfight. I swear I don't know what makes you tick. One minute you're the soul of concession, the next you can't be budged, especially if it involves something that gives you some kind of subcutaneous gratification."

"Can I help it if it's my mature period?"

"Oh, God, who knows what anybody is like!" she said, ignoring me. "Before a woman can begin telling you what a prince you are, you've become a pain. You know what I think? *I* think," she went on, warming to her subject, "you mask a genuine aggression under a façade of compliance, and vice versa — a sort of basic insecurity inside this husk of independence. You seem unable to divorce your societal from your ego drives, your gregarious from your competitional. . . ."

She can go on like that for days. Ah, well, it's an age of criticism, isn't it? It's nothing if not that.

THE INDEPENDENT VOTER
AT TWILIGHT

"Your lips are sweet." I said, "sweeter than dayspring to the shipwrecked in Nova Zembla. Now what?"

At six o'clock in the morning any husband looks like Early Man, and my wife considered the flowers growing beside the terrace where we sat scalding ourselves with coffee as she said, "Now, try to get a look at the sticker on Jack Bronson's car at the station *today*. This is the third time I've asked you, and I can't wait any longer if we're going to invite them."

The Bronsons were a couple relatively new to the neighborhood, living in a converted barn a quarter of a mile from

my own backslidden salt-box. They had had us for drinks
once, and the cocktail party we were giving a week hence
would be a convenient occasion to repay them, if their politics were right. My wife and I, though firm in our opinions,
are not intolerant of other people's, but some who would be
on hand at the party were. I am thinking particularly of Fred
Kitzbite. Fred is a hardened New Dealer who regards A.T.
& T.'s acquisition of outer space as a form of creeping capi-
talism, which gives you some idea of the way his wind sock
points An equally rabid, or even a lukewarm, Republican
present at the same party would make it one to which I
would not care to play host. Campaigns for the forthcoming
Connecticut elections had tempers almost as short as during
a Presidential year. Stickers declaring the loyalties of the
owners were sprouting on the windows and bumpers of cars
everywhere. My wife had seen one on the rear bumper of
the Bronsons' station wagon somewhere around town, but
not closely enough to make out the name on it. The mere
existence of the sticker seemed to indicate a firmness of con-
viction sufficient to make the thoughtful hostess brief herself
more fully on the Bronsons before throwing them in with
the Kitzbites.

"Bronson doesn't go in on the seven-ten," I said, rising to
shave, "so the car won't be at the station when I get there."

"But he comes home on a later train than you do, so it'll
be there when you get back. It's that big Mercury with the
squirrel tail on the aerial. Now, check it without fail."

Trying to catch a few extra winks on the train, I remembered something Disraeli had said on this whole tricky subject of entertaining. The exact quotation eluded me, but it
goes something like, "Anybody inviting a group of people
to dine in his house must first sit down and do some serious
moral bookkeeping."

Halfway in to the city, the air-conditioning broke down

— a bad augury for a day that promised to be a scorcher It was. When I got off the train that evening, one of a hundred toilers carrying their wilted coats, all I had on my mind was a shower and a cold bottle of beer. As I sped home with all the car windows down, I hoped that the clouds massing to the northwest meant that a good thundershower was on the way.

"Well?" my wife asked when I walked in the door. "What did the sticker say?"

"Damn," I said. "It completely slipped my mind."

After a rather sultry dinner, we sat on the terrace with iced coffee, watching those thunderheads building up in the distance like a mass of body bruises. We listened to the seven-o'clock news on a transistor radio. After the news came a gossip columnist who devoted his entire broadcast to a panegyric on the Princess of Monaco and the valor with which she has resisted the temptations of Hollywood.

"I, too, admire Grace under pressure," I said. "but doesn't each of us in his humble, everyday —"

"Last month you forgot to send the mortgage check and the bank had to call us. Last week you forgot to mail that letter I gave you," my wife said. "I found it in your pocket when I sent your suit out to the cleaner's. You'd forget your head if it wasn't tied on."

I lowered my head to my knees, so bowed down was I with the sense of domestic clichés, of absolutely abysmal platitudes in which a man seems at times engulfed. I was sitting like this when my sixteen-year-old son came out of the house and said, "Pop, can I have the car tonight? A bunch of us are going to the bowling alleys" He meant the car I drive to the station, my daughter having already gone off to the movies with the other.

My wife and I went around to the front of the house to see him off, with reminders to drive carefully and to go directly to the bowling alleys and stay inside while it stormed, if it did. We were standing at the head of the driveway watching him make off down the road when the Bronsons themselves rode by, waving, in the other of *their* two cars, a Dodge sedan with no visible propaganda.

"Out for the evening," my wife said. "That means the station wagon's at the house. Now's your chance."

"But I haven't got a car," I said.

"It's not that much of a walk You say yourself you need the exercise. If you want to be New Frontier, *be* New Frontier. Go ahead. It's cooled off now, and it won't storm for a bit."

It didn't, but I was delayed in my departure by a telephone call that took a good twenty minutes. Dusk was falling when I set out down the road, and it deepened into premature nightfall as thunder that had seemed distant suddenly began to crack overhead. The first scattered drops quickened my walk into a brisk trot. I tried to affect the long, easy stride of the cross-country runner, remembering also to enclose my thumbs tightly in my fists, which, as a boy, I had always been told would keep you from getting a stitch in your side.

The Bronsons' place lay just beyond a dogleg in the road up ahead. I surmised that I would have to take shelter in it till the storm was over. I rounded the dogleg, swinging along smoothly, and saw that the station wagon was not in the driveway. It was in the garage, which had room in it for only one car, the other being presumably left outside. The garage was in any case shut and locked for the night, I found when I galloped to a stop behind it and tried the handle.

I darted around the house in what was now a heavy downpour, and found a side door, luckily unlocked. I ducked inside. I stood there a moment getting my wind, and also my bearings. My eyes were not yet accustomed to the gloom of the interior, but a flash of lightning revealed that I seemed to be in a sort of utility room, or "dirty room," as it is sometimes called. I groped along the walls for a light switch, without success. Just then I felt something soft and living between my feet, and gave an involuntary jump. My start caused the cat — which a loud yelp from below proved it to be — to become more awkwardly entangled in my feet, so that I lost my balance and pitched to the floor, clawing the air and bringing down with me what seemed to be a loaded clothes rack, judging from the masses of garments among which I lay sprawled. I extricated myself and climbed once more to my feet. My spill had landed me clear at the other side of the room, where, after some more feeling along the wall, I finally did locate a light switch.

It was the Bronsons' utility room, all right, crammed with laundry apparatus and smelling faintly of creosote. It had two doors, one leading into the house, the other down into the garage. The cat was nowhere to be seen. After hanging the Mackinaws and things back on the righted clothes rack, I descended the three steps into the garage.

There was plenty of illumination from the utility room, but I still had no view of the rear bumper, which was a mere six or eight inches from the closed door. By putting my head into this narrow space, I could just barely catch a glimpse of the sticker and what seemed to be the initial "A." Whether that meant Abe Ribicoff, the Democratic candidate for senator, or any one of a host of other candidates for state and local offices was impossible to say. I would have to see more. And to do that I would have to open the garage door.

One thing certain about the Bronsons was that they lived in cramped quarters. With my left hand I reached down to the lock assembly midway of the door, turned the triangular knob of the latch, and heard the crossbars snap free. I grabbed the handle and slid the door up. Even then I had to go all the way outside to see. When I had popped out, another flash of lightning brought the sticker vividly into view. What I saw made me shake my head as I popped back in again

I reversed my actions, closing doors and snapping out lights, and as I reached the utility room again, the storm suddenly let up. Even the rain had stopped, I saw when I had stepped outside, and, pulling that door shut, I started for home.

I had forgotten the capriciousness of summer storms — their habit, so to speak, of taking unpredictable encores. I was no more than halfway back when there was a deafening peal of thunder followed by a downpour that had me soaked to the skin in two minutes. The only protection from the rain was the trees — to be eschewed, of course. Lightning had never seemed to me, till that night, the terrifying phenomenon it really is, probably because I had never been so nakedly exposed to it before. Now I was convinced it was splitting the trees on either side of the road up which I sped, splashing through pools already inches deep and muttering oaths for which I could ill spare the breath. Such of my hair as did not hang in my eyes was plastered to my ears. My legs felt like mangled rubber, and a nasty stitch was developing in my side, for all my care in keeping my thumbs clutched. I cursed all women and their social complications, and couldn't wait to get home and tell my wife what I had found.

As I came down the stretch in the driveway, I saw that she was standing in the front hallway waiting for me. She held the screen door open as I stumbled, gasping like a drowning man, over the threshold, taking a keen pleasure in the mud I tracked on the rug. I continued into the living room, where I sank into a deep chair. I sat there for several minutes, coughing and spluttering, my arms hanging over the sides. She stood with her own arms folded, watching the water drip from my clothes onto the carpet.

"You'd better get out of those wet things," she said.

I nodded. The storm was still crashing about the house, in a way that made one glad one had had lightning rods installed even while one reveled in the mad sense of "judgment" implicit in the blasting thunder, which gave one the momentary illusion of being, oneself, an angry god She would get what she had coming to her in a minute.

"Did you . . . ?" she began.

I nodded again, a single, curt nod, as of a man who cannot speak until he has caught his breath.

"What did it say?" she asked finally.

I rolled wild eyes at her, fixing her with them for a moment before answering " 'Ausable Chasm,' " I said.

She looked down at the floor, nodding. Then she gazed out the window, shifting from one foot to the other, her arms still folded. After a moment more, she took me by the hand and drew me out of the chair. "Come on upstairs, and I'll hang those clothes up for you and get you a fresh towel. Then I'll fix you a nice drink," she said.

Traipsing in her wake to the bedroom, I pondered again this terrible orchestration of people known as hospitality, and wondered whether the Kennedys sweat as much blood over their guest lists as the Disraelis and we.

"Why, what you found out tells us *something*," she said. "It's perfectly safe to invite them They probably don't care about politics one way or another."

You know the rest. How the talk at the party got around to travel and vacations, and where everybody had been and where they would like to go.

"Next summer, Joan and I want to go to Spain," Jack Bronson said.

You could feel Fred Kitzbite stiffen. "You mean and support Fascism?" he said. "You mean you think it's perfectly all right to bolster a regime like that with American dollars? To give it your moral as well as financial support by spending your money there?"

"Now, look here," Bronson said, and the free-for-all was on.

It was a shambles. It was a night to remember. Nobody we know has had the heart to get up a cocktail party since. Which is, after all, something.

THE CONVERSATIONAL BALL

I SUPPOSE it's true enough that women talk too much, and, conversely, husbands never listen. A proper conjunction of these two clichés of human conduct can produce a crisis of anything but trite proportions, as was proved by a recent incident of which I still bear the scars — or will as soon as the wounds heal. Even now I have this queasy apprehension that the worst is yet to come. The qualm before the storm, you might say.

I was drinking coffee in my favorite chair, one evening after dinner several weeks ago, when I dimly sensed that my wife was discoursing at length on something that perhaps required closer attention than, through the fog of abstraction with which I listened, I was paying it. She was in fact relating a dream she had had, but, like a late theatregoer who has missed an essential piece of exposition, I didn't learn that until it was too late. I thought she was talking about something that had happened to her that day, or maybe the day before.

"I was wearing my new slacks — you know, the pink ones with the flower print," she was saying, "and I was walking downtown. As I turned the corner and passed the library, I met Jack Brady We stopped a minute to talk."

"Oh? How is Jack?" I asked, showing some interest.

"What?"

"How is Jack?"

"All right, I guess. Why? What has that got to do with it? You see him on the train."

"Not every day. He doesn't even go in every day, as you know." I was only trying to keep the conversational ball rolling. "But go on. What then?"

"Well, suddenly he looked down at my slacks and started to laugh. He asked whether they were new, and I said yes, and he laughed again."

"Why, that son of a bitch," I said. "It's just like him, though. Jack likes to think he's the answer to every woman's prayer, but he's really a pain in the pancreas. So what happened then? What did you say?"

"Well, naturally I took offense, and asked him what he meant. He kind of looked away and said what he meant was that I was one of the few women who understood the art of dressing absurdly. He was trying to cover up, you see."

"He's a lout. Yet at the same time mealymouthed. Then what?"

"Then I left him, and hadn't gone far up Main Street when I was glad to run into Louise Maley, dressed in slacks, like me, and I told her what Jack Brady had said. Then we decided to have a cup of tea together. . . ."

Here my attention wandered again from an account of what was an apparently interminable ramble through town. Catching a word here and there to keep some vague connection with the thread of the narrative, I turned over in my mind the prospects of lunch in town the next day with an office colleague of tender years and notable charms. I mentally sorted out the various midtown restaurants from among which a choice might be made, occasionally turning to nod at my wife with the expression of an intelligent listener.

I forgot about the whole thing until the next morning when I caught sight of Jack Brady in the bar car on the way to the city, and I bristled. The bar car is not serving at that hour, of course, but Jack is one of the habitués who ride it then in anticipation of the evening return, when it is. His eyes seemed a little bleary now, probably the result of a heavy load the night before, and I hoped for his sake he had had a few when he had insulted my wife. I could clearly not let that pass, though obviously I would not stop to make an issue of it in public — even the low-consciousness public represented by the score or so of somnambulists slumped behind their *Timeses*. I returned his greeting with a curt snub, and went on through to a coach farther up front.

Settled down in a seat there, I found myself unable to concentrate on my own *Times*. The challenge I must raise, and the "satisfaction" I would positively require, hung like a cloud over my day. Well before we reached the city, I had decided to have it out the minute we pulled into Grand Central.

I was waiting for him at the train gate as he made his way along the station platform.

"Jack?" I said, accosting him.

"Hi," he said. "What is it?" He looked really awful, close up. His eyes were red-rimmed, and he was coughing into a handkerchief. He had evidently caught a heavy summer cold.

"I want to talk to you a minute. Let's step over here."

With a jerk of my head, I led the way back inside the train gate and toward a baggage cart, behind which it seemed to me we could most decently have this thing out. We both had on gabardine suits, and we were swinging attaché cases of the same shape, color, and size, and I had a brief, Surrealist vision of two commuters flailing one another to death with identical luggage — *reductio ad absurdum* of the Age of Conformity. Well, chivalry, at least, was not dead.

When we were out of view, I turned and faced him squarely.

"Look, fellow, I take exception to that crack you made to my wife," I said.

"What crack?" he said. "What are you talking about?"

"You know very well what I mean. The slacks. That seem to refresh your memory, Jack?"

His face was something to behold as he coughed again into the handkerchief, which he had not yet pocketed, looking away and shaking his head in puzzlement. "When was this?"

I opened my mouth to answer several times before a lull in his coughing fit permitted. The whole thing was like some dream. "Don't stall. It doesn't become you, and hardly serves to dignify this thing. You know very well when this was, and what it was. It so happens that I think my wife looks very good in slacks."

"Why, none better, man, but whah —?"

"Soft soap will get you nowhere. We don't behave toward women that way — that's the long and the short of it. I demand an apology, not to me but to her," I said, and added, tapping him on the chest, "and I demand it by tonight!" With that, I turned on my heel and marched out of the station.

As can be imagined, my day in the city was not in the least brightened by the relief of having spoken up and got that part of it over with. It was a rotten day, hardly improved when this office colleague of mine turned out to be busy for lunch. "I have a date with this, um, friend I met at the party in Teaneck I was telling you about," she said. She was apparently ignorant of the present-day vogue decreeing that young girls be seen in the best restaurants with older men, nor had I the time or the strength to try to bring her *au courant* just now. I

had a grilled-cheese sandwich sent up to my office, and relieved my solitude by munching it into suggestive shapes. It
had come uncut, and I was able, by careful nibbling from
the crusts inward, to mold it into a very satisfactory female
silhouette — which I immediately defaced into a lampoon of
this office colleague by adding the two pickle slices for big
feet, and making a funny hat of strands of the coleslaw that
accompanied the sandwich in a small fluted cup, complete
with disposable plastic fork. I had this composition laid out
on the wax wrapper on top of my desk, and was admiring
the effect as I sipped iced tea from a container when my telephone rang. It was my wife.

"What. In God's name. Have you done. Now?" she said,
spacing her words in the dramatically clipped manner of one
long burdened with the need for some device to express utter
and total exasperation.

"Why? What have I done now?"

"Jack Brady just called me, from the city —"

"As damn well he might. I buttonholed him this morning
and insisted on an apology."

"What for?"

"For that crack he made about your slacks. What else?"

"That's what I thought." There was a long sigh, after
which she said, "Now, look. Are you listening very carefully
now, for once? Because this time — What's that guzzling
noise? Are you drinking something?"

"Just some iced tea. In my office. But shoot. What's this
all about?"

"It's all about some more confusion created by your not
paying any attention to anything anyone tells you. But listen
very closely now. *That was a dream I was telling you about,*
not something that happened. Jack didn't say it to me, I
dreamed he did, that's all. Now have you got it straight?"

"Oh, good Lord," I said. "I'm sorry. I've made a mess of

things Poor Jack. And you, too. I'm terribly sorry. But I'll make it up to you, and I'll square it with Jack, too, tonight on the —"

"No. The best thing is to forget about the whole business. I think I handled it the only way. He really did call to apologize, figuring he *had* said something to me after a few drinks at that beach party the other night. It wouldn't be the first time he couldn't remember what he said to somebody. It's always happening to him. I just said that you had misunderstood what I'd told you — a mixup for everybody to forget as soon as possible. I didn't tell him the truth. Confusion now hath made his masterpiece, but I do think it's better this way, and lets him off just as well. So just turn it off if he brings it up, and buy him a drink. And maybe after this you'll listen when somebody's talking to you. Goodbye!"

The aftermath can be readily imagined. I listen attentively these days when nothing much is being said. The corrosive silences are, however, gradually beginning to diminish in both length and severity, and despite the occasional twinges of apprehension that the worst is yet to come, I hope that things will soon be back to normal. Meanwhile, there was a kind of epilogue to the whole episode that rounds it off in a rather neat fashion, I think.

This business colleague came into my office one day to announce that the courtship by the chap in Teaneck had proved to be whirlwind, and flashed a ring to prove it. She then hemmed and hawed a moment in a way that indicated she had a favor to ask.

"I don't know what to give him for a wedding present, personally, from me," she said, "and I was wondering if you might have any suggestions. Get the point of view of a man who's more, um, seasoned."

"If you're free for lunch, we can discuss it," I said.

I knew instantly what to suggest, but didn't spring my idea till we were well into our brandies. "By all means give him a leather club chair," I said. "A plain. Old-fashioned. Leather club chair is what every man wants but nobody ever thinks of getting him. Go to Macy's. I got mine there."

She nodded thoughtfully, while I smiled inscrutably to myself, knowing what she did not know but would soon enough learn: to wit, the sequel to the fairy tale that she was, for a brief moment, living. The princess is awakened from her sleep by the kiss of a true lover, all right enough, but that's not the end of the story by a long shot. Some of us are familiar with the fuller version, which is never told. How they get married, and how after dinner they sit down together and she begins to talk to him. And she talks and she talks, till at last his head nods on his chest, and he sleeps, forever, and ever, and ever.

ADVENTURES OF A PEOPLE BUFF

CALL ME a people buff. I like people. And among my favorites, at the moment, must certainly be ranked the Cox Thimble Drome people of Santa Ana, California, manufacturers of a line of model planes of which I recently bought their one-cylinder-engine SB2C, popularly known as the Helldiver. I had been medically urged to get myself a hobby a little more active than lounging around with a highball after a day in the city, mentally reviewing the human specimens, each more absurd than the last, that I had encountered in the course of it. "I mean that's all right," the doctor said when I told him what I did for hacks, "but it hardly tones up the system or provides any exercise. Also, you should get out more." So I bought this plane, of the sort I had seen people flying in open fields at the ends of guidestrings, apparently quite happily, and flew it — once. Its uncollected fragments lie in the yard beneath the living-room window — one of those picture windows composed of two panes of plate glass slightly spaced to provide insulation and called Twindows by an outfit also high on my list — and I have reverted to the tamer but safer pastime of stretching out with a drink to contemplate the clothed mammal.

The Helldiver people are wonderful. Contact with their product was brief and catastrophic, but I still spend many fascinated hours poring over the set of instructions in which they stated in plain English that it probably would be; and which seem to have been systematically devised, for that reason, to put any likelihood of a takeoff safely out of the purchaser's reach. Consider, for example, the errant charm of this paragraph, which the greenhorn encounters early on in the set of directions, after some preliminary portents of the total demolition in store for anyone fool enough to think he can get the upper hand·

"Your Thimble Drome Helldiver is much too beautiful and expensive to use as a training ship to learn to fly Trainer planes made for this purpose are much less expensive to learn to fly with because they are much less vulnerable to crash damage. It might be wise to buy a PT-19 Thimble Drome Trainer for learning to fly as this ship is especially built to absorb hard crash landings without damage. The catalog number is 5700 and the price is $10.00."

Now, an outlay of twenty clams for the Helldiver as a roundabout way of coming by the information that you should have bought something else instead is not, I think, exorbitant, as good advice is always worth paying for, and these people seem to know their business. I hurried out to buy the lesser model, but, unable to locate a merchant in town who stocked it, hurried home again to make do with the better. The briefing now sternly warned against the use of any fuel other than something called Thimble Drome Racing Fuel, so I put on my coat and hat again (observing to myself that I was certainly getting out more) and rushed off to buy a can of that. My mission this time was more fruitful, and I was soon home again, settled down to the phase having to do with fueling and starting the engine.

Here the Helldiver people's genius for frustrating their clientele proves to be at its most disarming. They speak tantalizingly of a carburetor needle valve, which you are supposed to close before you make another move, and direct you to Figure 4. But nowhere in Figure 4 is the nature of the part indicated or its location specified. Love that firm. I found out where the needle valve was, however, thanks to some drag I have at a local repair garage, of which the head mechanic is a friend of mine, and then, back home again for — let's see — the third time, with the engine fueled, I proceeded to the business of starting it.

The instructions said, "Squirt a few drops of fuel into the exhaust port. This is called priming." No exhaust port in Figure 4, either. Here I outwitted the makers by gathering up my model and taking it to the boy next door — a plucky lad of ten whom I had seen and heard flying a small plane similar to mine behind his house — and he showed me how to start it. I was now ready for the final stage of my preparations — the actual flying of the plane. Here I was dealt the worst blow of all. For a full comprehension of it, we must return briefly to my medical picture.

I happen to be subject to something known as Ménière's syndrome, a malfunction of the mechanism in the inner ear which is responsible for equilibrium, and which can convert the visible world into a carrousel without warning. Things become bollixed up firmament-wise, with attendant nausea.

People so afflicted tend by instinct to avoid sudden moves, especially those involving circular actions of the head. Friends never have to say to us "Don't look now," because long habits of deliberation would make us about-face slowly if told "There's a panther behind you." Even the quarter turn necessary to dismount a soda-fountain stool is enacted with caution for fear of starting a bout of vertigo, which might be described to the uninitiated as roughly resembling an undeserved hangover, or a kind of *mal de mer* on dry land.

It can be imagined with what dismay, therefore, I encountered this paragraph in the instruction leaflet:

"If you have no previous experience you must accustom yourself to turning around counterclockwise until you can turn 20 times or so without becoming excessively dizzy. This is necessary whether you start flying with this ship or any other Turn only 3 or 4 times the first time. Repeat after a half hour. Next day try 6 turns — repeat after a half hour. In a week or less you should be ready to fly."

To a man who can scarcely orbit a *smörgåsbord* table without losing his balance, not to mention his appetite, this is a crusher. It could be the coup de grâce to one not made of sterner stuff than the Helldiver people seem to take for granted. I thought first I might duck this entire problem by not revolving on my axis in conformity with the plane's overhead circles at all but simply standing still in the middle of a field, steadily passing my end of the guideline around myself from hand to hand, closing my eyes so I wouldn't see the plane, and trying not to retch. But this sort of thing will not work, as one glance at anybody flying a model plane will indicate. You have to move around, you have to keep your eye on things every second to maintain the steady rotating flight required. No, there was nothing for it, if I was determined not to be daunted, but to practice the pivoting exercises suggested, as prelude to any actual flying.

I picked a spot behind the garage where I would not be observed, closed my eyes, took a deep breath, and began. I rotated slowly, making a half turn first, then a full I took a rest, and after a few minutes decided to try for two. I was very gratified to note I could manage two, but my exhilaration was short-lived When I opened my eyes again, it was to find myself heading straight into a lilac bush The next time, I blundered into a wheelbarrow, thinking I was headed in another direction altogether, such was my disorientation. I decided to quit for the day and try again the next. I returned to the house, marveling, as I often do, at the spins executed by ballet dancers as a complete matter of course.

It occurred to me that there was no need to be practicing my rotations in the yard just because I would be flying the plane there, or hoped to. So I did them in the living room, the bedroom, even at the office, whenever I was alone and happened to have a spare moment. One Saturday morning, my wife entered the dining room in time to see me march into the side of a china cabinet, bruising my nose and flattening a cigar butt I happened to have clenched in my teeth.

"Why don't you give this thing up?" she said. "You know it's no use."

I rushed downstairs to the recreation room, where the plane was, snatched it up, rushed outside into the back yard, started it up, and let it go. I had read the instruction leaflet through in full two or three times by now, and, despite the manufacturer's obscurantism, had absorbed a few things about the care necessary in takeoff, both in terms of the plane and the guidelines attached to it (to the left wing, to command this counterclockwise circle), but I forgot all that now in my frenzy and just let the infernal thing rip. I can't say it went out of control, because it never was under control, nor did I pause to try to get it so The caution to make sure takeoff was downwind (in contrast to that of a real plane) was probably accidentally observed, for the ship rose with a rush. It shot off to the right until all the slack was out of the guidelines, at which point it snapped violently back, like a bolting animal on a leash, made several crazy gyrations as a crosswind caught it, and then, after describing one more erratic loop, came straight at me.

I dropped the guidelines and ran for the house, beginning to gag a little. My feet got tangled up in the lines, which was probably what saved my life, because I tripped and fell as the plane shot by where my head had just been. It went over with its insane whine, then must have got caught in a sudden updraft, for it rose with a jerk, leveled off, and made at full speed for the Twindow.

I heard but did not see the crash, being still bent on saving my own hide. I had recovered my footing, and now scuttled around a corner of the house. As a haven of refuge, however, this nook of the property left nearly as much to be desired as the open peril I had just fled. There is a short, abrupt declivity in the lawn there, and as I started across it my foot met a patch of residual winter ice, along which I shot precipitately, and with that slightly delirious sense of having to accelerate momentum on a slippery surface in order to keep upright. I rushed down the slope, arms out, swooped full-tilt across a narrow gravel walk, and wound up espaliered against the side of the garage.

Well, it was just such a calamity as the Helldiver people envisioned for tyros foolhardy enough to try the SB2C, and my hat is off to them. With the lengths of surgical gauze currently turbaning my brow, I can't wear it anyway.

I was stretched out on the living-room couch one Sunday afternoon shortly after washing out of the model air force when I began to hear the steady, rasping drone that meant the boy next door was outside flying his plane in the open

lot between our houses. I had decided to forgive the Helldiver people for their handling of the crucial element in my
fiasco. I know it concerned a defect in me, not in their mer-
chandise. Still, I think they should not have given the problem the emphasis they did in their leaflet, or perhaps even
brought the subject up, since by doing so they introduced a
note of anxiety and tension into a pastime that many people
take up precisely to relieve anxiety and tension Many au-
thorities consider the Ménière syndrome psychogenic anyway, and you only double the hazard by calling attention to
it. No, they should not have opened that can of peas.

I rose and went to the Twindow and stood gazing out of
it with my hands in my pockets The Twindow itself was,
fortunately, not broken.

The late-January day was bright and cold, and I could see
the plane circling in the clear air, just above the level of some
intervening treetops, round and around with absolute pre-
cision, like a bird against the blue sky. I had followed its
flight for several minutes when I began to realize something
very exciting. I was perfectly able to follow the plane with
my eyes, provided I myself remained motionless, and to do
this *without the slightest loss of equilibrium or orientation.*
This may seem a small matter to you, but it hit me with the
force of a revelation. The facts of the case are, paradoxically,
these: During an onset of Ménière's syndrome, my eyes tend
to slew around in my head (neutral observers have told me as
much), but when I slew my eyes around in my head deliberately, which should be asking for trouble, as many people
not normally subject to dizziness get dizzy when they try it,
why, I feel no ill effects whatever. It's some time since I've
been able to drum up any interest in myself, but this seemed
a phenomenon worth noting — indeed, a knack worth developing. Which is the upshot of the whole episode: the discovery of an unexpected skill.

I practiced swiveling my eyes around in my head till I was really quite adept at it. I can now rotate them clockwise at high speed, stop suddenly, and reverse to counterclockwise. I did this for members of my family till they were nauseated. Next, I took to doing my tricks for neighborhood kids, then at parties, finally on public conveyances. What I do is, I take a seat at the front or back of a bus, so that I am facing passengers on parallel seats, and then quite casually, with no other facial expression, go into my routine. The first time I did it, a man in a bowler hat turned green and changed his seat. He seemed to have to steady himself as he picked his way up the aisle toward the rear of the bus.

Since then, I have introduced many variations and refinements into my act. I will describe one in closing. I shut one eye, so that only the other is seen whirling around in my head, and simultaneously thrust my tongue deep into my cheek so that it makes a bulge, and whirl that around. When I reach that point in my repertoire, generally everyone is quite affected, and either moves or turns and looks out the window. As my skill grows, so does the percentage of people who rise and get off the bus altogether — and of course, as a confirmed people buff, I like to note exactly *how* they go as well as when they go. Soon, no doubt, I expect I shall be able to empty an entire coach with no trouble.

Why don't *you* get yourself a good hobby? You certainly look as though you need one, Mac, and badly.

HEART

I RECEIVED an unexpected phone call recently from my old friend Syd Cottonfelt. He was here on business from Kansas

City, where he works for a shoe-manufacturing company. He said he was sick of the fakes and phonies he had been running into in New York, and wanted to see some real people. So he arranged to come out to Connecticut and spend an evening with me.

Syd had met me some years before at the University of Chicago, where we were roommates. Kansas City was his home town, and he was all agog at the campus. "I never knew there were people like you in the world," he said.

"Well, there are," I told him. I had brains, charm, sensitivity, savoir faire, and a bag of bananas. Making a Saturday night of the bananas, in lieu of larger dissipations from which our squandered allowances momentarily barred us, we sat in our room talking until the small hours.

"You have a handsome profile," Syd said

"Well, as a matter of fact I have two," I said. "One on either side."

He laughed. "Swiftie," he said, calling me by my nickname, "you're one of those people who justify life."

Driving home from the suburban station, where I had gone to meet him on his arrival on the seven-two from New York, we naturally reminisced about old times. Then he asked, "How's Megs?" He had never met my wife, but he knew her name.

"Well, we're not getting on too well, actually," I said. "She's been seeing not one chap but several lately. Their names are Warshawski, Kosciusko, Chodkiewicz, and Brzaprazetski. So you can see we're Poles apart."

He flinched, for reasons I could not fathom at the moment but that became clear to me in due course. Syd Cottonfelt, I began to sense, had made little progress in that urbanity in which, in college days, he had expressed such envious determination to groom himself. He had, if anything, lost ground. He might just as well never have met me. Nothing of me had rubbed off on him — at least permanently. He is thickset, with a square head and close-cropped black hair. His nose is obsolete, recalling Louis Wolheim. He brought out presently that he had lost his wife a few years before. "It leaves an emptiness," he said.

Orders for highballs were taken swiftly, after my introduction of Syd to Megs, when we got home. "You two get acquainted," I said. "I'll get the drinks."

Since the room was an all-purpose living area, this consisted of little more than turning around to a bar at my back and pouring them. I prolonged the operation, however, in order to listen to the conversation between the other two. They seemed to hit it off instantly. Syd had lots of gossip to relate about the old bunch, but he addressed it all to Megs, who has never been to the University of Chicago at all but only to some women's college, the name of which I have never succeeded in extracting from her.

"Al Carter passed away, of course," he said. "Swiftie's probably told you about old Al. The salt of the earth. He left the world a better place to live in."

"That's good to know," I said, handing Syd and Megs their drinks. They both scowled at me. I got my own glass from the bar. "Cheers."

"Zimmerman keeps painting. Unfortunately, without much success."

"Hanging is too good for him," I said, and laughed.

Liquor seemed to increase rather than relieve Syd's native sobriety. He said, a little later, "You don't have any children?"

Megs relayed his gaze on toward me, as the one answerable there. "He's never wanted any," she said.

"Gee!" said Syd. "Isn't that the whole purpose of marriage? A family, a home? Don't you want that?"

"No," I replied "I consider the home an invasion of privacy."

There was another joint scowl at this. Then the two exchanged glances — Megs' an appeal for sympathy, Syd's the offer of it.

"What ever happened to Tod Willoughby?" I asked, to change the subject.

"Ah, thereby hangs a tale." Syd took a pull of his highball and set it down, making a point of putting it very carefully on a coaster so as not to stain the table finish. "Tod's been divorced. I heard the legal reasons, but I have my ear to the ground, and, believe you me, they're not the real ones. The fact is that Marion simply up and ditched him because he wasn't making enough money to suit her. Her and her uppity ideas! Can you imagine that? I mean, a woman leaving you just because you're only making ten thousand a year!"

"A little earning is a dangerous thing," I said.

Syd frowned and shook his head. "Divorce is a terrible thing," he said.

"Not always," said my wife, looking away with an odd expression I had never seen on her face before.

"Of course, you've got to support a woman," Syd went on. "I have no objection to that. But to make money your god to the point where it can ruin a relationship, then all I can say is, 'Where are we going?' I'd welcome the chance to work for a good woman again," he said, with another glance at Megs. "To, as the old-fashioned expression goes, lay all my worldly goods at her feet. And between you and me, I've had a little luck with certain investments lately."

"You have?" Megs said, with interest. "Swiftie won't bother his head about those things."

"Well, he should," Syd said. "Aside from providing for those dependent on him, a man should want to own a part of the growth of his country. Did you know that there are now fifteen million Americans who own securities and go to share-holders' meetings?"

"Stocks and bonds are the opiate of the people," I said, and wafted myself to the bar for a refill.

It was from here on that events moved with the speed at which, later, I was to marvel. As I set my empty glass down on the bar, I decided that what I wanted was a bottle of beer, and as I got it from the kitchen icebox, the sight of cold chicken and ham and whatnot in there made me realize that I was starved. I called into the living room to ask whether anyone wanted to join me in a midnight snack (hoping to communicate thereby my impression that that was how late the hour seemed), and they answered either yes or no — I couldn't make out which above the sound of phonograph music. I prolonged the solitary pleasure of slicing and butter-ing pumpernickel and spreading out a platterful of cold cuts and cheese, so it may have been as much as half an hour later that I carried it all into the living room, to find them dancing.

I sat watching them as I improvised a portmanteau sand-wich from the wealth of viands at my sole disposal, they hav-ing expressed no wish to join me. I sank my teeth into the sandwich (carefully calibrated for accommodation by the human mouth) just as the waltz to which they had been swaying, by now cheek to cheek, came to an end. There was a whispered exchange between them, and then Megs excused herself and disappeared. Syd Cottonfelt sat down to watch me eat, taking nothing himself except a stuffed olive, which he snatched from the platter just as I was reaching for it my-self.

"She's a real person," he said.

"Who?" I asked, doubling a flap of cold tongue over my own.

"Megs."

I nodded, mumbling assent through a quid of food.

The object of these encomiums reappeared in ten minutes or so, wearing a light coat and carrying two suitcases. "I'm leaving you," she said.

"Why?" I asked.

She set the bags down and heaved a long sigh, as one shouldering the challenge of a difficult assignment. "It's hard to put into words, at least into a few words, and it's not a decision I've reached on the spur of the moment. I've felt this way for a long time — meeting Syd just brings it to a head. Swiftie, you're not real. You're not a real person."

"No?" I said, selecting a morsel of Port du Salut from the assortment on the platter. I nodded to the archetypal and irreducible Cube, who had moved to her side. "Is he?"

"I see now he's what I want," she said. "Oh, you're brilliant, yes. Amusing, sure. But that's just the trouble. Nothing is safe from your wicked tongue. Nothing is sacred. Swiftie, life can't be lived on that level. You laugh at simple people, but they're what I need after seven years of you. I can't breathe this rarefied air anymore. I've got to come down to" — she turned and smiled at her Cottonfelt — "to earth. I need roots."

"Have some potato salad," I said. "Potatoes are roots, you know. Stop this nonsense."

But my voice became suddenly tinged with fear. I heard a rustle in the doorway where they had been standing, and looking up, saw that they were gone. I rose and rushed through the open front door to the porch, in time to see them hurrying toward a waiting cab. She had telephoned for one while packing!

"Give me another chance!" I called.

She turned at the curb. "It's too late. You had a sweetness and a freshness once, Swiftie, but that was long ago Remember —" In the light from a street lamp, I could see the sad half smile wreathing her lips as she went on. "Remember the corny little jokes you used to play when we were first married? You'd put things in my handbag — absurd little items I would find later and pull out, sometimes in public A can opener, a canvas garden glove, an egg timer. Once a handful of cranberries. Then I would laugh and love you. Do you remember all that?"

I nodded mutely from the top of the steps, tears spilling from my eyes. "I'll do all that again. If that's what you want. We can start fresh. I'll be like other people. You'll see."

"It's too late," she replied. "You never gave that side of you a chance, and now it's too late. You went the other way — too far to go back. You're a snob. Oh, you're the most fabulous thing going, and probably right for the right woman, but it's not me. Goodbye, Swiftie."

"Wait!" I cried. "We'll be like that again. I'll put stuff in your bag till hell won't hold it. I'll buy albums of the world's best-loved overtures. All that." I moved down a step, away from the empty house into which I now suddenly feared returning. I called one more thing. It was absolutely my last offer. "I'll whisper low."

She turned and hurried into the cab, into which the Cube had by now chucked the luggage. He climbed in after her, slammed the door, and they were gone. I went back into the empty house alone.

It was there that I did most of the hard thinking that occupied me in the days that followed. I had had my moment of truth: I was not a real person at all, as I had all along taken for granted, but something so far from it that for another man to be my opposite was sufficient recommendation in the eyes of the woman with whom I had been living. What a rude awakening! Radical changes were in order — in fact, a prompt about-face. I must seek new influences, and fast, before I became too recherché even for the few friends I had left and found myself completely isolated from the human race.

It was to this end that I took to spending my free evenings not in Greenwich or Fairfield or any of my other old haunts but in Bridgeport. There, one Saturday night, I met a girl named Rose in a bar-and-grill near the Bridgeport Brass Company. I lured her away from some girl friends, with whom she was clustered about a pinball machine, to a booth that became free just as we were striking up our acquaintance. She was a sturdy girl in her twenties, with that solid yet fluid firmness of line that is associated with Biedermeier furniture — a resemblance also furthered by her blond coloring. I was not surprised to learn she was of German extraction. In the course of our first Tom Collins together, she dug into a large wicker handbag for her cigarettes, removing from it a frazzled paperback reprint, which she set on the table to facilitate her search. It was the English version of a French novel I happened to have read in the original and disliked. I glanced at a few pages of it. "Fortunately, it's a poor translation," I would have said in the old days, and it was on the tip of my tongue now, but I checked it. I was not going to start this relationship with the kind of unilateral intercourse that had curdled another. Instead I said, noting the last of innumerable dog's-ears, "Well, you're almost finished."

"I am finished."

"May I borrow it?" I asked, putting it beside me on the bench.

She smiled at me through the smoke of her cigarette, to which I had also meanwhile managed to set fire for her. "Are you that hard up for something to read? Frankly, you look like you've read everything," she said, noting the peeved intellectuality of my face, as well, I imagine, as the tic that had developed in my right eye as the result of all these stresses.

"Frankly, I want to make sure I see you again," I told her. "I'll have to return it "

"I don't want it back. I read every spare minute I have — on the bus to and from work, when things are slack at the switchboard. That's what I do where I work. That's how come I always carry a paperback in my bag. My girl friends say I read too much — that I'll ruin my eyes, always with my nose in a book. I didn't care much for that one. I thought it drug in the middle, and I couldn't identify with the characters. I feel that's essential to the enjoyment of a book. Don't you?"

"But of course! We have so much in common," I said. "Can I take you to dinner next week if I promise to bring you a new book? You need one, you know. And I'll write you a poem. I am a poet, you know. My feet are Longfellows."

She blew a puff of smoke playfully into my face.

"I like the way you wrinkle your nose when you smile," I said.

"Fast worker," she said, permitting me to take her hand. "Say, your hand is like ice."

"Well, you know what they say about cold hands," I said. "How about Wednesday?"

"If you behave yourself tonight." She laughed, then rose and said she had to telephone her mother to say she would be home a little later than expected.

The instant she was gone, I reached for her handbag, which she had left behind after taking a dime from it. I quickly stowed into it the salt and pepper shakers, the lid of the sugar bowl, a beer coaster, and a pair of pliers left behind by a repairman who had been fixing the jukebox meter in that booth prior to our taking it. I buried them all well down in the bottom of the bag, so she would be sure not to see them till she got home, when she would proceed to extract them one by one and think of me with a smile of affection. I've got to have heart, and there isn't much time.

REQUIEM FOR A NOUN; OR, INTRUDER IN THE DUSK

*(What can come of trying to read
William Faulkner while minding a
child, or vice versa)*

THE COLD Brussels sprout rolled off the page of the book I was reading and lay inert and defunctive in my lap Turning my head with a leisure at least three-fourths impotent rage, I saw him standing there holding the toy with which he had catapulted the vegetable, or rather the reverse, the toy first then the fat insolent fist clutching it and then above that the bland defiant face beneath the shock of black hair like tangible gas. It, the toy, was one of those cardboard funnels with a trigger near the point for firing a small celluloid ball. Letting the cold Brussels sprout lie there in my lap for him to absorb or anyhow apprehend rebuke from, I took a pull at a Scotch highball I had had in my hand and then set it down on the end table beside me.

"So instead of losing the shooter which would have been a mercy you had to lose the ball," I said, fixing with a stern eye what I had fathered out of all sentient and biding dust; remembering with that retroactive memory by which we count chimes seconds and even minutes after they have struck (recapitulate, even, the very grinding of the bowels of the clock before and during and after) the cunning furtive click, clicks rather, which perception should have told me then already were not the trigger plied but the icebox opened.

"Even a boy of five going on six should have more respect for his father if not for food," I said, now picking the cold Brussels sprout out of my lap and setting it — not dropping it, setting it — in an ashtray, thinking how across the wax bland treachery of the kitchen linoleum were now in all likelihood distributed the remnants of string beans and cold potatoes and maybe even tapioca. "You're no son of mine."

I took up the thread of the book again or tried to· the weft of legitimate kinship that was intricate enough without the obbligato of that dark other: the sixteenths and thirty-seconds and even sixty-fourths of dishonoring cousinships brewed out of the violable blood by the ineffaceable errant lusts. Then I heard another click; a faint metallic rejoinder that this time was neither the trigger nor the icebox but the front door opened and then shut. Through the window I saw him picking his way over the season's soiled and sun-frayed vestiges of snow like shreds of rotted lace, the cheap up-ended toy cone in one hand and a child's cardboard suitcase in the other, toward the road.

I dropped the book and went out after him who had forgotten not only that I was in shirtsleeves but that my braces hung down over my flanks in twin festoons. "Where are you going?" I called, my voice expostulant and forlorn on the warm numb air. Then I caught it: caught it in the succinct outrage of the suitcase and the prim churning rear and marching heels as well: I had said he was no son of mine, and so he was leaving a house not only where he was not wanted but where he did not even belong.

"I see," I said in that shocked clarity with which we perceive the truth instantaneous and entire out of the very astonishment that refuses to acknowledge it. "Just as you now cannot be sure of any roof you belong more than half under, you figure there is no housetop from which you might not as well begin to shout it. Is that it?"

Requiem for a Noun; or, Intruder in the Dusk

Something was trying to tell me something. Watching him turn off on the road — and that not only with the ostensible declaration of vagabondage but already its very assumption, attaining as though with a single footfall the very apotheosis of wandering just as with a single shutting of a door he had that of renunciation and farewell — watching him turn off on it, the road, in the direction of the Permisangs', our nearest neighbors, I thought *Wait; no; what I said was not enough for him to leave the house on, it must have been the blurted inscrutable chance confirmation of something he already knew, and was half able to assess, either out of the blown facts of boyhood or pure male divination or both.*

"What is it you know?" I said, springing forward over the delicate squalor of the snow and falling in beside the boy. "Does any man come to the house to see your mother when I'm away, that you know of?" Thinking *We are mocked, first by the old mammalian snare, then, snared, by that final unilaterality of all flesh to which birth is given; not only not knowing when we may be cuckolded, but not even sure that in the veins of the very hantling we dandle does not flow the miscreant sniggering wayward blood.*

"I get it now," I said, catching in the undeviating face just as I had in the prim back and marching heels the steady articulation of disdain. "Cuckoldry is something of which the victim may be as guilty as the wrongdoer. That's what you're thinking? That by letting in this taint upon our heritage I am as accountable as she or they who have been its actual avatars. More. Though the foe may survive, the sleeping sentinel must be shot. Is that it?"

"You talk funny."

Mother-and-daughter blood conspires in the old mammalian office. Father-and-son blood vies in the ancient phallic enmity. I caught him by the arm and we scuffled in the snow. "I will be heard," I said, holding him now as though we might

126

be dancing, my voice intimate and furious against the furious sibilance of our feet in the snow. Thinking how revelation had had to be inherent in the very vegetable scraps to which venery was probably that instant contriving to abandon me, the cold boiled despair of whatever already featureless suburban Wednesday Thursday or Saturday supper the shot green was the remainder. "I see another thing," I panted, cursing my helplessness to curse whoever it was had given him blood and wind. Thinking *He's glad; glad to credit what is always secretly fostered and fermented out of the vats of childhood fantasy anyway — for all childhood must conceive a substitute for the father that has conceived it (finding that other inconceivable?)*; thinking *He is walking in a nursery fairy tale to find the king his sire.* "Just as I said to you 'You're no son of mine' so now you answer back 'Neither are you any father to me' "

The scherzo of violence ended as abruptly as it had begun. He broke away and walked on, after retrieving the toy he had dropped and adjusting his grip on the suitcase which he had not, this time faster and more urgently.

The last light was seeping out of the shabby sky, after the hemorrhage of sunset. High in the west where the fierce constellations soon would wheel, the evening star in single bombast burned and burned. The boy passed the Permisangs' without going in, then passed the Kellers'. Maybe he's heading for the McCullums', I thought, but he passed their house too. Then he, we, neared the Jelliffs'. He's got to be going there, his search will end there, I thought. Because that was the last house this side of the tracks. And because *something was trying to tell me something.*

"Were you maybe thinking of what you heard said about Mrs. Jelliff and me having relations in Spuyten Duyvil?" I said in rapid frantic speculation. "But they were talking about

mutual kin — nothing else." The boy said nothing. But I had
sensed it instant and complete: the boy felt that, whatever of
offense his mother may or may not have given, his father had
given provocation; and out of the old embattled malehood, it
was the hairy ineluctable Him whose guilt and shame he was
going to hold preponderant. *Because now I remembered.*

"So it's Mrs Jelliff — Sue Jelliff — and me you have got
this all mixed up with," I said, figuring he must, in that fat sly
nocturnal stealth that took him creeping up and down the
stairs to listen when he should have been in bed, certainly
have heard his mother exclaiming to his father behind that
bedroom door it had been vain to close since it was not
soundproof: "I saw you I saw that with Sue. There may not
be anything between you but you'd like there to be! Maybe
there is at that!'"

Now like a dentist forced to ruin sound enamel to reach
decayed I had to risk telling him what he did not know to
keep what he assuredly did in relative control.

"This is what happened on the night in question," I said
"It was under the mistletoe, during the holidays, at the Jelliffs'. Wait! I will be heard out! See your father as he is, but
see him in no baser light. He has his arms around his neighbor's wife It is evening, in the heat and huddled spiced felicity of the year's end, under the mistletoe (where as well as
anywhere else the thirsting and exasperated flesh might be
visited by the futile pangs and jets of later lust, the omnivo-
rous aches of fifty and forty and even thirty-five to seize
what may be the last of the allotted lips). Your father seems
to prolong beyond its usual moment's span that custom's
usufruct. Only for an instant, but in that instant letting
trickle through the fissures of appearance what your mother
and probably Rudy Jelliff too saw as an earnest of a flood
that would have devoured that house and one four doors
away."

A moon hung over the eastern roofs like a phantasmal bladder. Somewhere an icicle crashed and splintered, fruit of the day's thaw

"So now I've got it straight," I said. "Just as through some nameless father your mother has cuckolded me (you think), so through one of Rudy Jelliff's five sons I have probably cuckolded him. Which would give you at least a half brother under that roof where under ours you have none at all. So you balance out one miscreance with another, and find your rightful kin in our poor weft of all the teeming random bonded sentient dust."

Shifting the grip, the boy walked on past the Jelliffs'. Before him — the tracks, and beyond that — the other side of the tracks. And now out of whatever reserve capacity for astonished incredulity may yet have remained I prepared to face this last and ultimate outrage. But he didn't cross. Along our own side of the tracks ran a road which the boy turned left on. He paused before a lighted house near the corner, a white cottage with a shingle in the window which I knew from familiarity to read, "Viola Pruett, Piano Lessons," and which, like a violently unscrambled pattern on a screen, now came to focus.

Memory adumbrates just as expectation recalls. The name on the shingle made audible to listening recollection the last words of the boy's mother as she'd left, which had fallen short then of the threshold of hearing. ". . . Pruett," I remembered now. "He's going to have supper and stay with Buzzie Pruett overnight . . . Can take a few things with him in that little suitcase of his. If Mrs. Pruett phones about it, just say I'll take him over when I get back," I recalled now in that chime-counting recapitulation of retroactive memory — better than which I could not have been expected to do. Because the eternal Who-instructs might have got through to the

whiskey-drinking husband or might have got through to the
reader immersed in that prose vertiginous intoxicant and
unique, but not to both.

"So that's it," I said. "You couldn't wait till you were taken
much less till it was time but had to sneak off by yourself,
and that not cross-lots but up the road I've told you a hundred times to keep off even the shoulder of."

The boy had stopped and now appeared to hesitate before
the house. He turned around at last, switched the toy and the
suitcase in his hands, and started back in the direction he had
come.

"What are you going back for now?" I asked.

"More stuff to take in this suitcase," he said. "I was going
to just sleep at the Pruetts' overnight, but now I'm going to
ask them to let me stay there for good."

THE HOUSE OF MIRTH

THE COLLABORATION known as marriage could, I think, be
profitably extended from the domestic to the social sphere,
where a man and wife might brighten their contribution to,
say, the give-and-take of dinner-table conversation by preparing a few exchanges in advance. "It's simply the principle of
teamwork," I told my wife in partially describing the idea to
her one evening as we were dressing to go to dinner at the
home of some friends named Anthem. "For instance, tonight,
Sue Anthem being as hipped as she is on family trees, we're
bound to talk relatives at some point. Well, I'm going to tell
about my seagoing grandfather who's so wonderful. In the
middle of it, I'll pause and take up my napkin, and then I'd
appreciate it if you'd ask me, 'Was he on your mother's

side?' " (I planned to answer, "Yes, except in money matters, when he usually stuck up for my father." This wasn't much, but I was feeling my way around in the form, trying to get the hang of it before going on to something more nearly certifiable as wit.)

Dinner ran along the lines I had foreseen. Sue Anthem got off on kinship, and I launched my little account of this wonderful grandfather. I paused at the appointed moment and, glancing at my wife, reached for my napkin by way of a signal.

"I keep forgetting," she came in brightly. "Was he your maternal grandfather?"

"Yes, except in money matters, when he usually stuck up for my father," I replied.

A circle of blank looks met my gaze. I coughed into my napkin, and Sue picked up the thread of the discussion while I reviewed in my mind a couple of other gambits I had worked out with my wife, on the way over. One of these concerned a female friend, not present that evening, whom I will cut corners by calling a gay divorcée. She had just announced her engagement to a man so staid that news of the match took everyone who knew her by surprise. "Now, if the thing comes up, as it probably will," I had coached my wife, "say something about how you've only met him a few times but he seems a man of considerable reserve." I intended then to adroitly add, "Which Monica will get her hands on in short order." I expected that to go over big, the divorcée being a notorious gold-digger.

The gossip did get around to her soon after it left the subject of relatives, and my wife came in on cue punctually enough, but her exact words were "He's such a quiet, unassuming chap."

This time, I had the presence of mind to realize the quip was useless, and check myself. Another misfire followed almost immediately. In preparation for possible discussion of Italy, where Monica and her fiancé planned to honeymoon, I had primed my wife to tell about her own visit to the Gulf of Spezia, where the drowned Shelley had been washed up. "In a way, you know, he was lucky," I had planned to comment. "Most poets are washed up *before* they're dead." She told her story, but used the words "where Shelley was found," thus washing up *that* mot.

It was clear that I would have to explain the system to my wife in detail if I was ever to get the bugs out of it. I decided, in fact, that I had better reveal in each case what the capper was to be, so that she would realize the importance of delivering her line exactly as prearranged I did this while we were driving to our next party, several evenings later. I had ducked her questions about the failures at the Anthems', preferring to wait till I had some new material worked up to hammer my point home with before I laid the whole thing on the line.

"At the Spiggetts' tonight," I said, "there's certain to be the usual talk about art. Here's a chance for you to get in those licks of yours about abstract painting — isn't it high time painters got back to nature, and so on. The sort of thing you said at the Fentons'. You might cite a few of the more traditional paintings, like the portraits of Mrs. Jack Gardner and Henry Marquand. Then turn to me and ask — now, get this, it's important — ask, 'Why can't we have portraits like that anymore?' "

"Then what will you say?" she asked.

I slowed to make a left turn, after glancing in the rearview mirror to make sure nobody was behind me. " 'It's no time for Sargents, my dear.' "

My wife reached over and pushed in the dash lighter, then sat waiting for it to pop, a cigarette in her hand.

"Of course I'll throw it away," I said. "Just sort of murmur it."

She lit the cigarette and put the lighter back in its socket. "Isn't this a little shabby?" she asked.

"Why? What's shabby about it? Isn't it better than the conversation you have to put up with normally — doesn't it make for something at least a cut above that?" I said. "What's wrong with trying to brighten life up? We can turn it around if you like. You can take the cappers while I feed you the straight lines —"

"Lord, no, leave it as it is."

"Can I count on you, then?"

"I suppose," she said, heaving a sigh. "But step on it. We're supposed to eat early and then go to that Shakespearean little theatre in Norwalk."

My wife and I parted on entering the Spiggetts' house. I made off to where a new television comedienne, named Mary Cobble, was holding court with a dozen or so males. She was a small blond, cute as a chipmunk and bright as a dollar. The men around her laughed heartily at everything she said. It was well known in Connecticut that her writers, of whom she kept a sizable stable, formed a loyal claque who followed her to every party, but it didn't seem to me that *all* the men around her could be writers. I knocked back a few quick Martinis and soon felt myself a gay part of the group. Once, I glanced around and saw my wife looking stonily my way over the shoulder of a man whose fame as a bore was so great that he was known around town as the Sandman. Matters weren't helped, I suppose, when, presently returning from the buffet with two plates of food, I carried one to Mary Cobble and sat down on the floor in front of her to eat the other. At the same time, I saw the Sandman fetching my wife a bite.

Midway through this lap dinner, there was one of those moments when all conversation suddenly stops at once. Lester Spiggett threw in a comment about a current show at a local art gallery. I saw my wife put down her fork and clear her throat. "Well, if there are any portraits in it, I hope the things on the canvases are faces," she said. She looked squarely at me. "Why is it we no longer have portraits that *portray* — that give you pictures of *people?* Like, oh, the *Mona Lisa*, or *The Man with the Hoe*, or even that *American Gothic* thing? Why is that?"

Everybody turned to regard me, as the one to whom the query had obviously been put. "That's a hard question for me to answer," I said, frowning into my plate. I nibbled thoughtfully on a fragment of cold salmon. "Your basic point is, of course, well taken — that the portraits we get are not deserving of the name. Look like somebody threw an egg at the canvas."

Fuming, I became lost in the ensuing free-for-all. Not so my wife, whom annoyance renders articulate. She more than held her own in the argument, which was cut short when Mary Cobble upset a glass of iced tea She made some cheery remark to smooth over the incident. The remark wasn't funny, nor was it intended to be funny, but to a man her retinue threw back their heads and laughed.

Meaning to be nice, I laughed, too, and said, "Well, it goes to show you. A good comedienne has her wits about her."

"And pays them well," my wife remarked, in her corner. (Luckily, Mary Cobble didn't hear it, but two or three others did, and they repeated it until it achieved wide circulation, with a resulting increase in our dinner invitations. That, however, was later. The present problem was to get through the rest of the evening.)

We had to bolt our dessert and rush to the theatre, where

they were doing *King Lear* in Bermuda shorts, or something, and my wife and I took another couple in our car, so I didn't get a chance to speak to her alone until after the show. Then I let her have it.

"That was a waspish remark," I said. "And do you know why you made it? Resentment. A feeling of being out of the swim. It's because you're not good at repartee that you say things like that, and are bitter."

"Things like what?" my wife asked.

I explained what, and repeated my charge.

In the wrangle, quite heated, that followed her denial of it, she gave me nothing but proof of its truth. I submitted that the idea of mine that had given rise to this hassle, and of which the hassle could safely be taken to be the corpse, had been a cozy and even a tender one· the idea that a man and wife could operate as a team in public. "What could be more domestic?" I said.

"Domesticity begins at home," she rather dryly returned.

I met this with a withering silence.

SPLIT-LEVEL

I WAS hurrying down the main street of Westport one Saturday afternoon late last fall when I heard my name called, followed by the words "as Ah live and breathe." My friend Malcolm Johnsprang was coming toward me, hand extended. "Haven't seen you in ages," he said.

"Hello, Malcolm," I said. "How are you?"

"Fahn. How are *you?* Walking along with distraction's aspect, your ahs in a fahn frenzy rolling. What's up?"

"Oh, usual rat race, one thing and another." We stood on

the sidewalk, grinning disproportionately at each other. "Well, well. It must be six months since I've seen you, Malcolm."

"Come have a beer," he proposed, slinging an arm through mine "Just sold two houses and feel flush." He is a real-estate broker.

I agreed willingly enough, and as he steered me back half a block in the direction I had come from, I congratulated him.

"We living in a boom town," Malcolm observed, with evident mixed feelings. "The new atrocities are going like hot cakes and ruining the landscape fast enough to drive the old families out of their beautiful homes — which Ah love, but business is business, and we're here to turn over the split-levels along with the gems." The tavern for which we were headed now lay across the street, and we paused for a break in the traffic. "It's a tragedy. Connecticut is being laid waste. And Ah love mah state."

Malcolm Johnsprang is an ardent and even chauvinistic New Englander, if a naturalized one, with a native accent that is rather more than vestigial. He is a bachelor of about thirty, blond, handsome in a somewhat moon-faced way. None of our friends know where Malcolm was born, except that it was obviously below the Mason and Dixon Line. The subject is never mentioned. I once cited, in favorable comparison with the storied New England manors about which he is forever spouting lore, the great houses in Biloxi and Paducah, down around in there, and was met with a frozen stare. I sensed that I had struck a taboo, and thereafter watched my tongue in his presence.

"When you going to put that lovely salt-box of your own on the market?" he asked as we crossed the street. "It's a delightful place, but with four kids and only three bedrooms, you ought to let me get you out of there and into something with some room. Got a sweet old place up Wilton way with five bedrooms."

This was not a new gambit. For the two years since the birth of my fourth child, Malcolm had been dying to "turn over" my house, of which he remained an admirer despite my protestations that it was not authentically old but mostly additions around an original cottage. Its musk of venerability had impressed Malcolm, who took it for granted that the split-levels discernible from my parlor window were gall to my soul, when as a matter of fact they looked like the Promised Land, and it was my plan, if ever I sold my dank little gem, to move into one as fast as a van could get me there.

At the bar, I listened silently while Malcolm reeled off what he had in the way of sweet old properties. When he got around to the atrocities again, I pricked up my ears. He had just been through a model house that was to be thrown open for public inspection the following week. "The minute you walk in, you get that smell of *newness*, you know?" he said, turning to me as to a kindred spirit. I nodded, chewing a peanut from a bowl of them on the bar. "From the entrance hall, you step into a dropped living room, which, of course, has a 'dining ell,' " he continued amusedly, "and from there you go up two steps to a section where there's four bedrooms and a den. Downstairs, behind the garage, there's the half-aboveground playroom and utility room." He paused to finish off his beer. "I guess they O.K. for people of a certain taste and income."

I signaled the bartender for refills. "You say four bedrooms and a den. You could consider that five bedrooms, couldn't you?" I said

"You could. It's a lot of house for the money. Fifty-three five."

"My God!" I exclaimed in genuine surprise. "That *is* reasonable. I mean if the construction is good."

"Construction's O.K. Nobody builds them any better than Spontini. The house is sound as a nut, but, of course, totally devoid of chawm. You should see it!"

I let the subject drop. But everything Malcolm had said came back to me the following Saturday evening, when, out of a clear sky, my domestic life took a new turn.

The "clear sky" is more than a little figurative. As a matter of fact, it rained cats and dogs from Friday on. Saturday evening, one of the bedroom ceilings sprang a leak. With the water gathering in the saucepans — collecting simultaneously in the cellar, as I knew without having to look — my wife chose the occasion to announce that she was again expecting.

"Damn," I said sympathetically. "Well, we'll *have* to move now. We'll just have to."

No argument there, or over my vow that it would not be into another old house — she was quick to make that point herself. What I wondered was how far we would agree on what we *did* want. She knew I was sick of making repairs, and I knew she was sick of a Currier & Ives kitchen and too little room, but that was as far as we had ever compared notes.

After sitting abstractedly for some minutes in the living room, to which we had returned after the hullabaloo, my wife said, "I've been thinking. Houses of this kind weren't planned with children in mind. But you know the kind they build nowadays, with an extra sort of half floor downstairs for a playroom? So that end of the main floor is *raised* a little? So you have to —" She held out a hand horizontally at varying heights, apparently unable to bring herself to speak the words.

"Darling, you mean —" I began, getting out of my chair. "You mean you like split-levels, too?"

She nodded. "On days like this, you wouldn't have kids

tracking mud into the house. They'd come in downstairs, take off their muddy boots and things, and *stay* down there."

"All five of them," I said affectionately, tousling her hair. "Him, too, down there with the rest, out of the way. I love him already."

My wife and I looked at Spontini's house the next day, liked it, and put down a binder of five hundred dollars, applicable to the purchase of one quite similar to it, to be erected within four months on a nearby plot two acres in size.

The next step was to go home and pour a stiff highball.

"I know what you're thinking," my wife said, watching me make short work of the drink. "What if we don't sell *this* house in time? But we will. People do it all the time — buy and then sell, I mean. The market is humming, everyone says so, and besides we've got four whole months."

That wasn't what I had on my mind at the moment, though God knew it was No 1 on my list of headaches. My mind was on a hurdle that seemed scarcely less formidable — that of telling Malcolm Johnsprang what I had done.

I stewed about facing him for the better part of a week before it occurred to me how I might cushion the blow. I would specify him as the agent for the brokerage fee. This was shaving it pretty fine, since he had derided the premises rather than extolled them, but he *had* apprised me of their existence and told me to go see for myself, and technically that is all an agent need do to be entitled to the commission. Anyhow, it would be no skin off my nose, since it was Spontini who would have to pony up; it wouldn't actually be any skin off Spontini's nose, either, since houses are priced to absorb the brokerage. That, at the customary rate of five percent, would come to twenty-six hundred and some dollars. With this amount lining his pockets, I felt, Malcolm would be at least tolerant of my move — after, of course, recovering from the shock of having his Yankee sensibilities outraged.

Still, it was with dread that I contemplated the luncheon date I finally made with him for the following Saturday, and after calling for him at his office that noon I steered him toward a place where I knew they served liquor as well as food. Once installed in a booth with him, I quickly put down a couple of hookers, leaned back, and said, "Malcolm, you've sold me a house."

Our appetizers had arrived. Malcolm looked up from his shrimp cocktail. "What y'all talking about?" he asked.

"Those Spontini houses you were raving about the other day. I couldn't wait to get over and see for myself, and, by George, they're everything you said. My wife and I both felt they were just what we need, and we've put a binder on one."

Bent over my own food, I could sense his prolonged regard. At length, I was aware of a shifting movement in his seat, and then I heard him say, "Ah don't believe Ah showed you the property in question."

"An agent doesn't have to," I said firmly. "All he has to do to collect is tell a client about a place."

"Ah don't think Ah even did that, in the accepted sense of the term," he said.

"I've named you as broker," I said. This wasn't strictly true, but I intended to name him when I signed the contract, in a few days. "The law's the law. The money's yours. There's nothing you can do about it."

His left eye contracted slightly, like a clam under lemon juice. The movement seemed part of a faltering effort to get the situation — or, rather, me — into focus. "Business is business," he said presently, "but that also implahs —"

My dander was up. I leaned impulsively across the table and brought it all out. I said very rapidly, "I like newness. I'm sick of original beams and cobblers' benches. What's more, I never *did* like them. I've been living a lie for seven years — ever since I moved into Connecticut and did as the

Romans did Now I want out. I want something spanking new. I want to *smell newness when I walk in*," I went remorselessly on, and Malcolm stiffened against the back of the booth with his eyes shut, like a man being electrocuted. I threw the switch for another charge. "I like split-levels. I like rustproof aluminum combination storm windows and screens, that fit. I love plastics. I love plywood and Fiberglas and things that are extruded and laminated. I love asphalt tile and Vinylite and Formica And I can't wait to get them."

I sat back, breathing heavily. Eventually, Malcolm picked up his cocktail fork, which he had let drop, and resumed eating his shrimps There were two left. He ate them with a thoughtful air, as though he had now recovered At last, he set his fork down and picked up his water. He took a swallow and set the glass down.

"Have you seen Tom?" he asked.

"Tom who?"

"Tom Magazine. They have an article this week on the modern home, and there's a good deal in it on the split-level. You might read it." He moved his water glass around the tabletop, frowning a little "Why, sure, fellow, if you think that's the ticket for you, more power to you. There's probably a lot to be said for that type of house which us old mossbacks up heah don't appreciate. Sot in our ways, you know," he added, with an engaging grin. "Anyhow, Ah hope you and your good lady are going to be happy in your new home. Ah *know* you'll be."

That I felt like a fool isn't the point, or that I felt like a heel. The point is what the incident showed about Malcolm. I had never really seen anyone behave, after the first surprise, so instinctively like a gentleman, so naturally and effortlessly displaying what used to be called good breeding, particularly in another part of the country — specifically, in that part the dust of which he supposed himself to have shaken from his feet. "The South is ouah cross," he would say. "We heah up Nawth must bear it." Now Malcolm pushed his dishes aside and said, leaning forward with a broad smile, "The next order of business is to get your present house off your hands, which presumably you have to do to swing this?" I nodded. "Ah don't know whether you've set an asking price, but what do you think of fifty-one five? It's worth every penny of it, in mah estimation."

Of the scores of agents who brought prospective buyers to my house in the next few weeks, Malcolm was far the most articulate. He would enter explaining that the black band around the chimney went back to Revolutionary days, when the mark was the sign of Tory sympathies (news to me); he would leave praising the view. "Stony fields against gently rolling hills is one of the loveliest sights we have up Nawth," he would say.

He got me an offer of forty-eight thousand the second week. I turned it down, and overnight the market went dead. There were a number of reasons. First, bad weather and the approaching holidays made a seasonal slump. Second, the Penn Central Railroad went to hell just then, scaring off the New York commuting market. Third, repair work on the road my house was on made it impassable, and brokers couldn't get clients up to the house.

Weeks passed with only a smattering of lookers. The weeks became months. I woke up one morning to find myself twenty days from closing time on the new house and all my money still tied up in the old. Malcolm arrived that evening for a council of war. He advised me to ask Spontini for a month's extension, to reduce the asking price to forty-nine thousand, and to advertise in the New York papers. A classified ad, I knew, would, in addition to its own virtues, put me in the way of buyers who wouldn't involve me in an agency commission, and I could afford to sell my place to them for that much less.

I put an ad in the *Times* the next day. I went to Spontini and he gave me the thirty days' extension. Three more weeks passed, and I was into the period of grace. However, there were signs of spring in the air — the favored mating time of buyer and seller — and also signs that the Penn Central was pulling itself together. I had lots of answers to my ad, which I repeated on successive weekends. But now a new thing began to puzzle me. Malcolm almost never brought clients anymore, nor did he call up or come by to ask how we were doing, as he formerly had "Maybe he can't stand the sight of human suffering," I said sardonically to my wife, and added that he might be turning out to be a fair-weather friend after all.

The next week, we sold the house for forty-eight thousand dollars to a couple from Long Island, who came without an agent. It was a "sacrifice," as stated in ads, but I was off the hook. I phoned the news to Malcolm, whom, in the joy of relief, I found it in my heart to forgive.

"Hurrah!" he exclaimed. "Going to buy me a drink on that, aren't you? Let's have lunch. Ah'll be out of town next week, but how about a week from Saturday?"

"Swell. I'll call you that morning," I said.

Our buyers, a young pair named Mackay, came on the intervening Sunday to discuss some things with my wife and me, such as buying the draperies and the carpeting, and whatnot. Over drinks, we all became rather friendly, and at one point in the amiable haggling over the price of these extras Mackay laughingly suggested that we ought to throw them all in, since we'd saved the commission. "Lucky for you, your being outside the town limits," he said.

"What do you mean?" I asked.

"Being out of the agent's territory," he said. "He showed

us what he had in Westport proper, but then he said there was this charming salt-box we ought to look at before we made up our minds. It was just out of his legal territory, so we had to come without him."

We were outside the town limits but not, of course, outside any agent's limits. "Who was your agent?" I asked, as if I didn't know.

"Malcolm Johnsprang," he answered, making me feel like a fool for the second — and, I hoped, the last — time.

When I picked Malcolm up for lunch on Saturday, it was with a check for twenty-four hundred dollars, made out to him, in my pocket. As we stood on a curb on our way to the restaurant, waiting for a traffic light to change, I said, "How's everything, Malcolm?"

"Fahn. Well, ma's bloodshot."

"Ma's bloodshot?" I said softly as we started across the street.

He pointed to his right eye, which looked like a hot cinder "Better not get too close, in case it's pinkah," he said. "That's the most contagious thing on earth."

"It looks too red to be pinkeye," I said, springing out of the path of a truck. "Hard to say what makes an eye get red like that."

There was a constraint on his part as well as mine, or so it seemed to me as we settled ourselves at a table. We both ordered Old-Fashioneds. As we sipped, we got on the subject of a book he had been reading, and from there onto the state of current literature in general At one point, he looked at me and asked directly, "What do you think of William Faulkner?"

"Oh, I don't know," I said, hating all the stalling. "He seems to me easier to reread than to read." I didn't really know what that meant, except vaguely that Faulkner seemed better the second time around, and rewarded study, and so on. Malcolm merely grunted in a neutral way and dropped the subject, satisfied, I suppose, that no issue had been taken with his disapproval of the South When our second drink had arrived, I drew the check from my pocket and laid it on the table in front of him. "Here," I said. "I believe I owe you this "

He read it with convincing blankness. "Ah don't believe Ah quite —"

"Now, look, let's not go through all *that* again," I said. "You gave the Mackays some nonsense about the place being out of your territory to spare me having to shell out. God knows how many people you did that with, because you knew I was going to take a licking —"

"Boy!" Malcolm said, with a laugh. "If you knew what it meant to me to get those Mackays out of my hair! That *very afternoon*, Ah picked up another client and sold him that sixty-thousand-dollar place Ah was telling you about, in Weston. You keep your money," he said, shoving it back across the table.

"I will *not* keep it," I said, pushing it back again. "*You'll* keep it."

For a while, the check went back and forth between us like a puck between hockey players.

"I don't want charity," I finally snapped, and at that Malcolm picked up the check and pocketed it, laughing again.

"All right, but Ah won't cash it just yet," he said. "You'll need seven hundred dollars' worth of screens alone on that house, boy, unless you're aiming to spend the summer nights swatting bugs."

I knew he would never cash it (just as I knew he would never take the commission from Spontini). He couldn't revoke a fine gesture any more than he could make a bad one. Such a thing would have gone against his innate sense of form, or what I might as well unabashedly call Honor. It was on this score that I experienced my most complete sense of frustration with Malcolm.

I didn't object to his being come-lately, of course. The naturalized are often the most patriotic, just as converts are the most pious, and New England has had its illustrious share. Robert Frost came from California to adopt it, and Mark Twain came from Missouri to adopt it, and many of Malcolm's and my friends have come from other parts of the country to adopt it, and it seemed just too dreary to have to say that it was what they brought that counted, not what they got. Nevertheless, in Malcolm's case I should have welcomed the chance to make the point. I wanted to shake him by the shoulders and say, "You're the flower of the South." I wanted to shake him and say, "You're the most perfect example of a Southern Gentleman I've ever seen." But I couldn't; he was too touchy on the subject for me to be able to risk that. Instead, the only polite thing for me to do was to sit and let him race his motor.

When the waitress came up and thrust menus at us, he consulted his for only a moment. His face lit up and he said, "Ah, the New England bawled dinner today. Bring me that, please, ma'am?"

"Make it two," I said, handing my menu rather wearily back to her.

TILL THE SANDS
OF THE DESERT GROW COLD

I RECENTLY found myself with a wedding anniversary coming up, my nineteenth, with the usual attendant problem of a gift for my wife. I had been racking my brains intermittently for the better part of a month when I suddenly remembered a Broadway play she had mentioned particularly wanting to see. So I bought her a ticket to that. She gave me a shuffle sander, a small power job for use in my woodworking, and as we sat admiring our presents we polished off a bottle of Veuve Clicquot and talked of old times.

"Nineteen years," I said. "It seems much longer somehow. Twice that."

She regarded me across her champagne glass, sipping.

"So packed with incident, so rich in experiences shared," I went on. "This whole business of time and tedium is very little understood, as Thomas Mann points out in the passage in *The Magic Mountain* where he goes into it, you may recall. It is only over the short haul that a crowded interval seems short — an eventful day, say. When it comes to a long span looked back on, the more there's been in it the longer it seems. Monotony stretches the passing moment while pleasure makes time fly, yes; but over a past viewed in *retrospect* this illusion is reversed. Lack of content will shrink the interval, eventfulness expand it. What is true of time is also true of space. An empty room will seem smaller than a full one. Remember how we left the house on Woolsey Lane when we had it on the market? Furnished, so it would look bigger to clients. What a chapter that was, eh, ducks? Well, here we still are, all right, and so here's to us again. Cheers."

She was tickled pink with her ticket, and implored me to help her remember the evening for which I'd got it — a Saturday eight weeks hence — lest it slip by unnoticed, as things often do when planned that far in advance. We did not forget. I had the car gassed up and ready in plenty of time, for she had decided to drive in from the suburb where we live, rather than take the train. I saw her off with every good wish, waving to her from the driveway as she rounded the bend toward the Merritt Parkway. I heaved a sigh of pleasure for her before turning back to the house in anticipation of my own evening there.

First, I opened a can of beer, and then I sat down to watch a little television. Then I got Proust off the shelf to reread some of that "Overture" and see how his narrator was making out with the jellied madrilène or whatever the hell it was. Then I paged through the local phone book till I found an Upjohn, dialed the number, and asked the man who answered, "Are you Upjohn?," and when he said "Yes," replied, "At this hour?," and was hung up on in a thoroughly satisfying manner. Then I wandered into the kitchen, where I got out of the refrigerator all the meats and cheeses I could find and made myself a proper three-decker sandwich (lingering with special affection over the slices of Kraft's Genuine Switzerland Swiss cheese) I ate it slowly, with another can of cold beer. It was now around eleven o'clock. I looked at television for another hour, this time hitting a revival of an old Jimmy Stewart and Rosalind Russell movie that I remembered with particular fondness. Very charming, very cute. When it was over, I turned in.

My wife got home around 2 A.M. She woke me up when she entered the bedroom and snapped the light on. I smiled drowsily from the bed, scratching myself and yawning. "How was it?"

Her dress was awry, her stockings were twisted, and she must have been trampled by more than the normal quota of latecomers, judging from the expression with which she sat nursing her feet after removing her shoes. The havoc wrought to her person suggested even a spot of audience participation. Her cheeks wore a vivid flush. Her hair offered the final testimony to an exciting evening in the theatre.

"Well, it's not something you're supposed to *enjoy*," she said.

"Of course not."

"You're galvanized, you're shaken to your roots, you're repelled. When you come out, you feel you've been through it all *with* the characters."

"What was this one about?"

"Well, there's this couple going through a crisis. They hate each other, but it's not enough. At one point, she empties the garbage pail on his head while he's sitting reading Pascal."

"Why?"

"Well, they're sensitive people, which puts a special strain on them, and on their marriage, too, I suppose."

"What happens next? What does he do?"

"He throws up his hands."

"I understand there's quite a lot of vomiting in *Who's Afraid of Virginia Woolf?*, too. There's a new vital theatre, they tell me Out there. Well, come to bed. You look as though you've been pulled through a hedge backward."

She joined me inside of five minutes. I slung an arm around her in the dark and nuzzled her ear. "Marriage is a give-and-take," I said. "Each doing his part, each respecting the other's individuality. I'm sorry those two couldn't make a go of it."

She took my hand and laid it on her brow. "Splitting headache," she said. She was given the expected soothing strokes by way of ministration. I knew well that Merritt Parkway katzenjammer, the product of fatigue and oncoming headlights, that sets the homebound suburbanite to wondering whether the train wouldn't have been better — just as the Penn Central inaugurates the reverse line of thought.

"I love you," I said "You're a jewel. I love you and I'm going to tie you down with good stout cord and suck out your eyeballs with the muzzle of the vacuum cleaner to show

I care. To show I'm not indifferent. What else happens in the play? Are her feelings reciprocated?"

"Tomorrow. I'm too dead now." After a moment, she murmured, "Glad I went, though," stirring pleasurably against me.

"Makes a person appreciate their home more when they get back to it." I yawned, and mumbled, "Love is the ideality of the relativity of the reality of an infinitesimal portion of the absolute totality of the Infinite Being."

"What was that noise?"

"Hegel."

Her breathing became slower, and more measured. But after a few minutes she raised her head and said, "Do I smell smoke?"

"That's the stuff. A woman should smell smoke. When a woman smells smoke, you know everything is all right, everything is in order. You go right on smelling smoke God, what a doll."

She was soon asleep, and then I turned over and dropped off again myself, as, like a loose hubcap, the old earth spun on toward morning through the perilous and promissory night.

FROM THERE TO INFINITY

(After reading "From Here to Eternity," by James Jones)

We all have a guilt-edged security.
—Moses

"STARK ROMANTICISM" was the phrase that kept pounding through his head as he knocked on the door of Mama Paloma's, saw the slot opened and the single sloe plum that was Mama Paloma's eye scrutinizing him through the peep-hole. "Oh, you again," the eye grinned at him, sliding back the bolt of the door. "The girls are all pretty busy tonight but go on up " A dress of sequins that made her look like a fat mermaid with scales three-quarters instead of halfway up tightly encased the mounds of old snow that was her flesh. She glanced down at the must-be-heavy-as-lead suitcase in his hand as she closed the door. "I don't dare ast how many pages you're carting around in that by now," she grinned.

He mounted the steps with that suffocating expectation of men who are about to read their stuff, the nerves in his loins tightening like drying rawhide, the familiar knot hard in his belly. Shifting the suitcase from one hand to the other, his head swam into the densening surf of upstairs conversation, above which the tinkle of the player piano was like spray breaking all the time on rocks. Standing in the upper door-way, he reflected how, just as there can be damned senseless pointless want in the midst of plenty, so there can be the acutest loneliness in the midst of crowds. Fortunately, the thought passed swiftly. The whores moved, blatant as fla-mingos in their colored gowns, among the drinking-grinning men, and his eye ran tremulously swiftly in search of Dorine, gulpingly taking in the room for her figure moving erectly womanly through it all.

"No Princess to listen tonight," Peggy grinned toward him. "The Princess went away."

He could have slapped her It puzzled him to find that beneath that hard, crusty exterior beat a heart of stone. What was she doing in a place like this? He turned and hurried back down the stairs.

"Come back soon, there's listeners as good as the Princess," Mama Paloma laughed jellily jollily as she let him out into the street.

With Dorine not there he couldn't bear Mama Paloma's,

and he didn't know another place. Yet he had to have a woman tonight. Another woman would have to do, any woman.

Colonel Stilton's wife, he thought. Why not? She was from Boston, but there was no mistaking the look of hard insolent invitation she gave him each time she came to the Regimental Headquarters to ask if he knew where the Colonel had been since night before last. He hated Stilton's guts, or would if he, Stilton, had any. Hated that smirk and that single eyebrow always jerking sardonically skeptically up, like an anchovy that's learned to stand on end. Why not transfer out, why be a noncom under that bastard? he asked himself. I'm a non-compoop, he thought. He tried to make a joke of it but it was no good.

He knew where the Colonel lived from the time he'd taken him home stewed. He got out of the cab a block from the house. As he approached it walking, he could see Mrs. Stilton under a burning bulb on the screened terrace with her feet on a hassock, smoking a cigarette. She had on shorts and a sweater. Her slim brown legs like a pair of scissors made a clean incision in his mind. He went up the flagstone walk and rapped on the door.

"What do you want?" she said with the same insolent invitation, not stirring. He was aware of the neat, apple-hard breasts under the sweater, and of the terse, apple-hard invitation in her manner.

"I want to read this to you," he said, trying not to let his voice sound too husky.

"How much have you got in there?" her voice knew all about him.

"A quarter of a million words," he said, thickly.

She came over and opened the screen door and flipped her cigarette out among the glows of the fireflies in the yard.

When she turned back he caught the screen door and followed her inside She sat down on the hassock and looked away for what seemed an eternity.

"It's a lot to ask of a woman," she said. "More than I've ever given."

He stood there shifting the suitcase to the other hand, the arm-about-to-come-out-of-its-socket ache added to that in his throat, wishing he wouldn't wish he hadn't come. She crossed her arms around her and, with that deft motion only women with their animal confidence can execute, pulled her sweater off over her head and threw it on the floor. "That's what you want, isn't it?" she said.

"You with your pair of scissors," he said. "When you can have a man who's willing to bare his soul." He gritted his teeth with impatience. "Don't you see how much we could have?"

"Come on in." She rose, and led the way inside. Nothing melts easier than ice, he thought, sad. He watched her draw the drapes across the window nook and settle herself back among the cushions. "I'm all yours," she said. "Read."

The female is a yawning chasm, he thought, glancing up from his reading at the lying listening woman. He found and read the passage explaining that, how she was the inert earth, passive potent, that waits to be beaten soft by April's fecundating rains. Rain is the male principle and there are times for it to be interminable: prosedrops into rivulets of sentences and those into streams of paragraphs, these merging into chapters flowing in turn into sectional torrents strong and hard enough to wear gullies down the flanks of mountains. After what seemed an eternity, he paused and she stirred.

"What time is it?" she sat up.

"A quarter to three."

"I never knew it could be like this," she said.

Each knew the other was thinking of Colonel Stilton

"He never reads anything but *Quick*," she said, rolling her head away from him.

"The sonofabitch," he said, his fist involuntarily clenching as tears scalded his eyes. "Oh, the rotten sonofabitch!"

"It's no matter. Tell me about you How did you get like this?"

Bending his head over the manuscript again he readingly told her about that part· how when he was a kid in downstate Illinois his uncle, who had wanted to be a lawyer but had never been able to finish law school because he would get roaring drunk and burn up all his textbooks, used to tell him about his dream, and about his hero, the late Justice Oliver Wendell Holmes, who in those great early days of this country was working on a manuscript which he would never let out of his sight, carrying it with him in a sack even when he went out courting or to somebody's house to dinner, setting it on the floor beside his chair How his uncle passed this dream on to him, and how he took it with him to the big cities, where you began to feel how you had to get it all down, had to get down everything that got you down: the singing women in the cheap bars with their mouths like shrimp cocktails, the daughters-into-wives of chicken-eating digest-reading middle-class hypocrisy that you saw riding in the purring cars on Park Avenue, and nobody anywhere loving anybody they were married to. You saw that and you saw why. You had it all figured out that we in this country marry for idealistic love, and after the honeymoon there is bound to be disillusionment. That after a week or maybe a month of honest passion you woke up to find yourself trapped with the sow Respectability, which was the chicken-eating digest-reading middle-class assurance and where it lived: the house with the, oh sure, refrigerator, oil furnace and all the other automatic contraptions that snicker when they go on

— the well-lighted air-conditioned mausoleum of love. She was a better listener than Fillow, a middle-aged swell who had eight hundred jazz records and who would sit in Lincoln Park in Chicago eating marshmallow out of a can with a spoon with gloves on. Every time he tried to read Fillow a passage, Fillow would say "Cut it out." Fillow was a negative product of bourgeois society just as Stilton with his chicken-eating digest-reading complacence was a positive one, whom his wife had and knew she had cuckolded the minute she had let the suitcase cross the threshold.

"It'll never be the same again, will it?" she said fondly softly, seeing he had paused again.

He read her some more and it was the same. Except that the thing went on so long the style would change, seeming to shift gears of itself like something living a hydramatic life of its own, so that side by side with the well-spent Heming-way patrimony and the continental cry of Wolfe would be the seachanged long tireless free-form sentences reminiscent of some but not all or maybe even much of Faulkner.

The door flew open and Stilton stood inside the room. His eyes were like two wet watermelon pips spaced close to-gether on an otherwise almost blank plate (under the an-chovies one of which had learned to stand on end).

"So," he said. The word sailed at them like a Yo-Yo flung out horizontally by someone who can spin it that way. It sailed for what seemed an infinity and came back at him.

"So yourself," she said. "Is this how long officers' stags last?" she said.

"So he *forced his way in here*," the Colonel cued her, at the same time talking for the benefit of a six-foot MP who hove into view behind him.

Realization went like a ball bouncing among the pegs of a pinball machine till it dropped into the proper slot in his mind and a bell rang and a little red flag went up reading "Leavenworth." He remembered what he'd heard. That an officer's wife is always safe because all she had to do was call out the single word rape and you were on your way to twenty years.

Why did he just stand there, almost detached? Why wasn't his anger rising from his guts into his head and setting his tongue into action? But what could you say to a chicken-eating digest-reading impediment like this anyhow, who with all the others of his kind had gelded contemporary literature and gelded it so good that an honest book that didn't mince words didn't stand a chance of getting even a smell of the best-seller list?

"This is my affair," he heard her say coolly, after what seemed a particularly long eternity.

The Colonel lighted a cigarette. "I suspected you were having one," they saw him smokingly smirk, "and since Klopstromer was seeing me home from the club I thought he might as well —" He stopped and looked down at the suitcase. "How long does he expect to *stay?*"

"I have something to say," he said, stepping forward.

"*Sir.*"

"I have something to say, sir," he said, picking up the suitcase to heft it for their benefit. "When Justice —"

"You'll get justice," the Colonel snapped as Klopstromer sprang alertly forward and bore down on him and wrested the suitcase from his grasp. "If you won't testify," the Colonel went on to his wife, "then Klopstromer at least will. That he assaulted a superior officer. It won't get him Leavenworth, but by God six months in the stockade will do him good."

"But why?" his wife protested. "You don't understand. He's a writer."

"Maybe," they saw the Colonel smirkingly smoke. The anchovy twitched and stood upright. "Maybe," he said, mo-

tioning to Klopstromer to march him out through the door
to the waiting jeep, "but he needs discipline."

OVERTURE

As MY WIFE lay writhing contentedly into wakefulness in the
next bed, I lay quietly in mine trying to evolve some morning
pleasantry with which to greet her, some dallying, com-
panionable nonsense. Not, I reminded myself, that is
easy; nonsense may be one of the lowliest of the arts but it is
certainly one of the trickiest, since the penalty for its failure
is silliness.

My wife lay on her side with one leg bent over the other,
an arm outflung on her pillow. Think of the languorous
organization of power in a woman's limbs, I said to myself:
how unlike a man's body, which in repose suggests only
latent locomotion. Latent locomotion and power in repose
indeed! I told myself. This is rubbish — where's the nonsense?

I sorted through the probable events of the coming day.
These would include the planing of the front door by a
handyman named Mr. Crèvecoeur. A long spell of humid
weather had warped and swollen one door after another, and
now Mr Crèvecoeur came every Saturday to plane something,
always bringing a tin of stain to coat over the newly exposed
surface. But the damp always got into the wood again, and
for a week now I had had to heave the front door shut at
night with my shoulder. Soon the winter would come and
the dry furnace heat would shrink the doors back hopelessly
short of the jambs, so in the end they would probably all
swing clear, like the doors of saloons. I examined these facts
as raw materials for some usable jest, turning once to glance

at my wife, who had kicked the covers down to the foot of her bed.

Settling my hands under my head, my fingers laced, I looked up at the ceiling and spoke. "When Mr. Crèvecoeur comes," I called over softly, "when Mr. Crèvecoeur comes, and he insists on painting the planed part the deep-mahogany stain that is all he ever has, that I keep telling him doesn't match the light finish we've got on the rest of the wood, if he refuses to pay any attention to me and does the same thing over. I'm going to say to him, 'Go away, and never darken my door again.' "

There was an extended murmuring as my wife stretched, pleasurably curling her fists over her shoulders and mingling with the act a nod of domestic agreement. She singled the sheet from the blankets at the end and drew it up to her chin, after which reorganization of her nest she lay momentarily at rest once more

"Why," I tried again, putting a riddle, "are these things — these botherations with a house in the country — like a tin can tied to a dog's tail? Because they're bound to occur."

I heard no sound.

"Bound to a cur," I said.

I had passed into general humor with no more detectable profit than in the case of nonsense, and I lay reflecting that next in order — supposing I wished to continue this double-or-nothing pursuit through levels of subtlety — was the calculated anecdote. I presently saw that my wife had rolled her head on the pillow and was now gazing past me with a dreamy imprecision at the wall, a moist tendril of hair pasted down her forehead like an inverted question mark I smiled now as, with fresh resolve, I sat up in bed and, looking through the window and across the intervening lot to the Shepherds' garden, told a funny story.

"I will not ask you to believe I know a man named De

Peyster," I began, "but I do. Harry De Peyster. Well, I was having a beer at Micklejohn's, across from the railroad station, one evening several weeks ago when in walks this Harry De Peyster. 'Harry De Peyster!' I said. But he was in no mood for gaiety, and after a few drinks he told me he was having trouble with his wife. Oh, nothing serious enough for a divorce or anything – luckily, because," I went on, very carefully, as though feeling my way through the task of assembling particular ingredients, "otherwise you would have De Peyster seeing de shyster. Well, anyway, I said, 'Harry, why don't you take her some flowers tonight when you go home?' When he protested that there were no florists open in town at that hour, I said, 'Steal some. Why not? A lyric idea – flowers stolen for her by moonlight from somebody's garden.' 'Whose?' he said. 'Anybody's. The Shepherds',' I said. 'People next door to me. They've got a garden with some beauties. Win prizes every year at the flower shows. Come on, we'll pile in my car and drive over.' So we did. I parked a hundred yards or so down the road. 'Now, right on this edge of the garden, in back there, are some phlox that are out of this world,' I said to Harry. 'You go on help yourself. I'll wait here in the car.' So he slipped over, keeping in the shadows as much as possible, and picked himself some of those giant blue phlox – that special breed that's the apple of the Shepherds' eye. When he had a good armful, the kitchen door opened, the porch light went on, and a man's voice – I don't know whether it was Old Man Shepherd or one of the sons – called out, 'Who's there?' Harry dropped the flowers and high-tailed it for the car. He got in and slammed the door and I started off. 'What the hell did you go and tell me to do that for?' he said. He was panting and puffing. I shifted the car into second, then into high, and settled back behind the wheel. 'Oh,' I said, 'I just wanted to show you how Shepherds watch their phlox by night.'"

My wife had commenced her morning ritual, and was brushing her hair. She did it, as usual, sitting on the edge of her bed, from which she could see her reflection in the dresser mirror. Perched tailorwise on mine, I could see it, too.

"I think it's 'special' myself, but that's no matter now," I said. "Maybe you don't like the merely acoustical pun — think only the pun with a point or meaning is worth while. Well, how's this one for size? 'Sweet are the uses of perversity.' You don't have to laugh," I went on, when she didn't. "The humor I'm in now isn't really humor, but more like wit. Intellectual."

She changed hands and did the left side of her hair. Getting off the bed, I drew on my robe, which had been hanging on the back of a chair, and tied the cord. I walked over and stood behind her, watching her ply the brush with leisurely, deliberate strokes, fluttering the ends of her hair upward at the conclusion of each one. "The next level," I said, "is formal epigram."

She rose and set the brush down on the dresser and went over and reached into the closet for a dressing gown, murmuring something into it that was indistinguishable but that seemed to me to resemble the single word "God."

"God," I said, "like Alfred Hitchcock, vouchsafes us only glimpses of Himself. I have often thought of this. And also that we make a game of trying to spot Him in this scene and then that, till we've squandered the revelation of the whole instead of simply accepting and enjoying what He has created. We're in philosophy now. I hope," I added sardonically, "I'm not keeping you up."

She drifted by, trailing the shred of a smile, which seemed to linger in the glass where I caught sight of it like a skein of smoke. She brushes her teeth before breakfast, too, and as she brushed them now I stood at the mirror and combed my hair, which was mashed in every direction, like grass after a storm.

My wife emerged from the bathroom, spruce, with a brisk yawn. I set the comb down and followed her out of the bedroom and downstairs to the dining room.

"As I see it, there's only the last level — Ultimate Beauty," I said. She turned with an expression of concern, which I overrode. "The hell with that now. If you're going to fall on your face, it might as well be from the top of the mountain. There Truth is Beauty and Beauty Truth," I continued, following her on into the kitchen. "There the mathematician resorts to letters and the poet uses numbers Think of the New England mathematician who covered the blackboard with abstract theorems while tears were streaming down his cheeks. So the juice that flows from visceral laughter is squeezed from the brain as well."

I watched her set coffee to brew and halve a honeydew, which she carried on two plates into the dining room. This had the quality of a feat of balancing, from which I tried to extract some hope of collecting and coordinating the fragments of the morning.

"It's an old joke of your own — correct me if I am mistaken — that if my nose were a quarter of an inch shorter, I would look like Cyrano," I said. "As I remember it, not the least of his accomplishments was the ability to improvise in strict verse forms." I closed my eyes and drew a deep breath. "I'll take — the sonnet."

When I looked again she was at the window. She twitched a cord, and the draperies flew apart with a dwindling swirl like that of a dancer's skirt. I pointed an arm toward the window, and began:

> *The flash of drapes that lets the morning in,*
> *Smartly adjuring us to be about,*
> *Gives tacit promise of its better twin —*
> *The pensive pull that shuts the evening out;*

> *When we may listen for, eventually catch,*
> *The sound of guests for dinner and for talk,*
> *Music for which there is no earthly match,*
> *Save that of their departure down the walk.*
>
> *For this there crow apocalyptic cocks!*
> *This rigmarole of Time, for which we heed*
> *The ticking gizzards of monotonous clocks.*
> *O Vanity! At least you spell my need:*
> *The strength to keep, for my ephemeral doom,*
> *One candle nourished on eternal gloom.*

Having paused to listen, she now paused a moment longer to assess my expression and find it in correspondence with what I had uttered. Then she came over to me. All woman, she put a hand to my cheek, and when her two arms slipped around over my shoulders, her embrace no less than her voice was that of one who had never shirked her obligation to encourage, comfort, and sustain. "Darling, that's nonsense," she said, drawing my head down to hers. Her fingers on my face and through my hair conveyed the most delicate sense of ministration. "It really is, you know, it's perfect nonsense."

I had done it at last.

REUBEN, REUBEN

WE KNOW NOW that everything is the opposite of what it seems — that lavish tipping conceals a niggardly nature, filial devotion the wish to do one's parents in, and sexual athleticism a basic doubt of one's masculinity — but we did not always know it, and the knowledge has enormously widened our horizons. My own doubt of my sexual adequacy dates back some years to a wild Saturday night party where I found myself messing around with two women at once. This is what happened.

I had taken a shine to a tall brunette who wore a red silk dress and a perfume that must have cost fifteen cents an ounce. She was a model, though scarcely of intelligence, and soon tiring of the canoodle with which we had been further-ing our acquaintance on a corner couch, I drifted out to the terrace for a breath of air — carrying her spoor with me evidently. Because the girl with whom I took up out there drew back at one point and, sniffing, asked, "What's that you're wearing?" I had to admit that the fragrance adhering to the folds of my clothing had been picked up in a canoodle with another woman a few minutes previous.

"Well, wear it in health," she said. "Because you're not ad-mitting — you're bragging — and when a man does that it's for a reason."

"What?"

"He's got to prove something he isn't."

Her name was Peggy Schotzinoff — there was no doubt about it — and she was a dancer in a ballet troupe. They were exponents, not of the classic ballet, but the more modern variety of which the dances, spastic, vital, are often con-cerned with the depicture of contemporary phenomena such as slum clearance or the installation of high tension wires through valleys in which people have hitherto lived in peace.

A phonograph playing jazz had started up inside the house, and I said, "Shall we?" After I had propelled her for some measures around the pebble floor of the terrace, she leaned back and said, "You're very graceful." I shrugged and began to wag my shoulders in an exaggerated fashion to indicate that this was not unqualifiedly true, or indicated at best a merely primitive zest for rhythm. "How about dinner tomorrow night?" I asked, still dancing.

"You certainly lay it on fast."

"Well, then, later in the week."

We did eventually have dinner, and afterward went up to my place. There, after some hard-breathing importunities in shirtsleeves on my part, she forced me gently back and said with an understanding laugh, "Don't struggle so hard, Goof." It was the nickname by which I was affectionately known in my set in those days.

"You're the one who's struggling," I said

"I don't mean that way. I mean don't fight so hard to prove what you feel this need to prove — that you're a man."

I rose and put on my coat.

"Listen, macushla," I said, "there are plenty more names in the little old black book. More than you can shake a stick at."

"You see?" she said, spreading her hands. "That's what I mean."

I called the girl of whose essence I had reeked in the first instance, when all this had got started, and asked her for a date. She was evidently in more black books than I could shake a stick at, because it was a good month before she could "tuck me in on Friday," by which time word had gotten around that Goof was racing his motor, and why. In the cab, after dinner, I seized her in a passionate embrace and began to devour her with kisses, gobbling her throat, her arms, her shoulders — everything in sight. She wriggled free of my grasp after a moment, and sat back to tidy herself.

"We all admire the way you're fighting homosexuality, Goof," she said.

I nodded, looking out the window. "We'll go up to my place and talk about it," I said.

I became more and more disturbed, emotionally, as what knowledgeable friends seemed to see as evidence of some deep-seated conflict continued to mount. It was a vicious circle, of course, with each attempt to allay the fear serving merely to offer more grounds for it. I became by turns moody and irritable. It was then that I met a woman such as a man with a problem like mine is bound to meet sooner or later a woman keen for the challenge to straighten him out.

Her name was Ada Purchase, and a nicer person I have never come across. She had straight auburn hair, drawn into a biscuit behind, and sturdy, well-cut features, especially on Saturday when she would drive me out to the beach in her car and explain things to me that I didn't see because they were under my nose. She had a wide knowledge of all the things that make people tick, with a vocabulary that made the intellectual in me's eyes pop.

"This health club that you belong to," she said one day as we were sitting on the sand, "and those daily exercises that you do. Why do you think you go in for all that?"

"To keep fit?"

"No. To cut a figure. To cultivate a masculine ideal that inwardly you don't feel you measure up to."

"Shall I quit?"

"Of course not. Just recognize why you have the obsession. The important thing is to have insight into ourselves." As she spoke, she would often pound the sand with the heel of her shoe, which she had taken off, to emphasize some point, while I nodded and listened. I remember that the shoe was "sensible."

Things got worse before they got better, as they usually do in cases of this kind where increasing insight at first stirs up a corresponding resistance, much as a medication sent in to fight a disease temporarily "muddles" it. They came to a head, rather unexpectedly one night, as Ada and I were sitting in a bar not far from her place, drinking beer. I had by now thrown away the black book and was seeing only her, which showed in itself an increasing confidence in my prowess with women.

We were occupying a booth near the front of the tavern. At the bar itself were one other couple, a middle-aged woman in a trench coat and a thickset man with a red neck which overflowed his shirt collar in a series of small tires. In a lull in both strains from the jukebox and our own conversation, we listened to what he was saying to the woman. He was explaining the meaning of the term laissez faire to her. "David Niven has got it. Rex Harrison. Actors like that," he said. "Means suave. Man of the world." There was an exchange of arch references to himself, after which he laughed and, spreading a beefy arm around her, gave her a woolly hug.

"Well," I observed to Ada, "there's no doubt *he's* hetero-sexual."

My remark had the misfortune of falling into a general silence, and he heard it. He turned around, gave me a look, and walked the few steps over to our booth.

"Was you referrin' to me, Bud?" he asked.

"Why, yes," I answered with an ingratiating smile, rising to my own feet as a gesture of courtesy. "I just said you were heterosexual."

"That's what I thought." He gave his trousers a hitch and his chest swelled up like a blowfish. "Care to back up them insinuations with a little action, and maybe see if there's any truth in them?"

"Apparently you misunderstand the term." I laughed good-naturedly at our little contretemps, at the same time evaluating the inch of forehead, or less, that separated his thick black hair from his beetling brows. "It simply means that in your case things are exactly as they seem. Canoodling with every confidence in self, and with great laissez faire I might add —"

"Hell business is that of yours? Hell do you think you are anyway, coming around here giving people angles on theirself? I'm just as normal as you any day, as I said I'm ready to step outside and prove — or stay right in here if you'd rather." He gave his belt another truculent hitch.

"But of course! That's precisely the —"

"Look, Bud, I don't care to hear any more about this particular wrinkle tonight. If you're so sure you're in the clear about all them fancy names your sort likes to go around calling people to show they're educated, maybe you're ready for that little demonstration. Or maybe if I flatten that nose of yours you won't have so much trouble keeping it out of other people's business."

With that he let fly with a hefty sock.

It was here that my daily exercising at the health club paid off. I not only worked out with the barbells and the wall pulleys in the gymnasium there, I also took boxing lessons from an old ex-pro the club had around for members interested in learning something of the manly art of self-defense. My right had been developed to a point where all I needed, among the violent but rather wild swings into which my assailant now threw himself, was one solid uppercut. Good footwork and the knack of finely timed ducking sufficed to elude those intended haymakers, which could be seen coming a mile off and which wore nobody out but himself. I had youth on my side, at least in those days, and he the disadvantage of a life that may very well have been sedentary — like truck driving. I saw my chance in a momentary pause in the snorting and flailing, and let him have it.

My punch caught him squarely on the jaw and sent him backwards into the jukebox, down whose decorated slopes he slid to the floor, where he remained in a sitting position. Dazedly, he raised a hand, not to the chin I had clipped, but to the back of his noggin. He had evidently struck it on the chrome trimming of the jukebox, making that contraption very much my ally. I murmured a word of anxious inquiry over him and then helped him to the bar. A goose egg seemed in the making, but nothing more serious than that. At this point his lady friend took over, and I looked around for mine.

Ada was standing in the doorway, poised for flight. "For God's sake let's get out of here," she whispered. I dropped a dollar on our table and hurried out after her.

We walked rapidly down the street, Ada holding my arm, first with one hand, then both. I sensed a subtle, but unmistakable, change in her attitude. It was an attitude of pride in her escort.

"You did all right in there, I must say," she said. "You handle yourself beautifully."

I shrugged, and said it was nothing. Her apartment was only three blocks away. When we reached it, I said goodnight to her in the hall

"Don't you want to come in?" she said.

"No," I said, "not tonight."

I was developing more and more self-confidence. I didn't call her that week or the next. The week after that, she called me.

"Would you like to go to the Higginsons' party?" she asked.

"I don't care if I do," I said.

We went, and had a very good time.

She called me again the following week and invited me to a dinner which she would cook herself. We were married toward the end of that year, and now live in a cottage in the country. The grass goes uncut in the summer and the snow unshoveled in the winter, and the house is generally a mess, but she never badgers me about chores. She knows I'm a perfectionist, and can't get started for fear of failure.

TOUCH AND GO

(With a low bow to
Elizabeth Bowen)

"TENNIS, ANYONE?"

The face thrust in at the library door had the square, animal good looks that are encountered in photographs of men examining niblicks in their underwear. It was in fact among the mail-order advertisements that it had first acquired an anonymous familiarity, but Londoners now recognized it — as did Angelica here — as something more recently seen in an antic glare, under a tilted bowler, above glib feet and a twinkling stick. "I say, isn't that that comic at the Palace?" she said to Mt. Auburn, as its owner disappeared strumming a racquet which he held as a banjo. "Aunt Aurora said he might push round."

Mt. Auburn, who had turned to the doorway to smile negatively as at a vendor, now murmured affirmatively to Angelica and resumed what he had been doing: browsing along the shelves His movements betrayed that incarcerated stress he always felt as a weekend house guest. The books were packed so tight it was like pulling bricks out of a wall: which to that extent appeared to give him something to do. Watching him open and close several, cracking the spines of some, the tip of his tongue visible between his teeth like a morsel of pimento, Angelica asked: "Did we come in here to be together or just to get away from the others?"

"I'm fond of you," he said with the touch of asperity that usually accompanied this declaration. "You know that. I mean why take on? . . . This has some interesting things in it," he

went on of an anthology he was holding. Two pressed roses
and a tasseled dance card fell out of it to the floor: he retrieved and returned them with deploring clucks, and wedged
the book back in its place, with the same old effort. None of
this had been thought through. She said: "Mt. Auburn, why
don't you take another out before you put one back? That'll
give you more space." They were both at the mercy of
impromptu irritations, and now Mt. Auburn, suddenly splay-
ing out the fingers of his hands, in that gesture one makes
when one draws on gloves, walked to the window and looked
out toward the west at a mass of clouds he knew to be darkening there. He had for a moment that expression which doctors wear when they are reading X-rays. "It'll rain," he murmured. "Then we shall all be trapped and huddled."

They had been trapped and huddled last night, not due to
rain: their host, Angelica's Uncle Malcolm, had read, in mus-
tard-colored tweeds and an oppressively interpretive voice, at
length from the Victorian poets. Traditions, like people, are
bellicose in youth and then again in age. Uncle Malcolm and
Aunt Aurora and their friends had a sense of cutting ice only
among themselves· together, their voices had the ring of
musketry, their gestures the gallantry of old alliance; but
single, pausing for instance in the doorway to a room in
which they would presently become anachronisms, standing
thus a moment in their flowing velvet and with their verdant
old moustaches, they had a kind of forlorn vehemence, like
exclamation marks that have got detached from their sentences.

"I suppose you're still done up from last night," Angelica
said. "But remember, *their* poets led the way."

"How?"

"They were the first to grope." As though that ended the
matter, Angelica turned to press the point with a forensic

gesture — which died in midair at the sound of approaching footsteps.

"Your aunt?" Mt. Auburn asked quickly.

Stiffening against the library table where she stood, Angelica reminded herself how she had resolved henceforward to meet sensibility: by remaining sensible. What after all could Mt. Auburn expect but to be asked down and trotted out for these relatives and those? Once lovers are declared or even suspected to be such, there is scarcely a move made in their direction that is not tribal in intent. The community is instantly ready with the shelter of its institutions, kin with their blessings; but the price of security is enclosure, that of benediction, tedium. Lovers have no more than kissed than society is busy defining the trellis on which their roses may sprawl. Now Mt. Auburn had got to look at family snapshots.

Sensing him to have darted a glance toward a nearby corridor, as though it were a side street up which he might run, Angelica said evenly. "Mt. Auburn, stay."

Aunt Aurora, who had over the years evolved a pattern of rigorous solicitude for her guests, had got herself up with formidable casualness in a suit of brown houndstooth, crowning which with a tweed porkpie, presently, she would go for a stride with whomever she could recruit. She entered the room as though she were already on the open heath.

"Hullo, hullo, hullo," she said. "Don't you two look knit up in here." She unslung from her shoulder her voracious camera, and hooked it over a chair. "Well, you wanted to see some pictures, didn't you, Harry?"

It is equally the plight and the safeguard of the sensitive that it is not easily known when they are at bay. Mt. Auburn, who disliked the use of his first name in even the closest of bonds, stood in the corner beside the final pleat of a curtain and watched her bear down with a rehearsed despair, but gave no sign. We are surprised at the collapses of the placid, not knowing when a preserved calm is merely the means of the overkeyed for keeping themselves illegible. Mt. Auburn's rather geometrically good-looking features did not "represent"; his face fleetly suggested an abstraction that had been mutilated by the addition of a second eye. Aunt Aurora stalwartly fancied herself as being able to take him in her stride, not dreaming it was she who must be taken in his. He could not exist in a plasm of overall sociability, and a siege of hospitality as robust as Aunt Aurora's took more out of him than the usual weekend. Aunt Aurora was assertive even in repose; occupying a chair, she did so with an affirmative quality, as though she were sitting on luggage.

She dug from the table drawer several packets of new snaps awaiting plastering and dating in her albums, and fetched them to the sofa. "There's heaps of Angelica I took last month, and soon there'll be heaps of you. We'll save *the* family album till tonight — a good look, long as you want to get knit up with us." She sat in the middle of the sofa and spread palms on either side of her. "Now let's make ourselves comfy."

Not least among the tensions of civilized intercourse is that of sitting beside. Taking a seat next another, and being sat next, are sharply different degrees of one sensation, and their demarcation is often the threshold of distress to the distilled consciousness. Angelica knew this made an ordeal of solitary train rides for Mt. Auburn. He did not, once possessively organized in a seat with a window to look out of, prohibitively mind being joined: what he could not do was join. Which was what Aunt Aurora was haling him into now, over and above the tribulation of whatever pictures were to come his way. Nor was this all. Angelica started across the floor with a qualmy deliberation, then began to

172

put herself outside the tension in this room, arriving at the sofa in that somnambulism which is a kind of blessed detachment about what is going to happen to us in a crisis. She took her place on one of the patted ends. Then suddenly her aunt heaved herself over to the other and with all that woolly good will smacked the middle cushion and said: "Here with him!"

Women, under strain, crumple from the shoulders, men from the knees. Mt. Auburn rounded the massive oak table with that peculiarly bowlegged gait of exhausted types who are being required to sit between. Goading herself to with an effort, Angelica thought how all about them were ranged Dickens and Thackeray, Hardy and Meredith, Smollett and Sir Walter Scott and Bulwer-Lytton, rank on rank. Nothing in her aunt's tradition equipped her to comprehend that at this very moment in her house events were boiling to a climax. Angelica's choice of alternatives was pellucid: get rid of her aunt, or explain to the woman that action was neural.

She was not long in taking the easier course.

"Look, Aunt Aurora, it may rain and I shan't have you missing your walk. We *insist.* I'll take Mt. Auburn on a rummage through these. Anyhow, think of your hovering about not letting me weed out the awful ones of me." Somehow her aunt was bundled out the front door, tucking on the porkpie and readjusting the camera looped once more on her shoulder.

Returning to the library Angelica saw Mt. Auburn inspecting a lesion in a lighted cigar. He sat on the end of the sofa next the table, one ankle on a knee, a hand flat on the tussock of envelopes which Aunt Aurora in rising had tumbled on the center cushion. He hummed a few measures of something and plucked a loose thread from his trouser cuff, with an air of imposture. "I mean there are relatives who want a chap on toast," he said.

Angelica picked up the envelopes and sat down with them. With a meticulous inefficiency she opened one and slid out the contents. She was a while sorting them in her lap. Mt. Auburn, the coal of his cigar pointed at the ceiling, took in the rather dental grimace of a bearskin rug at the other end of the room. At length Angelica passed him a sheaf. He shuffled through it with a frown of response.

"But these are negatives," he said.

"I did so not want to be obvious."

The sensations of love had always set themselves forth to Angelica as those of something delicious eaten in anxiety. She pursued it with a guarded ecstasy, a kind of wary bliss, which made it natural for her now to watch with her head lowered and out of the tail of her eye, watch with a keyed readiness as Mt. Auburn reached a hand to her and brought his fist down softly on her knee several times, as though he were trying to invent a new impulse.

She said· "You say you're fond of me. I don't suppose you could say 'I love you'?"

"That's not fair. There are things it would break all the teeth in a chap's head to get off."

Putting aside the pictures she rose and went to the mantel to which she clung as though to an escarpment. Yet when she brought her brow to rest on the back of one hand she gave an effect of almost languid thought. She was thinking how the perils of intimacy had, among the over-evolved, in our time, made the double bed give way to singles, these in turn to separate rooms. "I suppose," she said, "you figure we could each have our own —" He spared her having to bring out "room."

"Yes, I've been thinking, now that you mention it, I mean

I don't imagine two smallish flats would be terribly more than one large — Oh, in the same building of course . . ."

When she straightened and turned, she gave her head a toss, like one who has just broken water. She had never realized how much of the maternal there was in her feeling toward Mt. Auburn till now when she wanted to lead him somewhere, conceivably back to London, by one ear. Instead she commenced a search among the shelves for something, running a finger along the titles as if it were a divining rod that might help her locate what it was.

"Angelica, what are you looking for?" he asked.

"I don't know," she answered. She had the certainty she would know it when she came to it· just as she had recognized, simply in coming to it, the end of "them" — and, in all of this, the end of youth as well.

Youth comes to an end in the afternoon. Middle age arrives in the evening, with the first book one rereads, but youth draws to a close in the afternoon, particularly a Friday afternoon in autumn. There is a premonitory chill in the air where lately summer may have lingered in a blue and gold reprieve, a ripple of shadow while it is still light, twisting the hearts of weekenders. The country dallier, knowing he must return to the city, tastes in advance those dumb, velvety, smothered moods of early dusk, when against the looming gray buildings the rain seems a liquefaction of light — subtly distinguishable from the twilit texture of spring whose light appears rather a rarefaction of rain. Even the uninstructed spirit senses, for all autumn's quickened tempo, this transposition to a minor key. But if one has suffered the asphyxiation of some hope — not necessarily a grief but at least a recession of outlook — then this seasonal drawing in symbolizes a larger human contraction: the intimation that we live, after all, not on the earth but in the world, a world of betrayal and complicity. The images that have been singled out and prized by memory — slants of early snow, a tree tweaked by wind, street lamps blooming alight — and that have come to reiterate a fixed emotion, like hieroglyphs, will now sharply gain in venerability, like, to alter the metaphor as well, coins that have acquired a numismatic value.

Angelica foresaw herself walking the streets and entering lighted rooms without Mt. Auburn. Mt. Auburn was the Individual: and that was a squeezed orange With him, one would go quite to bits. There was nothing for it but to start fresh from the other end: if one could not humanize from above, then refine from below. She was thinking of the wire-haired ad model who had popped his head in a while ago, and it was with him intruding on the edge of her mind that she was searching among the shelves. Her finger, as if indeed a dowsing wand with a discernment of its own, came to rest on a volume of poetry. She drew it out with a smile — This poet was the very golden mean of British taste: as *de trop* to the likes of Mt. Auburn as he would be elevating to one still wanting in criteria.

She turned and started out of the room. She paused over Mt. Auburn, whose cigar had perished on the rim of an ashtray where he had left it. She looked down at it with that mild bemusement of people contemplating a leftover piece of something they have taken apart and put together again. Then she went on out of the library and out of the house, to the lawn. The book she clasped gave her a sense of having split the British Isles down the middle, yet with a gesture as simple as Mt. Auburn tidying the cleft in his Homburg, "escaping."

There was a mixed-doubles match in progress on the court, but Ad Model wasn't even watching, let alone playing, so his gallop through the house asking for players had been humorous. He was with a group on the grass, sitting each in a halo of gnats. She marched through a gap in the privet and continued toward them. She let her eye rest for the merest moment on his, as, wagging the volume aloft, she said, approaching, smiling:

"Tennyson, anyone?"

FALL GUY

I WAS STARING, chin in hand, out of the window of my usual morning train to the city when a man sitting beside me turned and said, "Commuting with nature?" I murmured something noncommittal. He was a smoking-car acquaintance named Shenstone, who customarily got on the train at Darien. He had taken to joining me whenever he found me alone, and drawing me into conversation on themes laid down by himself. These themes had a kind of unity, for it was Shenstone's wont to air his private affairs in the third person, as though he were talking about somebody else, and to clothe them in terms abstract enough to make them sound like algebraic problems. I wondered what might be on his mind this morning.

"Family A is related to Family B by marriage — the wives are sisters — and they take turns having each other over for Sunday dinner," he said presently, though I had unfolded a *Times* that had lain in my lap since I got on the train at Westport. "Family A will have B over one Sunday, and then a month or two later, say, B will do the honors. Fair?"

"Fair," I said.

"But A has two children while B has five," he went on, "so for each time B feeds four mouths, A has to feed seven." Shenstone amplified this with such pique that I had no doubt

I was talking to the head of A. "*Now* is it fair?" he asked.

"Not if you look at it that way, it doesn't seem fair," I replied.

"I mean if you were the head of A, wouldn't you think it was a racket?" he persisted. He turned his round, leathery face abruptly to me with a kind of truculent sociability. "I mean year after year?"

"Definitely," I said, and spread my paper wide.

Several mornings later, Shenstone joined me in the smoker again. He slung his topcoat and hat on the luggage rack, hiked up his trouser legs, and sat down. He set fire to a cigarette and dropped the match in the aisle. "Well, I repeated what you said the other day," he remarked.

"Repeated what? To whom?" I asked.

"About the two families trading dinners, remember? I told the fall guy's wife that a friend of mine had said the whole thing struck him as definitely a racket for the family with the most kids, and, boy, your ears must have been ringing." Shenstone's face was wreathed in sardonic amusement.

I slid up in my seat. "I don't think I said that, exactly," I answered. "If I did, I was just agreeing with you."

"Think nothing of it," Shenstone said. "This woman is on the defensive because the one with the five kids is her sister." He shook his head ruefully. "That whole thing is only rub number one in this man's family."

I began to unfold my *Times*.

"The family sphere is the be-all and end-all of a woman's life, but it's only part of a man's," he said. "That's why you get arguments, ructions, and hell and high water. Of the other spheres in a man's life," he continued, "I'd put business second. Sphere Three is sports and recreation. Sphere Four, stag society. Of course, some of these spheres overlap. Anyhow, I happen to know that in this case there's a definite conflict between Sphere One and all the rest." He looked at me. "What's this guy to do?"

"That's hard to say unless you know the person himself," I replied.

"Names I can't mention," Shenstone said. "Suffice it to say he's no knothead — fellow with a systematic mind, and a good provider, though all he gets it in is the neck from all sides. I happen to be close to this family — too close for comfort, I sometimes think. The complaints against him range from objections to his using curse words to why doesn't he get into some other line of work. Now I ask you, how long can a man go on letting people sandbag him out of what he wants?"

"It seems a problem," I answered cautiously. After an interval, I asked him, "By the way, what do *you* do?"

"I'm trying to get out a beer-vending machine," he said. "It's got a lot of bugs in it, but I'm hopeful. But getting back to this fellow, shouldn't a man insist on living his own life?"

"Absolutely," I said, and got behind my paper.

There was a bug in *that* device; spreading it open to get behind it more or less put Shenstone there with me. He turned and said in a lower tone, "It means all of Sphere One, including relatives, will crack down on him."

This had the effect of plunging us both into gloom for the remainder of the journey. "I'll probably be seeing you again soon," I said apprehensively as we parted in Grand Central Terminal.

Soon enough, it turned out.

As I was climbing the stairs to the Forty-third Street exit of the station some days later, Shenstone trotted up and fell in beside me.

"Well, you blew things higher than a kite that time," he announced.

"In what way?" I inquired.

"This fellow took your advice and laid it on the line about how everybody has an absolute right to live his own life, let the chips fall where they may. And, brother, are they falling!" He took my elbow and steered me through the doorway into the Biltmore and toward a coffee shop. "Come on, let's have a second breakfast," he said. "I'll fill you in."

He did this over coffee and my protestations. Sphere One, he explained, was now trying to overflow and dominate all the others, in order to snuff out certain wants and wishes in a man. To that end, more and more relatives had been getting their two cents in. He had it on good authority that an ultimatum on the domestic front had been given this chap, who very much needed advice — friendly advice. Shouldn't the man defy the ultimatum and make a stand for his integrity and independence even if it meant pulling out?

"Out of the *house?*" I said.

"Wouldn't *you?*"

What was this game Shenstone played with himself, I wondered, of extorting sanctions for courses of action already cut and dried? Now he was trying to wangle out of me a recommendation that he walk out on his family — unless, of course, I was mistaken in my surmise that it was his own grievances he had been so deviously hashing over. I gingerly put out what I thought might be a test question. "If you won't tell me who this chap is, at least tell me something more about him," I said. "What's he like?"

"He's a fool," Shenstone answered.

This took me by surprise. "How do you mean?" I asked.

"He lets people walk all over him. He's patient to a fault." Those words and a subtle alteration in his skin tones, as he looked away, confirmed my original assumption. "Isn't it an outrage?" he presently demanded, fishing angrily for my blessing.

"Isn't *what* an outrage?" I asked, growing indignant myself "For instance, what are some of these wants and wishes? What are some of the things they're trying to sandbag him out of? And so on."

"Things a man has a right to," he retorted, and when I said nothing, he continued, "Well? Isn't it an outrage, from where you sit?" I maintained a stout silence. "Aren't you going to give your opinion of this rank imposition?"

I chose my words carefully.

"There are times," I said, wrapping a finger around the ear of my coffee cup, "when a man has to be firm."

"I'll buy that," said Shenstone.

The next day, I spotted him getting on at Darien with two Gladstone bags. This was really too much! So when I saw him peering, in search of my face, from the vestibule of the car I was riding in, I quickly unfolded my *Times* and put my face behind it. I sat crooked and well down in the seat, with the newspaper forming a right angle so that one side of it screened me from the aisle. Remaining motionless, like a deer in cover, I was able to escape detection and was joined by nothing worse than a woman in tweeds who passed the journey violently editing business reports with a blue pencil. In Grand Central, I succeeded in ducking unsnared out of the train onto the station platform, and was congratulating myself on having, as I thought, melted into the crowd, when Shenstone materialized on my left and, breathing heavily, said as he drew abreast. "Well, you weren't just flapping your lip that time — you damn well laid it on the line. There *are* times when a man has to be firm."

"Where do you think you're going?" I asked, glancing down at the bags

"To the Waldorf."

"Then it was you all along — not a friend," I said.

He set down the suitcases to secure his grip on them. I did not offer to help him with them. "I've barked my shins on enough," he said, picking up the bags and toiling up the ramp beside me. "They asked for it." He had on a corduroy hat that was Alpine in derivation, and a light-colored topcoat of such length as to resemble a deliveryman's duster.

"We're going to have a second breakfast," I said, "and a little talk."

"*First* breakfast," he corrected me sardonically, "speaking for yours truly."

"A plain, straight-from-the-shoulder talk," I said.

"Check," said Shenstone.

Following him through the door into the coffee shop, I said in commanding tones, "You're going to stop this nonsense and go back home!"

He banged his way among a congestion of tables to a corner, where he dropped the luggage and said "Whew!" We hung up coats and hats and, that done, stood waiting for a table to be cleared, and then for impurities to be flicked from chairs. I cursed the day I had ever laid eyes — or, to be more accurate with a locution that is at best untidy, ears — on Shenstone. But at last we were seated. I nursed a cup of coffee while Shenstone had a double orange juice, ham and eggs, toast, marmalade, and coffee, eating as though revolt had rendered him ravenous. He brooded into his orange juice in a way that give it the quality of a highball, hunching over the table and moving the glass around between his hands. "You see, there's a new intruder at the house, which I'll call Factor X," he said. "It's a familiar joke about married life, only it's no joke. It's a certain somebody that's like a bagpipe — nice in the distance."

"Like a bagpipe — nice in the distance," I put the words to myself, like a riddle. Then I thought, Mother-in-law. She's moved in and he's moved out. The last straw. This was, of course, pure guesswork, but it had the merit of conferring coherence and shape on the lather of ambiguities I had been fed. So, keeping his problem in that focus, I lectured Shenstone, while he ate, on the frailty and folly of running away. "Now, I want to see you on that evening train," I concluded sternly, though we never met riding back from the city — only going in.

He shook his head. "Wait till things settle down to a dull roar," he said. "I left everybody steaming under the collar this morning, including Factor X."

"I hope you didn't mention my name," I said, running a finger under my own.

"Oh, you've been a great help — I mean getting me to take a straight, hard look at the facts, at the way things are with me and mine," he said. "Let's hope it all comes out in the wash, but meanwhile, since I won't be seeing you on the train" — he dug in a pocket for a pencil — "give me your phone number in the city here, so I'll know where I can get in touch with you."

"I'm going on a trip," I quickly fabricated. I tumbled a quarter onto the table for my coffee, and rose.

As I got into my coat, Shenstone shook his head reminiscently. "I told them plenty when I packed up and got out," he said.

"What did you tell them?" I asked.

"That a man's home is his castle," Shenstone said.

It was difficult to know how to meet this. Resentful as I was at having been made free with, I nevertheless felt that in parting I ought to *volunteer* a word of wisdom. I said the only thing that came into my head. I intended something austere, but it didn't come out that way. "Well, you've got to pick a rope apart before you can splice it," I said. I had no idea what it meant.

Shenstone told me, about a month afterward. I was taking a seven-o'clock train home from New York — later than my

usual one. It was still standing in the station, and I was reading the evening paper, when I heard a familiar voice say,
"Well, well, look who's here!"

Shenstone grinned down at me. He was holding a package
of bakery goods from Schrafft's in one hand, and in the other,
a conical parcel in green paper that could only be a bouquet
of flowers. He seemed in good spirits. "I've been looking for
you, but I don't take the same train in the morning now," he
said. "I take a later one." He stowed the Schrafft's package
on the luggage rack with his hat and coat, and sat down
with the flowers in his lap. "I want to thank you."

"So you do go back and forth," I said.

Shenstone nodded, in thoughtful contemplation as much as
in reply. "You were right that last time," he said, sliding
down in the seat and hiking his knees up on the back of the
seat ahead. "You sure as hell hit the nail on the head *that*
time."

"Oh? How so?" I asked

"When you said how you have to tear a broken rope
some more before you can splice it. You were right at every
turn, but you said a mouthful that time. Things had to get
worse at our place before they could get better."

"They're better now?" I asked, gratified.

He nodded again. "Certain elements could only be cleared
up by being cleared out," he told me. "Well, concessions
have been exchanged, things have canceled other things out.
The step I took was the thunderbolt that cleared the air. If
I hadn't made an issue out of it, like you told me, why, we'd
probably have gone along with what the doctors call a low-
grade infection, just enough to make you feel lousy but not
enough to make your system get cutting on it. But my boiling over brought things to a head and put the fire out."

"I see," I said, dazed by the variety of metaphors that
could be adduced in this connection.

"A bone is strongest where it's been broken," Shenstone went irrepressibly on, "and that's us. I want to thank you." He beamed with such warmth that for a moment I thought he was going to give *me* the flowers.

"You're entirely welcome," I said, mentally adding yet another metaphor to those we had amassed, one perhaps more apt than any of the others — namely that they grease the wheel that squeaks. Shenstone's profile, at which I presently stole a glance, showed the composure of demands met rather than the strains of arbitration undergone, and I did not ask what latitudes had been given or taken, what had become of Factor X, or how things stood between Families A and B. Those were sleeping dogs.

That was the last I ever saw of Shenstone, for our commuting orbits no longer cross at all. I am, somehow, confident he will not return, streaking erratically, like a comet, back into mine. I make a practice of reading books on the train now, principally criticism and meaty biographies. I have learned that a newspaper is at best a tentative and imperfect bulwark, and that one is less liable to invasion behind something like *In Search of Chopin* or *Four Hundred Centuries of Cave Art*.

Often, again, if my seatmate is immersed in literature of his own, or seems otherwise a safe risk, I let what I'm reading drop into my lap and commute with nature. I'm glad things have settled down to something better than a dull roar for Shenstone and his, and also that I am regarded, at least by Shenstone, as having been instrumental in their repair. Despite the obliquity of my impressions and the prejudice through which they were filtered, I feel, as the saying goes, that I know his family. But there's a disquieting side to that. It causes me qualms when I think that I might someday run into Shenstone when he's with one or another of them, and have to be introduced. They probably feel, and a good deal more strongly, that they know me, too.

YOU AND WHO ELSE?

PALEY was planning to tell his wife he was mixed up with Mrs. Tatum. Ten months before, they'd been thrown together on a citizens' study committee for improvement of the town museum, and, the committee's work done but their relations rooted, he had managed a series of fairly regular rendezvous since, simply by telling his wife he was out bowling at Pfemister's Greater Alleys — a ruse that had cost him nothing but the sacrifice of that recreation. Now Mrs. Tatum didn't feel she could go on in this clandestine and demoralizing way, it was time, she thought, that he brought matters to a head and made a choice one way or another. She herself happened to be a divorcée.

Watching his wife carry her sewing paraphernalia to the living-room sofa after dinner, Paley thought he ought to break the news before she got to work on a suede blazer of his that was included in a pile of garments she had collected to mend. But she took up a blouse of hers first, and he sat silent. He watched her yank off a loose button preliminary to sewing it on securely. The act seemed to establish their evening tableau, and the tableau to define the limits of their bond. Where this left off, the other began, just beyond the circuit of conventional cooking and remembered buttons lay the sour-cream dishes and worldly inflections of Mrs Tatum.

"What are you trying to do, hypmatize me?" his wife asked, with no apparent need to raise her eyes to know his own were fixed on her.

Hypmatize, he thought. How, having been exposed to Mrs. Tatum's wave length, could he be satisfied with a woman who kept port in the icebox and said "hypmatize"? Still, telling her would not be easy. Mrs. Tatum said a woman was like the mandrake, which, according to legend, shrieks when uprooted.

He went to the kitchen for some ice cubes, and while carrying them to the cellarette in the living room and mixing up a highball, he looked back on the sixteen years of his marriage. He reviewed the little private jokes, the household shorthand. There had been, from the first, an imaginary Mr. Quackenbush, who represented overtime. "I've got to see Mr. Quackenbush, so don't expect me home for dinner," he would phone from the city to say. "Well, get rid of him as soon as possible," his wife would answer. "Allardyce never did this." Allardyce was her mythical first husband — a device she would use to chide him whimsically. "Allardyce never spilled ashes on the rug," she would say. These things now made him wince. The names were all wrong — he could see that.

He finished making his drink and sat down with it, remembering other things. Sometimes he had come home with a crazy story, such as the announcement that he had been embezzling funds at the office, and they would make a rigmarole of that. He gave a shake of his head, as though this might shed the plague of reminiscence.

"What's the matter with you?" his wife asked.

"I'm having an affair," he said.

"Oh?" she said. "You and who else?"

"Mrs. Tatum." He rose, walked over to a stand of plants near the window, and inanely inspected a bloom. After some moments of silence, he looked over his shoulder, and saw that his wife was holding up the blouse in both hands, for scrutiny, and smiling absently.

"And you want your freedom," she said, in a tone familiar to him as the one with which she had always fallen in with his folderol. A slight chill raised the hairs along the back of his neck. She settled herself with a cozy wriggle. "So she is now the light of your life, the object of all your dreams," she went on, with excruciating zest.

Standing in the middle of the room, with one hand in his trousers pocket, Paley finished off his drink in four swallows, letting the ice cubes slide against his teeth as the last of the liquid trickled through. The cubes dropped with a clunk when he lowered the glass. "Right," he said. He set the glass down on the coffee table.

"Well, you owed it to me to tell me, and I appreciate that," she said. She selected a sourball from a dish on the table and poked it into her mouth. He picked up his glass again and headed for the cellarette.

"I was with her on that study committee, you know. We were thrown together a lot," he said. "Well, the committee disbanded. and, finding we had to see each other, we did so secretly."

"Real clandestine," she said, bringing Paley's problem to further focus by stressing the first syllable of the word.

"Real clandestine," he echoed, by way of bearing down on an aching tooth.

His wife grinned, the sourball tucked in one cheek. "She still say 'an hardware store'?" she asked. She paused to reflect. "Where was it we stopped to talk to her and she told us about the 'warranty' on her gas stove that she couldn't get any satisfaction on?"

"At the tobacconist's," he answered.

Mrs. Paley bobbed her head in fresh mirth. " 'Tobacconist.' That's right. Another one of her words. Little old Sontag and his cigar store. A tobacconist." She savored this, then continued, musingly, after a moment, "Old Somerset."

He dropped another cube of ice into his glass with a clack. "Old what?"

"Oh, one of the women at the bridge club calls her that. She says 'somerset' for 'somersault.' "

"She doesn't say 'somersault' for 'somerset,' " he said tersely.

"How about it?" she asked. "You used to that walking-on-eggs way she has of talking yet, through all the nights of love?"

He was almost more aware of the clatter of the candy in her teeth than of her words. He debated waiting till the sourball had dissolved before trying to get a grip on the discussion. But he poured bourbon over the ice, splashed in some sparkling water, and plowed ahead. "She doesn't say 'wreckanize,' " he said, in a voice that had gained in tension what it might have lost in volume.

Mrs. Paley raised her head and looked at him. She watched his back as long as he stood with it turned to her. "She says 'Friday next.' " She also spoke in a just perceptibly lowered tone. "She says 'Friday next,' and 'bet your boots,' when even Englishmen say 'betcha boots.' "

He turned around, and her head dropped again over her work.

"She doesn't say 'hypmatize,' " he said, crossing the room with the glass in his hand. "And she doesn't say 'ap-pricot' and 'dark-complected' and 'umpteen.' " He stood beside the window. "And you don't have to tell me her diction is good. I know that."

She ground up the candy with her teeth and then was a while swallowing the fragments. "We used to call it elocution," she said when the crunching had died away. She held the garment at arm's length once more for inspection. "I will say she was good at teaching it to the kids for graduation exercises and all, whatever name you want to call it by,"

Mrs. Paley said fairly. "But then her appearance is in her favor. I always said it was imposing, with those large, dark, horn-rimmed glasses."

Standing at the window looking out, Paley took a sip of his highball. "Mrs. Tatum is the only woman in this town you can get conversation out of, as distinguished from just talk," he said.

"Can you remember any, offhand?" Mrs. Paley picked snippets of thread and stored them on her tongue.

He brushed a speck from the sill with his little finger. "Once she said, 'One gets what one pays for in cheap restaurants, just as one pays for what one gets in good ones.' " He turned to regard his wife for the effect of this.

She worked the tips of her pinking shears around an inside seam, drawing her lips taut in the effort. "What else?"

He could recall other minor but perceptive remarks Mrs. Tatum had made, such as the observation that all business colleges are on the second floor and that realtors sit in their offices with their hats on, but he saw no need to squander them in this discussion. "She's a woman of refinement," he said. "She's got over three hundred classical phonograph records."

"Not alone that, she puts 'ish' behind more things than anybody." His wife drew a fresh length of thread from a spool. "I sat next to her at a table at the country-club dance for a half hour, and in that time the weather was goodish, the orchestra was fairish, and — let's see, what else? — she had to go because it was oneish."

"What if I asked for a divorce?"

She broke off the thread and wet the end of it between her lips. Paley stooped to fish a handful of salted nuts from a dish on a table near him. "I suppose," she said, aiming her thread at the eye of her needle, "that you were gadding around with her all those nights when you told me you were out with Quackenbush "

"Quackenbush hasn't got anything to do with this!" he said, spreading his arms. "Let's leave Quackenbush out of it!"

"*Well!*" she said, dropping her hands in her lap with elaborate distress, for she had no intention of being lured into the key he was striving to pitch the colloquy in. "A divorce." She resumed threading the needle. "Just leave me your shirt," she said, pulling the thread through and knotting the two ends with a single movement of one hand that always impressed him "The same as I got out of Allardyce, you know. No need for any trouble that I can see. The car is in my name, I co-own the house, and the bank account is joint." She rummaged in the pile of clothing beside her on the sofa and brought up the blazer. "I'll fight to the best of my ability to save you from yourself, the same as I did with Allardyce, and if it's no go — why, I'll have plenty consolation."

Paley had once tried to stand up in a hammock. He and several others had had a sort of contest to see who could stay longest on his feet He had kept his balance for a few moments, swinging violently from side to side, and finally pitched off. He had a sensation of rocking similarly now.

"I think I'd like a drink, too," Mrs. Paley said, settling the blazer on her lap to sew a button on that also. He started for the cellarette. "No, some port. There's a bottle in the icebox."

Now he pitched out of the hammock. He had long ago pointed out that putting port on ice was ridiculous, that nobody did it, only to have her dig out a women's magazine with an article about drinks in it. It contained the statement "A few drinkers know that the English occasionally chill port, mostly for use as an apéritif." He had gnashed his teeth at the ground this lost him — at the hopelessness of ever explaining that only by the purest fluke had she hit on this thing, that you had to know enough *not* to chill port before you did chill it You reached a point where you said "swanky," then passed it. She had reached it; he had passed it.

Paley got the port without audible protest, poured a glass, and set it beside her. "What consolation did you mean a minute ago?" he asked. "Holding me up for the house and all?"

Having disposed of the hoard of snippets in an ashtray, she sipped the wine, then put it down with a gratified exhalation. "That and the alimony," she said. "There are lots of ways of getting a man's shirt, you know."

He snickered carefully into his glass, which he had picked up again. "That's what they're all after," he said. "That's the last word these days."

"It's mine." She continued her sewing. He sat with his elbows on his knees and his drink in his two hands. She glanced up presently. "So when shall I see my lawyer?" she inquired brightly, resuming the rigmarole.

A married friend of Paley's named Bethune had once strayed into an affair. At a crucial moment, when he had had to decide whether he was going to go ahead whole hog or drop the thing completely, he had summarized his feelings to himself with unexpected simplicity. Oh, the hell with it! was the sum of his thinking. "It's just too much bother," he'd said to Paley later, assessing the passion. "It's just — too — goddam — much — bother." This, and not conscience or integrity, Bethune claimed, kept 90 percent of the faithful husbands out of affairs and got 90 percent of the others out after they were in.

Almost simultaneously with recalling this conversation, Paley thought of something else — his last phone call to Mrs. Tatum. "Have you talked to her yet?" she had asked. "I can't go on like this — sub rosa."

"Well, all right," he'd said. "I'll just feel things out Then I'll decide."

"And after that I suppose it will be told in Gath and published in the streets of Askelon."

Paley had paused, settling the receiver more securely against his ear. "What did you say?"

"I say, I suppose it will be told in Gath and published in the streets of Askelon," she had repeated, in modulations with which he had the sudden illusion of long familiarity — unless it was the warning premonition of it. "Can you understand me?"

"Not quite," he had answered, after a prolonged silence. "Maybe this is a poor connection."

"Well, come as soon as you've news," she had said. "Wednesday would be good. Eight-thirtyish."

His wife's voice broke, preternaturally, into this rumination.

"I wonder why her first husband left her," she said. "It was desertion, wasn't it?"

Paley rose with a heavy sigh and dusted his hands together, though it was some time since he had eaten any nuts. He strolled toward the mantel, where his eye lit speculatively on a pair of heavy brass candlesticks. "I could kill you," he improvised.

She laughed responsively, wound the thread deftly around the button a few times, fastened it on the underside, then snapped it off with her teeth, glancing up at him. "There," she said, throwing him the blazer, which he caught. "I think you'll find that's on for keeps"

A short time later, Paley left the room abruptly and went to the front closet. "I'm going out," he said.

She leaned to one side to see through the vestibule doorway and watched him. "Going bowling?" she called.

He reached into the closet for his hat. "I can't tell you where I'm going," he said. "I can't say." She rose and went out to the vestibule. He put on his hat and opened the front door. "I'll be back later," he said, and went out and down the steps.

She stood in the lighted doorway as he walked to the driveway, got into the car, started the engine, and drove off. She watched till he was out of sight, then went back inside and closed the door slowly.

Paley continued for several blocks to a highway. He turned left on it, and presently saw come into view the lights of Pfemister's Greater Alleys. He pulled in there and parked his car on the lot, which was crowded. Standing outside the car, after he'd locked it, he looked at the building and drew another long breath, this time of resumption and relief — as though it were his first free one in a good while. He regarded the lighted windows a moment, watching the shadows moving about behind them and wondering who of his friends would be on hand tonight. Then he hurried toward the wide, open doors, through which he could hear the rich, inviting thunder of the pins.

NOBODY'S FOOL

*(A character or two over-
looked in Miss Katherine
Anne Porter's shipload)*

"THE CHARACTERS are all at sea," Mrs. Haverstick was explaining to them with her usual bitter charm, "and the reader is given the most vivid possible experience of being there with them. Yes, that will be the scheme of the book. I see that more clearly with each chapter that I finish."

Herr Gottschalk, seated beside her at the Captain's table, wondered only when she would finish the book. In one pocket of his coat was a radiogram from the publishing firm for which he worked, reading, "If you don't get it this time don't bother to come back," in the other a small phial of pills whose bitter taste was ever on his tongue, either in memory or anticipation.

He watched her pale hand — what exquisite hands she had, how many men in times past must have been struck by them — gesturing over her plate, then over his, as her description of the grand plan of the novel broadened out, it waved like a sea frond under his nose, mesmerizing him till his eyes crossed. He aspired to be her editor, therefore he sighed carefully, but the belt around his fat middle creaked like a ship's timber. What a symbolism! For ten years he had pursued her from one tropical paradise to another, each paradise a worse hell than the last, driven by the rumor that she was again at work on the book, lashed by the bitter dream that it might at last be his He often saw himself as an Ahab on the track of a legendary whale. "There are times when I hate it," she said As if he didn't!

"Our author, then," the Captain broke in. He sat with his napkin tucked under his pink gills, his fists on the arms of his chair, as though he were going to punch them all in the nose for having come. He had heard for ten days from their lips nothing but names like Nietzsche, Schopenhauer, Kierkegaard, and Weltschmerz — he knew the last was not the name of a writer but of some German dish, perhaps a good deal like sauerbraten He did not want to hear any more about the characters in the book, for the time being, but he wished to give the beautiful English lady her head so that Herr Gottschalk would not start one of his lectures on the inherent goodness of man. "Our author then has mixed feelings about the human race?"

"Oh, yes. We cannot forever loathe. We must swing back occasionally to simple dislike. In this way a balance is kept."

Mrs. Haverstick's reply was designed not so much to answer the Captain, who was in any case a swine and in no need of conversion, as to torture Herr Gottschalk a little. Whom she now considered with a lazy malice, leaning slightly away from him in her chair. "Though every prospect pleases, and only man is vile. Eh, Herr Gottschalk?" she teased in her rather bitterly musical voice. Gottschalk was seized with the wish to rap her knuckles with the butt of his knife, but instead squeezed over them the juice of half a lemon intended, in point of actual fact, for his sole. That would teach her to deny the inherent nobility of man, his action seemed to say.

Almost instantly there writhed across his lips the apologetic smile for which he was in fact more famous than for such independent deeds. Mrs. Haverstick remained smilingly quiet; her tawny eyes, so like bees darting this way and that, took on a momentarily sated look. He had met her standards, for the time being.

Yet revolt was not entirely gone out of him. "I'm nobody's fool," he muttered, forlornly.

"You should find someone," Frau Hindendorf spoke up. She had finished gobbling her fish and was now ready to catch up on the conversation in a more intelligent fashion while she waited for dessert. She wore a plain blue linen dress and white beads, and on her arm an amorous bruise. "We all need someone to belong to in this world. To . . ."

The ship's saloon was filling up rapidly after dinner, and as Herr Gottschalk rounded the doorway into it his nostrils encountered the bitter smell of individuals. He hoped to find

Mrs. Haverstick alone at a table. When he did his heart sank. "May I . . . ?" he began apprehensively.

"Of course. Please sit down."

Seated across from her, he felt a familiar dew gather on his brow. She seemed, herself, now, prepared to put him at his ease. She drew from her bag a bottle of Cointreau, unscrewed the cap, and began to pour the contents over her bare arms. She let it trickle along her wrists to her elbows, rubbing it gently, pleasurably into her skin, at the same time inhaling its fumes with a lost air, her eyes voluptuously closed. Was she inviting him into the ornate privacy of her life, if you could call it privacy? But it was the book he wanted, he reminded himself sternly, the prize for which he had given up a decade of even the simple pleasures, let alone the exotic. Yet she was a woman and he a man, so that chase also had something of the bitter duplicity of love — about which no one knew more than this woman. He tried to affect a lover's nonchalance as he pressed the bell for the waiter. God, the energy that went into indifference!

The waiter came to take their orders. "Have you any cologne?" she asked. Herr Gottschalk became now quite terrified. He heard to his relief the waiter say no, with gratitude saw him go off with their orders for highballs — and return in two minutes with no further words spoken at their table. Herr Gottschalk raised his highball and with a flustered "*Adios*," which was what the South Americans seemed to be saying all the time, drank it down as though it were a glass of water, he was quite parched.

Now he would make the pitch. It was all very well for the damned unwritten book to be a legend in her lifetime, but his was drawing to a close. Down the arches of how many years had he not followed her, not like the Hound of Heaven any more than a Captain Ahab, to be sure, but rather like some tireless meek mongrel trotting at her heels? The end of the book receded eternally before you like the horizon, and while she might be only forty-five and could wait ten more years, making it twenty in all, he was fifty-eight and could not.

Mrs. Haverstick, who did not miss a trick even with her eyes closed, had seen the flush go up his face and misunderstood his emotion. Seeing through people sometimes made her miss what was inside them, but that was the price one paid for the gift of penetration. She thought he was still smarting under the incident at dinner. Men never know when to quarrel, she thought: how to spare, against a hungrier day, the still uneaten portions of the heart.

"There is something I must say tonight," Herr Gottschalk began, his voice gaining an unexpected octave in pitch. She saw him fidget in his pocket. He was nudging the cap off his own little bottle with a thumb, so as to have in readiness one of the tablets which had so often saved his life and might be called upon to perform the same role tonight. "You are getting off at Port-au-Prince, they say, to finish another chapter."

"I hope to finish another chapter there," she said, kneading the aromatic liquid into her wrists, working it well down into the crevices of her fingers. "A page or two a day is all I can manage. Sometimes not that. It's slow going."

"Of course. It is so rich. How far through it are you?"

"Oh, a third. Perhaps a little less. Why?"

He cleared his throat hoarsely and, reaching between his thighs with his free hand, hitched his chair an inch closer to the table. "I am too old to make advances to beautiful ladies, but I am still fortunately in a position to give them." The dog's smile writhed across his face again as he joked. "I am in a position to offer you a check for ten thousand dollars for what you have of the manuscript."

She stopped kneading her hands and dropped them on the table, resting the undersides of her wrists against its edge. She looked at him quite blankly. "What manuscript?"

"The — the Book."

"You seem to be under some misconception, Herr Gott-schalk," she said. "This is not a book I am writing. It is a book I am reading."

Herr Gottschalk sat like something molded out of cheese, staring at the table as if into a pool of sharks. His head went forward, slowly, like that of a man descending willingly into whatever it was transfixed his gaze, not falling helplessly.

"I'm a slow reader, and the book is long. And a masterpiece. One is sometimes discouraged, but one knows that what's there is worth staying with." She seemed to have forgotten Herr Gottschalk, and began to speak as though she were talking to another woman with whom she was gossiping about a third. "She's a genius, of course, and genius always has the right to bore us now and then, for the sake of what's up ahead. And why does characterization for a woman so often consist in having someone's number? Let me tell you about . . ."

His fingers relinquished the bottle in his pocket. It was the great, really quite blissful Letting Go that he had always dreamed it would be. Even before his head struck the table he had the sensation of sinking leagues through peaceful waters already far below the ship, into cool fathoms where he could rest forever among waving fronds and the great tides already tolling in his ears like a dim, delicious, distant bell. . . .

Mrs. Haverstick saw his head come to a stop among the litter of glasses, ashtrays, and spilled nuts on the tabletop. Rising, she reached across him and rang for the waiter.

"Clear these things away," she said in her most pleasant manner.

BLOCK

On one of her trips between the kitchen and the dining room, as she was gathering up the breakfast things, Mrs. Dunstable happened to glance into the living room and saw that her husband was sitting there in his chair, still in the bathrobe in which he'd left the table. "Better get a move on," she called. "You'll be late for work."

"I'm not going to work," Dunstable answered.

Mrs. Dunstable went over and stood in the living-room doorway, with a stack of dishes in her hands. "What's the matter, don't you feel good?" she asked.

"I feel all right," he said. "It's not that."

"Then what is it? Because it's after eight," she said.

Dunstable was a moment replying. "To tell you the truth," he said, "I've developed a sort of emotional block about the office. I'm not going there."

Mrs. Dunstable returned the dishes to the dining-room table. Then she went into the living room. "Is it that play we saw, about living beautifully and doing what you want?" she asked.

"Oh, for God's sake!" Dunstable crossed his legs. "I'm trying to tell you, I've got this emotional block. Maybe you don't know what that is."

"Of course I know what it is." Mrs. Dunstable had last encountered the term only a few days before. In a daytime television serial she listened to, there had been an artist, a painter, who'd had an emotional block about his work and had been unable to turn out any stuff till he got straightened around. "But an emotional block — about *office work?*" she said.

"Certainly," said Dunstable. "Why not? What's wrong with office work? I suppose you think I sit there all day with an eyeshade on, and cuff dusters. And that nobody like that could have an emotional block."

Mrs. Dunstable removed last night's paper from a chair, laid it on a table, and sat down in the chair "Just how do you feel?" she asked. "Can you tell me more about it?"

"I'm tied up in knots, is all," he said. "You know what *that* is."

"Is everything all right at the office?" she asked sharply. "Are you on good terms with your boss?"

"You mean Steve Smith?" he said, smiling ironically. "You heard what I said to Smith when we ran into him on the street during my vacation that time — 'And how's Mrs Smith and all the little Smithereens?' You heard that. What better terms do you want?"

"Then what —" she began.

"I'm trying to tell you, if you'll sit still and listen a minute," he said. "I'm all bottled and jammed up. I couldn't turn out a decent tap of work if I *did* go back. I've gone absolutely stale. I've got to lie fallow for a while."

"Oh, that!" Mrs. Dunstable smiled with relief. "Everybody gets to feeling that way," she said encouragingly. "Why, you can get it about running a house. Absolutely sick and tired of it."

"It's not the same thing," Dunstable said tersely, looking over her head and out of a window behind her — a window that offered him a view of successive suburban bungalows not perceptibly different from his own.

"Yes, it is," she said. "But a person can't just stay home because of it. Supposing I woke up tomorrow morning and said

I couldn't possibly fix another breakfast? What would you say?"

"I'd say you were having a block just because I was," Dunstable answered. "You belittle this just the way you belittle everything I have. Belittle and pooh-pooh. The way you belittled that lumbago I had last week. You seem to begrudge me everything — even that little lumbago."

"That's not true," Mrs. Dunstable said. "It's not belittling. I'm only trying to keep your spirits up. What's a wife's duty if not to keep her husband's spirits up?"

"Running his ailments down is no way to do it," Dunstable said.

"All right. Let's let that part of it pass," she said. "But tied up in knots! When you put it that way, I think you're making a mountain out of a molehill. Why, everybody thinks of you as being as steady and sound as they come."

"There you go belittling again," Dunstable said. "Why can't I be tied up in knots? Who do you *call* tied up in knots? Fred Quayle, I suppose. You think he's so wonderful and interesting, always talking about what makes him tick and all. But outside of him name somebody you think is tied up in knots. Maybe we just don't talk the same language."

Mrs. Dunstable said nothing for a few moments. Watching her keenly, Dunstable went on, "I suppose you think I'm a simple person."

"Oh, not necessarily," she said.

"Yes, you do. It's amazing," Dunstable observed, "how two people can live together for years and not have the slightest idea who they're married to. You, for instance. You take me for something easy, say, in the key of C" — his eyes narrowed — "when all the while maybe I've got five sharps."

Mrs. Dunstable looked from her husband to her hands in her lap. "All right," she said. "Maybe you have this block and are tied up in knots. There's a lot of that going around."

Dunstable began to search for his pipe, which he found under the paper his wife had laid on the table. He gave it a suck to check the draft but did not immediately fill it. He circled the room chewing the stem, one hand in the pocket of his robe, and Mrs. Dunstable found that the words to pursue the discussion came readily enough.

"Why can't you go down to the office?" she asked. "Is it for fear of failure?"

"Or of success, maybe. Of crystallizing," Dunstable said, hitching up the braided cord of his bathrobe. "Why, even lunch has gotten to be a ritual."

"How?"

"It's not just that I go to the same restaurants and order the same things in rotation," Dunstable said. "It's more than that When I eat a sandwich, it's the same as the way you may have noticed I eat a piece of toast in the morning. I eat it so the bites come out even with the coffee. I want to break all that up."

"But aren't you stirring this up just to maybe make yourself out a person, or even to break the monotony, or to . . ." She permitted the sentence to expire, remembering that this was ground already conceded him. "What do you suppose is behind this ritual?" she resumed. "Do you suppose you go through it for some hidden reason? Or just because you've got five sharps?"

"It might be a feeling of guilt," he said. "Or a tension about something else. Anything. A human being is like an iceberg, two-thirds under water."

"Or he's like a soil that needs turning over now and then," she said, to show that such metaphors were at her own fingertips. "What will you do about all this?"

"Think things through till I can get myself squared away," Dunstable said.

"What do you mean, squared away?"

"Get straightened around," he said. "Get back some perspective in my attitude toward my work."

"Which I suppose you figure will take time." Mrs. Dunstable sighed acquiescently. "Well, if that's the way you feel, that's the way you feel, I guess."

He turned presently and, with a look of complete surprise, watched her go slowly back to her chores.

Mrs. Dunstable's motions were automatic. She was unaware of the dishes in her hands as she carried them into the kitchen and washed them. She frowned as she worked, not in disapproval but in thought. Once, she stepped to the doorway and looked into the living room. Dunstable was back in his chair, one foot on an ottoman, the pipe now kindled. He held it characteristically, a forefinger curled around the stem just behind the bowl, and he twitched his jaw muscles as he gazed through the clouds of smoke. She watched him while she dried a glass, then returned to the sink. By the time she had finished the dishes, the frown had left her face. Purposefully, she dried her hands, hung the towel on its rack, and went back into the living room.

"The quickest way out of this thing is straight through it," she said, sitting down in the same chair as previously. "I think you should go to an analyst."

He removed his pipe and looked at her, waving the smoke away to clear his view. "Really?" he said.

She nodded. "I'm sorry I said you weren't tied up in knots, a while ago," she went on. "Actually, I feel that you're one of the most complicated men I know."

Dunstable gave the gratified grunt of one flattered beyond a more articulate reply, and dropped his eyes.

"I don't believe in letting an emotional block go," said Mrs. Dunstable. "I'd feel better in my own mind if you did something definite about getting straightened around, rather than just trying to work it out in *your* own mind."

Dunstable slid himself upright in his chair, propping his elbows on its arms. "It beats chasing your tail around in a stew," he assented.

"Now, then," his wife said. "Do you know of a good analyst?"

Dunstable rapped out his pipe in an ashtray on his left. "Well, Carmel Edison — she's the woman who used to do our advertising layouts — went to a man named Fanshaw that she swore by. I suppose I could see him."

"Do that," Mrs. Dunstable said. "If he comes highly recommended, then see him." She sighed again, this time to express relief. "I'm glad that's settled. I think you ought to get busy on it as soon as possible."

After a moment's silence, Dunstable rose. Picking a thread from her skirt, Mrs. Dunstable asked, "How much does this man charge?"

"I think Carmel said thirty-five dollars an interview," he answered.

"Thirty-five smackers!" she said. "Isn't that a lot of money?"

He smiled charitably. "Not for an analyst," he said. "And for a good analyst it's cheap. Of course, I wouldn't go but once a week or so. That ought to do it."

Mrs. Dunstable shook her head dubiously. "Even so, thirty-five dollars a week extra expense, when you're not working. I don't know —" She broke off and got up herself, walking over to a window sill where there was a row of plants. She bent to scrutinize an avocado pit suspended in a tumbler of water by means of four toothpicks thrust into its sides — like the spokes of a wheel — and set on the rim of the glass. "Well, for heaven's sake, what do you know?" she said. "This thing is going to sprout after all!" She peered at it a while longer, then straightened. "Why, I mean there you are," she said. "You want an analyst to get you back to work, but you need an income to pay the analyst."

"Like the Butterscotchmen," Dunstable said. "Couldn't run till they got warm, and couldn't get warm till they ran." He flapped a hand, as though to ask what greater proof of intricacy was required.

Frowning in helpful thought, Mrs. Dunstable said, "Of course, there's one way out."

"What?"

"Well, if you're really set on this thing, hold on to your job," she said.

Dunstable turned this over in his mind. "While I'm getting organized. Well, that figures," he said, nodding to himself.

Mrs. Dunstable glanced at the clock that sat on the mantel. "Call it working temporarily till you begin to feel you've settled back in the groove on a permanent footing again," she said. "Emotionally. It might even be wise to take that inventory overtime they offered you. That would cover the added expense nicely."

"That'd more than cover it," he said.

"Well, tell them you'll take it, then," she said. "And, look — don't let on about this. Do you hear?"

He laughed indulgently at her. "Will you quit worrying about how solid I stand at the office? Steve — or my boss, as you call him — has a habit of letting his hair grow for weeks. I keep implying it's because he's so tight. When it's starting to curl around his ears, I say to him, 'Well, Steve, been around to the barbers lately getting estimates?' Does that sound like anything to worry about?"

"Well, just don't let on to anybody there that you're tied up in knots," she said sharply.

"Oh, for God's sake, stop worrying," Dunstable said. "You worry too much."

Mrs. Dunstable pointed at the clock. "It's twenty-two to nine," she said. "You'd better get a move on. You can still catch that quarter-to bus"

Her husband went into the bedroom, pulling off his bathrobe. He had, as usual, shaved before breakfast, so it wasn't more than five minutes before he emerged in a blue pin-stripe suit, buttoning up his vest.

"I think you're doing much the sensible thing," Mrs. Dunstable said

Dunstable looped a watch chain through the middle buttonhole of his vest as he hurried to the vestibule closet. He put his hat on and then pulled a topcoat from a hanger. "This way, he can analyze me while I'm treading water," he said.

Mrs. Dunstable had produced a stamped-and-addressed envelope. which she held out to him as she opened the front door. "You'll get a better chance to mail this than I will," she said. He took it as he was still hunching into his topcoat. "Don't forget it, now," she said as he went out the door and started down the front steps to the sidewalk. "Do you hear?"

"Yes, yes," he answered, without turning. At the foot of the steps, he broke into a trot to race an approaching bus to the corner. His loose topcoat billowed out behind him.

"Be sure to tell them you'll take that overtime!" she called after him.

"All right, all right!" he called back.

He thrust the letter into a pocket as he sprinted down the sidewalk alongside the slowing bus. He drew abreast of it at the corner, where it stopped. Mrs. Dunstable watched him get on the bus and the bus door close behind him. Then she shut the door of the house, went back into the kitchen, and, with noticeably more than her normal spirit, resumed her interrupted housework.

DOUBLE OR NOTHING

WHEN MacNaughton's wife went up to Maine for two weeks
to help her sister get settled with a newborn pair of twins,
MacNaughton was left alone in New York. Wandering past
Gramercy Park one evening, after a solitary dinner in a
Twenty-third Street restaurant, he ran into a girl he'd known
in an office where he'd worked before his marriage. Her name
was Mapes. They chatted for a while, dropped into a neighborhood bar for a drink, had several, then went for a nightcap to Miss Mapes's apartment, where, one thing leading to
another, MacNaughton kissed her.

It left him with a nagging conscience.

Instead of abating, in the days immediately following, Mac-
Naughton's remorse grew worse. It was especially keen in the
house, where his wife's blank pillow and empty bed, the
framed family photographs on the mantel, the clock ticking
into the silence drenched with absence filled him with a sentimental regret. This state of mind continued until he found
himself in an endless round of wishing he had the delinquent
evening to live over again.

So obsessed did he become with the idea of having another
chance that he finally began to ask himself, Why not? Why
couldn't he relive that evening? It should be perfectly simple.
He would reproduce as far as possible the circumstances under which he had erred, lead up to the point where he had
succumbed, and then not succumb. This, he felt, would be
not a mere ritualistic repair of his spirit but an actual moral
victory, since the same physical indulgence would be open to
him in the second instance as in the first.

The urge to make this token demonstration of fidelity prompted him at last to phone Miss Mapes and ask her for a date.

"Why, I'd love to," she responded brightly.

"How's tomorrow evening?" MacNaughton asked. "Maybe we can have dinner."

"Tomorrow night is fine, and I'd love to have dinner," she said.

"Well, swell," MacNaughton said. "Suppose I pick you up at seven."

"Okie doke."

They ate at Keen's Chop House. Miss Mapes looked her full twenty-eight years, but, dressed in a tan gabardine suit, canary-yellow blouse, and floppy brown felt hat, all of which advantageously set off her amber skin and brown eyes, she was attractive company. She chattered sociably over a dinner of mutton chops and a bottle of Burgundy. Racked overhead in the grottolike interior were the thousands of clay pipes familiar to patrons of Keen's, and once, glancing up at them, she said they looked like "stalactites running sideways "

"That's pretty good," MacNaughton said. "That's one for the book."

After a dessert of *babas au rhum*, MacNaughton ordered two ponies of Bénédictine-and-brandy.

"Plying me with liquor?" Miss Mapes asked amiably.

When he finished his B.-and-B., MacNaughton set his glass down and said, "Let's go up to your apartment."

She waved her still unfinished drink back and forth across her nostrils and closed her eyes. She sipped, assuming a grave expression. "I've been thinking, after the other night," she said.

MacNaughton leaned back in his chair and looked away. Resistance was the last thing he had reckoned on. If she was going to play hard to get, he reflected, they were faced with a hopeless stalemate — she withholding what he would wait forever for the opportunity to decline. Yet without the act of moral reclamation the evening would be a total waste. He turned over the check, which the waiter had left, reaching for his wallet with the other hand. "Getting strait-laced?" he murmured as he read the check, which was close to thirty dollars. The waiter trotted up in answer to his summons, and trotted off with the check and two twenties.

MacNaughton looked across at Miss Mapes again. "Ah, come on, let's go up there," he said.

She closed her eyes and shook her head with a playful smile.

"What if I said it meant a lot to me?" he asked.

She dug into her bag for a cigarette. "What if I said it meant a lot to me not to miss a picture that's running in the Village?" she asked. "*The Third Man.* Have you seen it?" MacNaughton shook his head. "Everybody says it's wonderful, and I missed it the first time around. It goes on at nine-eleven. I checked. Do you mind?"

"Not at all," MacNaughton said.

The picture absorbed them both. Halfway through it, Miss Mapes peeled off one glove and slipped her hand through MacNaughton's arm and down along his wrist. They sat holding hands till the end of the movie. Then they walked to her place, which was only a few blocks away. In the street vestibule, she extended her hand. "Thanks for a marvelous dinner and one of the best movies I ever saw," she said.

"Not at all," MacNaughton said, removing his hat and shaking her hand. "I enjoyed it, too."

"Will I hear from you again?" she asked.

MacNaughton had once seen a film in which Walter Pidgeon stalked Hitler at Berchtesgaden with a rifle, drawing a bead on *der Führer* from a cliff overlooking the castle

entrance. It was a mock assassination, modeled scrupulously on the stalking sport of the English countryside, in
which the hunter does everything but actually fire at the
game. To take the risk of prowling at Berchtesgaden with a
loaded weapon, aiming, putting one's finger on the trigger,
and then not pulling it — that was the code as Pidgeon had
cleaved to it. MacNaughton was familiar enough with terms
like "guilt feeling" and "compulsive ritual." But he felt that
the image of Walter Pidgeon, representing a thousand years
of British decency as he sighted down the unfired rifle, was a
perfect symbol of the sort of thing he was driving at himself.

"Maybe you'll be free some evening within the next week?"
he said.

"Come on up," said Miss Mapes.

He mounted the dark stairs behind her, swinging his hat in
his hand.

MacNaughton put his hat and coat on the seat of a tiny
chair in the entrance hall as Miss Mapes switched on a light
and closed the door. Her quarters consisted of a small living
room, a Pullman kitchen, a bedroom, and a bath. She switched
on a table lamp in the living room and disappeared into the
bedroom, taking off her hat. "Fix us a drink," she said. "You
know where everything is."

MacNaughton mixed two bourbon-and-water highballs in
the Pullman kitchen and carried them to the coffee table in
front of Miss Mapes's studio couch. He wiped his wet fingers
on a handkerchief he took from a rear trouser pocket and
put back, still folded into a square. He sat down on the couch.
He heard, somewhere in the building, the muffled sound of a
door shutting. He glanced nervously at his wristwatch. It was
eleven-thirty.

Miss Mapes returned in a satin dressing gown of ice blue
and joined him on the couch. She reached for her drink and

settled back with it, lounging, partly turned toward him, with one shoulder against the back cushion of the couch.

MacNaughton was aware of the intimate sibilance of negligee and of his senses drowning in perfume. " 'Stalactites running sideways' is good," he said. "I suppose you're one of those people who can never remember which are stalactites and which are stalagmites?"

"I've given up hope of keeping *that* straight," she said.

"Well, here's a simple rule," he said. "Just remember that 'stalactites' and 'ceiling' both have a 'c' in them. That way, you can remember stalactites hang down from above."

"But how will I remember the rule?" she asked.

MacNaughton laughed, a soft laugh of private security. The whole thing had resolved itself into a kind of double or nothing, so to speak, and her apparent willingness to have him stay the night would leave him with a substantial moral balance in his favor. Cautiously he tested his position. Running the ball of his right forefinger around the rim of his glass, he asked, with a tongue grown surprisingly dry, "What time is breakfast around here?"

"Breakfast is any time before anybody has to get to work," she said. "But it won't be around here. Not with a Schrafft's nice and handy across the corner."

MacNaughton finished his drink and waited a few minutes more. Then he stood up. "Look, I think I'd better be getting along," he said.

But the retrieval of his self-respect brought about something for which MacNaughton had not bargained — the loss to Miss Mapes of her own. "Well, will you make up your mind?" she said, her eyes brighter than he had yet seen them flash. "Is this a habit of yours — flipping through samples till you find something that strikes you —"

"No, it's not that at all," MacNaughton said.

Miss Mapes rose. "I'd like to know exactly who you're trying to make a fool of," she said, tucking the lapels of her dressing gown together in a gesture not without truculence.

"Myself, I guess," he said. "I'll probably hate myself for this in the morning," he went on, attempting a humorous subtlety that he did not quite comprehend himself.

"Just what the devil does *that* mean?" she asked.

MacNaughton smiled and looked down at the rug. There was a moment of silence. "It's just that I think you were right earlier in the evening, back in the restaurant," he said. "People shouldn't lose their heads."

"They shouldn't blow hot and cold, either," she answered.

"You've a perfect right to call it that," he said fairly. He shook his head reflectively. "Sex," he said, as though the grievance and the weariness were equally his.

It was MacNaughton's apologetic air rather than his philosophical one that somewhat mollified Miss Mapes. "Well, I won't keep you," she said presently. "I was going to ask you whether you'd care to go to a party Friday night. There'll be some of the old bunch from the office I thought you might like to see again."

MacNaughton was momentarily clawed with panic. Had she been talking about him at the office where he had worked? It was time for plain words. "Look, I'm married, you know," he said. "I thought you knew I got married since I worked there."

"Well!" she said. "Married!" She took a few steps to the window. There she turned around and, folding her arms, regarded him. "Will you kindly tell me what this is all about, including the double-talk?" she said.

MacNaughton drew a long breath and looked at the ceiling, as though mentally preparing the analysis that had been asked for. "I've seen you twice," he began. "The first time was accidental, as you know, and a case where — well, one thing led to another, as those things do. I was sorry for it."

213

"I'll bet you were sorry, the time it took you to call me back," said Miss Mapes.

"I'm coming to that," MacNaughton said. "You see, I wanted a chance to prove to myself I was of better stuff. And besides, I felt I owed it to my wife."

"What about what you owed me?" she said, tucking shut the neck of her negligee with the same resentful gesture. "When are we coming to *that?*"

MacNaughton was like a man who, thinking to pluck up a negligible strand of briar, finds he has hold of a mile of twisting root.

"Do you know what I think *I* owe *you?*" she said, starting toward him with deliberate steps.

MacNaughton shot a glance at a vase on a nearby table. "Did you ever see a movie where Walter Pidgeon goes to Berchtesgaden to stalk Hitler?" he jabbered in a dry voice, backing toward the door.

"I can think of a lot of things to do to you —" Miss Mapes said, still advancing.

"Think of my intentions!" MacNaughton protested. "I might as well have come up here to put you on a pedestal."

"— but they're all too good for you. Like hanging," she continued, ignoring his rebuttal as she had his parallel.

"*Man Hunt,*" MacNaughton said, feeling for the doorknob behind his back. "That was the name of the picture. George Sanders was in it."

"I could call a cop to say you're annoying me, or the janitor to throw you out," Miss Mapes was saying. "I could —"

MacNaughton opened the door, snatched his hat and coat off the chair, and scurried for the stairs. He picked his way down them gingerly but at high speed, hearing behind him the sound he had so diligently striven to expunge the thought of deserving — the sound, shrill, formidable, and sustained, of a woman wronged.

JOURNEY TO THE CENTER
OF THE ROOM

THERE WAS an earthquake in Los Angeles last July Fourth, the day I arrived there on vacation with my wife and brood. I don't imagine a series of tremors registering no higher than four or five points on the seismographic scale is worth more than passing notice to Californians used to living along the great San Andreas fault, but for me, who had never been in anything like it before, the experience was a notably vivid one, complicated as it was by an additional, and rather special, set of circumstances.

I was alone in my hotel room when the shocks began. My wife and children were all downstairs, splashing about in the pool in what seems, in retrospect, a sort of Babylonian frivolity second only to the sybaritic ease in which I had just stretched out in my lounging robe to savor, in all frankness, their momentary absence. Judging from my Los Angeles *Times* of the next day, which placed the first of the temblors at five-thirty-six in the afternoon, it must have been shortly after five-thirty that I advanced toward the bed, freshly shaved and showered, and smacking my lips over an Old-Fashioned just sent up by room service. As I drew back the counterpane, I noticed, from a small metal plate riveted to the wall just above the pillow, that the bed was one of those deluxe affairs equipped with an electrically vibrating spring designed to give you a body massage — fifteen minutes for a quarter. I slipped a twenty-five-cent piece into the meter and lay down with a grateful sigh.

The bed quivered pleasurably beneath me, oscillating at just the right speed and frequency for the back rub that, now, made my bliss complete. The low hum that accompanied its chiropractic ministrations added to my peace. Lacing my hands under my head, I closed my eyes, the better to relish this brief respite from the strains of travel *cum* family, assorted occupational worries, and the barren vulgarity of a coin-operated civilization.

This last could hardly be exaggerated. It had hounded me from coast to coast in the form of children, and even a wife, unremittingly bugging me for chicken feed to shove into this vending machine and that in return for — I couldn't hope to name it all. Candy bars, soda pop, and chewing gum are only the beginning of what is now available in these contrivances. They yield pocket combs, packets of Kleenex, copies of the New Testament, nylon stockings, key chains, tubes of spot remover, ice-cream bars that leave spots, paperback novels apparently written by other machines in turn, nail scissors — and, so help me, shrunken heads. My youngest son had got one of those from a novelty machine somewhere in the bowels of Grand Central while we were awaiting the first of the trains that were to take us across the country from New York. Yes, trains indeed. I am not blind to the merits of air travel — how I can board a midmorning plane at Kennedy and be in Havana in time for lunch — but I prefer railroad journeys. I like the hypnotically unwinding scenery, the meals in the diners, the placental snugness of the berths.

It was of the gently rocking rhythms of Pullman sleepers that those of the Massage-O-Bed now in fact reminded me. I smiled dreamily, by turns closing my eyes to shut out all distractions and opening them again to gaze at the ceiling. One crack running its length reminded me of the letter Z dear, in long sequences, to comic-strip cartoonists depicting slumber in their subjects. I found the fancy lazily amusing. I closed my eyes and, with a little burrowing wriggle, hollowed out a slightly more comfortable position for myself upon the bed.

It was then that I first sensed the action beneath me to have become noticeably more brisk, as of something shifted from low gear into a higher. "Say, these things are all right," I murmured to myself. I had scarcely more than made the observation than the bed began to swing violently from side to side in a manner not to be construed as an intended graduation of voluptuous pleasure. It also started to bounce up and down, and even to dance about the room, like a table at a séance. I sat bolt upright. Almost instantly all this extreme behavior subsided, and, after a somewhat puzzled sip of my cocktail, which I had beside me on the nightstand, I lay back again, shrugging to myself. The bed resumed its normal, soothing hum. I could feel the muscles of my back relaxing once more, my nerves unwind.

This sensation of only briefly interrupted euphoria lasted for several minutes — nine, to be exact. Because my *Times* goes on to report that it was precisely at five-forty-five that the second tremor occurred, far more severe than the first. To that I can attest. The licentious shimmy of my Massage-O-Bed escalated steeply. In a twinkling, it was pitching and heaving beneath me like a skiff in stormy waters, overturning me as I reached out for another drink and dumping me out onto the floor, where I landed with a thud on all fours.

My first thought was that the bed had gone bananas. Not, that is, *qua* bed but as a piece of machinery got punitively out of hand, a piece of machinery balking at the perverted uses to which it was being put by a decadent civilization. I had been chosen, by blind chance or otherwise, as the sacrificial victim. I had blundered into one of those science fantasies in which man-made inventions go berserk, turning on their creators and bringing them down in their Luciferian pride. That sort of thing. That such allegorical speculations had indeed shot into my head is, in any case, certainly proof of the wild bewilderment in which they were entertained. It should further be realized that in my lotus-eating trance I had really been half asleep. The obvious never entered my head, either for these reasons or possibly because I had struck it on a corner of the nightstand on my way out of beddy-bye and been rendered momentarily incapable of rational thought.

The Old-Fashioned had fallen to the floor, too. I snatched up the empty glass and ran as fast as I could toward a closet, where I swiftly refilled it from a flask of bourbon dug from a suitcase. Warily skirting the bed, I scuttled past the foot end of it to an armchair that was as far from it as I could get. There I sat, staring at it. It hadn't itself overturned, but stood more or less in its place, its agitation back to normal. My own certainly exceeded it. The bed throbbed quietly on without its occupant. I watched and listened till the quarter-hour interval for which I had paid had run its course. After that it stopped, leaving the room in silence. Even then I sat there, nursing my drink and the goose egg on my head.

Into this tableau my welcome children burst, swinging their towels and shouting, "Hey, Pop, did you feel that? We were in an earthquake!"

Dazed inquiries revealed a chandelier to have been seen swaying in the lobby, a few pictures to have been knocked askew on their hooks. The water in the pool had sloshed about, like tea in a cup. A room-service waiter had trundled his cart into a wall. That was about the size of it, for all the *Times'* front-page streamer reading, "ROLLING QUAKES JAR SOUTHLAND." I had probably not been dumped out of bed by the temblor at all but fallen out in my frantic haste to get away from what I thought was a piece of machinery running amuck. That I had not understood what I was in the thick of is proof of both the vividness of the episode and the mixed-up state in which it was experienced. Further evidence, I must uneasily report, lies in the length of time it seems to be taking for this mixed-up condition to clear up, and my wits to return to normal.

For there are aftereffects. For one thing, I detect in myself a tendency to *post-hoc* fallacies of a kind to which my thinking has never been prone. An example of this was the eerie suspicion, entertained for just a split second when the truth did penetrate such head as I could boast of, that I had myself caused the earthquake by putting a quarter in the meter slot and starting that bed on its obscene little hula. Why not? We speak of the single pebble that precipitates a landslide. Why not of the last hemidemisemiquaver that, added to the pulsations already bombarding earth, sends the poised rock shelf on its thundering course?

But there are subtler and therefore more disturbing signs. I find I have difficulty in following any conversations but those of the most rudimentary order, trouble in grasping implications and allusions, even the familiar ones bandied about at the family board. I took it on the coco again on the trip home, my Burlington upper giving me a tumble-dry your coin Laundromat couldn't begin to deliver, let alone a Massage-O-Bed, and this without so much as asking for a two-bit piece — proof again of the strides the railroad people are making in their efforts to kill off the last remaining passenger travel simply by letting tracks and rolling stock both go to hell. But this is not a berth trauma that I'm talking about now. No, I'm talking about symptoms left over from my Los Angeles adventure and that first appeared there, without a doubt. The scene in the hotel dining room after the earthquake is typical, and will suffice to illustrate what I mean.

Perhaps if I relate it exactly as it happened you will see what it is I apparently missed, or get what I don't quite understand, in my current reduced comprehension.

Everyone was still joking and laughing about the shakeup when we sat down to dinner. One of my children said, "What I don't get is why people live in a place like this when they know what may happen any time."

"They become loyal to their part of the country, not just used to it," my wife said. "Chauvinistic, you might say. They become blindly attached to it, resentful of criticism. Even possessive."

"It's their own fault," I said.

I can't for the life of me figure out what they all roared about. Maybe it was the way I missed when I tried, just then, to drink from my Planter's Punch. The straw went down alongside the glass, on the outside of it, instead of into it. Which leads me to suspect there may very well have been still a third temblor, unrecorded by the *Times*, or even the seismograph, but not lost on your more sensitive type. Even one, if so it be, permanently addled.

DIFFERENT CULTURAL LEVELS
EAT HERE

When the counterman glanced up from the grill on which he was frying himself a hamburger and saw the two couples come in the door, he sized them up as people who had spent the evening at the theatre or the Horse Show or something like that, from their clothes. They were all about the same age — in their early forties, he decided, as they sat down on

220

stools at the counter. Except for them, the place was empty. At least, the front was. Al Spain, the proprietor, was sitting out in the kitchen working on a ledger.

The counterman drew four glasses of water, stopping once to adjust the limp handkerchief around his neck. He had been whistling softly and without continuity when they entered, and he kept it up as he set the water glasses down.

"Well, what's yours?" he asked, wiping his hands on his apron and beginning with the man on the end.

"Hamburger."

"Mit or mitout?"

The man paused in the act of fishing a cigarette out of a package and glanced up. He was a rather good-looking fellow with dark circles under his eyes that, together with the general aspect of his face, gave him a sort of charred look. "Mit," he said at length.

The counterman moved down. "And yours?" he asked the woman who was next.

"I'll have a hamburger, too."

"Mit or mitout?"

The second woman, who had a gardenia pinned in her hair, leaned to her escort and started to whisper something about "a character," audibly, it happened, for the counterman paused and turned to look at her. Her escort jogged her with the side of his knee, and then she noticed the counterman watching her and stopped, smiling uneasily. The counterman looked at her a moment longer, then turned back to the other woman. "I'm sorry I didn't get that," he said. "Was that mit or mitout?"

She coughed into her fist and moved her bag pointlessly on the counter. "Mit," she said.

"That's two mits," the counterman said, and moved on down to the next one, the woman with the gardenia. "And yours?"

She folded her fingers on the counter and leaned toward him. "And what would we come here for except a hamburger?" She smiled sociably, showing a set of long, brilliant teeth.

"Mit or mitout?" he asked flatly.

She wriggled forward on the stool and smiled again. "May I ask a question?"

"Sure."

"Why do you say 'mit or mitout'?" Her escort jogged her again with his knee, this time more sharply.

The counterman turned around and picked up a lighted cigarette he had left lying on the ledge of the pastry case.

He took a deep inhale, ground the butt out underfoot, and blew out the smoke. "To find out the customer's wish," he said. "And now, how did you want it?"

"I think mitout," she said. "I like onions, but they don't like me."

"And yours?" he asked the remaining man.

"I'll have a hamburger, too," the man said. He fixed his eyes on a box of matches in his hands, as though steeling himself.

"Mit or mitout?"

The man fished studiously in the matchbox. "Mitout."

The four watched the counterman in complete silence as he took the hamburger patties from a refrigerator and set them to frying on the grill. They all wanted coffee, and he served it now. After slicing open four buns, he returned to his own sandwich. He put the meat in a bun and folded it closed, the others watching him as though witnessing an act of legerdemain. Conscious of their collective gaze, he turned his head, and scattered their looks in various directions. Just then the phone rang. The counterman set his sandwich down and walked past the four customers to answer it. He paused with his hand on the receiver a moment, finished chewing, swallowed, and picked up the phone.

"Al's," he announced, his elbows on the cigarette counter. "Oh, hello, Charlie," he said brightening, and straightened up. "How many? . . . Well, that's a little steep right now. I can let you have half of that, is all. . . . O.K., shoot. . . . That's nine mits and three mitouts, right? . . . Check. . . . That'll be O.K." He consulted the clock overhead. "Send the kid over then. So long."

He hung up and was on his way back to the grill when he became aware that the woman with the gardenia was whispering to her escort again. He stopped, and stood in front of her with his hands on his hips. "I beg your pardon, but what was that remark, lady?"

"Nothing."

"You passed a remark about me, if I'm not mistaken. What was it?"

"I just said you were wonderful."

"I was what?"

"Wonderful."

"That's what I thought." He went back to the hamburgers, which needed attention.

As he turned them in silence, the woman regarded him doubtfully. "What's the matter?" she asked at last, ignoring the nudging from her friends on either side.

The counterman's attention remained stonily fixed on his work.

"Is something wrong?" the woman asked.

The counterman lowered the flame, stooping to check it, and straightened up. "Maybe," he said, not looking at her.

She looked at her friends with a gesture of appeal "But what?"

"Maybe I'm sore."

"What are you sore about?" the woman's escort asked. "She only said you were wonderful."

"I know what that means in her book."

"What?"

The counterman turned around and faced them. "We have a woman comes in here," he said, "who everything's wonderful to, too. She's got a dog she clips. When she hits a cab driver without teeth who doesn't know any streets and you got to show him how to get to where you want to go, he's wonderful. Fellow with a cap with earlaps come in here with some kind of a bird in his pocket one night when she was here. He had a coat on but no shirt and he sung tunes. *He* was wonderful. Everything is wonderful, till I can't stand to hear her talk to whoever she's with any more. This lady reminds me a lot of her. I got a picture of *her* all right going home and telling somebody I'm wonderful."

"But by wonderful she means to pay you a —"

"I know what wonderful means. You don't have to tell me. Saloons full of old junk, they're wonderful, old guys that stick cigar butts in their pipe —"

"The lady didn't mean any harm."

"Well . . ."

There was a moment of silence, and the charred-looking man signaled the others to let well enough — or bad enough, whichever it was — alone, but the other man was impelled to complete the conciliation. "I see perfectly well what you mean," he said. "But she meant not all of us stand out with a sort of — well, trademark."

The counterman seemed to bristle. "Meaning what?"

"Why, the way you say 'mit or mitout,' I guess," the man said, looking for confirmation to the woman, who nodded brightly.

The counterman squinted at him. "What about it?"

"Nothing, nothing at all. I just say I suppose it's sort of your trademark."

"Now, cut it out," the counterman said, taking a step closer. "Or you'll have a trademark. And when you get up tomorrow morning, you'll look a darn side more wonderful than anybody *she* ever saw."

The charred-looking man brought his hand down on the counter. "Oh, for God's sake, let's cut this out! Let's eat if we're going to eat, and get out of here."

"That suits me, bud," said the counterman.

The commotion brought Al Spain from the kitchen. "What seems to be the trouble?" he asked, stepping around to the customers' side of the counter.

"She said I was wonderful," the counterman said, pointing. "And I don't see that I have to take it from people just because they're customers, Al."

"Maybe she didn't mean any harm by it," the proprietor said.

"It's the way she said it. The way that type says it. I know. You know. We get 'em in here. You know what they think's wonderful, don't you?"

"Well," Al said, scratching his head and looking at the floor.

"Hack drivers that recite poems they wrote while they cart fares around, saloons full of old —"

"Oh Jesus, are we going through that again?" the charred-looking man broke in. He stood up. "Let's just go," he said to his friends.

"We'll go into this quietly," Al said, and removed a toothpick from his mouth and dropped it on the floor. "We're intelligent human beings," he continued, with an edge of interrogation, looking at the others, who gave little nods of agreement. He sat down on one of the stools. "Now, the thing is this. This man is fine." He waved at the counterman, who stood looking modestly down at the grill. "He's a great fellow. But he's sensitive. By that I mean he gets along fine with the public – people who come in here from day to day, you understand. Has a pleasant way of passing the time of day, and a nice line of gab, *but* – different cultural levels eat here, and he doesn't like people that he thinks they're coming in here with the idea they're slumming. Now don't get me wrong," he went on when the woman with the gardenia started to say something. "I like all types of people and I'm tickled to death to have them come in here, you understand. I'm just saying that's his attitude. Some things set his back up, because he's like I say, sensitive." He crossed his legs. "Let's go into this thing like intelligent human beings a little farther. What prompted you to pass the remark – namely, he's wonderful?"

The charred-looking man groaned. "Oh, Christ, let's get –"

"Shut up, Paul," the woman with the gardenia said. She returned her attention to the proprietor. "It was just – oh, it all starts to sound so silly. I mean it was a perfectly insignificant remark. It's the way he says 'mit or mitout.'"

Al was silent a moment. "That's all?" he asked, regarding her curiously.

"Yes."

"It's just a habit of his. A way he's got." Al looked from her to the counterman and back again.

"You see," she said, "it's making something out of nothing. It's the way he says it. It's so – so offhand-like and – well, the offhand way he evidently keeps saying it. It's so – marvelous."

"I see. Well, it's just a sort of habit of his." Al was studying her with mounting interest.

"Of course, we're sorry if we've offended him," said the woman's escort.

"We'll let it go that way," the counterman said.

"Fine! We'll say no more about it," Al said, gesturing covertly to the counterman to serve up the sandwiches. "Come again any time," he added, and went back to the kitchen.

The two couples composed themselves and ate. The counterman went and leaned on the cigarette case, over a newspaper. The door opened and a small man in a tight gray suit came in and sat down, pushed his hat back, drew a newspaper out of his pocket, and spread it on the counter. The counterman dropped his, drew a glass of water, and set it before the customer.

"What'll it be?"

"Two hamburgers."

The two couples stopped eating and looked up, and there was a blank silence for a moment. Then they bent over their food, eating busily and stirring their coffee with an excessive clatter of spoons. Suddenly the clink of cutlery subsided and there was dead silence again. The counterman wiped his hands on his apron, turned, and walked to the refrigerator. He opened it, took out two patties, set them on the grill, and peeled off the paper on them. He sliced the buns and set them in readiness on a plate. Standing there waiting for the meat to fry, he cleared his throat and said, looking out the window at something in the street, "Onion with these?"

"No. Plain," the customer said, without raising his head from the paper and turning a page.

The two couples hurried through their sandwiches and coffee, crumpled their paper napkins, and rose together. One of the men paid, left a dollar tip on the counter, turned, and herded the others through the door, following them himself and closing the door rapidly and quietly. The counterman shoved the cash register shut and went back to the grill without looking at them or glancing through the window as they unlocked their car at the curb, got in, and drove off. He served the man his sandwiches. Then he came around the counter and sat on a stool with the paper.

The door flew open and a big fellow in a bright checked shirt came in, grinning. "Hello, paesan!" the newcomer said "Loafing as usual, eh?"

The counterman jumped off the stool and held out his hand. "Louie! When did you get back?"

"Yesterday."

"For God's sake!" The counterman went back behind the counter. "Glad to see you."

"Glad to see you, too, you lazy bastard."

"How many, Louie?"

"I'm starved. Fry me up three."

"Mit or mitout?"

"Mit!"

THE MAN WHO READ WAUGH
(After rereading a great
deal of the same)

WHEN the two British archaeologists excavating for relics in African Numania accidentally discovered gold, they were arrested for prospecting without a license and thrown into prison. They were found guilty as charged and sped back to the expedition site, this time bound in chains.

"They're taking us back to the dig," said Miles Butter. "They figure it for a mine now that we've stumbled onto that bloody ore."

"To be worked by convict labor," said Peter Paltry. They

had both learnt to speak without moving their lips, in the manner of ventriloquists, since, like everyone else in Numania with gold fillings, they lived in constant fear of having their mouths confiscated by the state; impounding inlays being the most recent of the monetary reforms undertaken by a regime in chronic fiscal straits.

Toil in the bonanza that the archaeologists had struck — to which other convicts were now hustled from every corner of the realm — was as arduous as might have been expected, but while delving for state metal they could at least keep an eye peeled for the spearheads and cooking pots for which they had originally been sent by the British Museum. One day Peter Paltry found a coin bearing the date 339 B.C.

"A novelty shop gag no better than that can mean only one thing," he said.

"Viscount Discount is in the country," Miles Butter said. "Having us on."

They were in any case not surprised to have their shackles hammered off and the poultry lorry that doubled for a police van whisk them back to the capital, over streets through which a state procession had recently passed. The air still smelt of the bath salts which, in lieu of flowers strewn before the royal car, were poured by cheering throngs into the rain pools standing everywhere at that time of year.

At the palace doors they were turned over to a series of eunuchs, who with their great paunches bumped them softly down a corridor to the throne room. There the ebony King Bismuth lolled on a lake of cushions, a red cummerbund circling his equatorial middle and a fez perched on his head. The fezzes, everywhere seen, were part of his program of Westernization; they had taken his fancy on a recent visit to New York during a Shriners convention. He had instituted numerous portfolios and periodically proclaimed cabinet crises modeled on those of the European commonwealths. He awoke from a doze and said, "Discuss it with my Prime Minister."

Viscount Discount grinned richly from a nearby divan, his cleaver face more reminiscent than ever of George Arliss. He was smoking a churchwarden, the stem of which at intervals he poked down to scratch the back of his throat, which tobacco irritated though soothing his nerves.

"Hello, Paltry. Well, Butter. It's been a long time."

"Hello, Vi," said Peter Paltry. "We lost track of you after Lord Wobleigh brought the action over the hotel stink. So this is where you've landed."

"Wobleigh had no cause. It was in the lobby that I autographed Lady Wobleigh's stomach, in perfectly plain view of everyone. You were there. Not that you came to my defense, either of you. . . . Well, it's down here that I've learnt the secret of political power today. It's electric power."

He pressed a button and zephyrs from three air conditioners gently swept the room. "Then we've vacuum cleaners, dishwashers, even a deep freeze, all thanks to me. Disposalls are promised for early delivery by a connection I have in the States. You see, London isn't all I electrified." Touching another button he directed their gaze to a cabinet of polished teak from which after a few moments of soft mechanical clatter issued the shattering strains of a Dixieland jazz band. "His Majesty has just discovered African rhythms," Viscount Discount said, "and has a standing order in at a New Orleans record shop for all the latest releases. Paltry, that'll be one of your jobs, to keep him happy there. I remember the gramophone you used to keep us awake with at Balliol. As a prisoner of Numania your collection has been confiscated, but it's safe for you to catalogue into the Palace library."

"Eddie Condon, Big Spiderbecke, all like that," said the monarch, snapping his fingers as he writhed with closed eyes among the pillows. "Who's on vibes?"

"What he wants is tutoring in the fine points," said Discount. "The real from the fake, that sort of thing. Some treacle by a Lawrence Welk got mixed up in the shipment last week. After all, the rest of us have to listen to the damned stuff all day long, too."

"And then all the pretty little statues," said the King, clawing a jujube from a packet concealed in the folds of his sash.

"Oh, yes, the African primitives. He's on that kick, too. There's a steady stream of figurines from Bond Street and Madison Avenue. All that wants overseeing. And now finally," Viscount Discount said with a gleam of genuine interest, "there's the cuisine here. It's worse than the truck we got at school. You're a gourmet. Repeat some of the miracles you performed on your little hot plate. You'll find all the herbs you need in the kitchen."

"We are not jade sophisticates," said the King, "but we like peachy things. We have been civilized since my dynasty got conceived by God in 1066."

Miles Butter broke in, impatient with the obvious. "How about you, Vi? Playing the power behind the throne is all very well, and this is a snug place to hide out from London subpoenas, but how do you keep yourself amused? You often threatened to slit your throat from boredom at Balliol."

"That, my dear Butter, is where you come in."

At the touch of a final button a bar reversed itself to disclose a tier of congested bookshelves.

"That's *my* side of the wall dividing Bismuth's digs from mine. All my old favorites are there — I needn't tell you what they are. I like reading aloud well enough, but have grown tired of the sound of my own voice. I remember now the cool beauty of yours, that mentholated baritone, reading your papers at the literary clubs. I see pleasant evenings stretching ahead of us, months, maybe even . . . Paltry, it's no good gaping out the window. The packet has sailed and won't be back till autumn. You chaps cooperate and I'll see that your mouths aren't confiscated."

Peter Paltry's gaze was fixed not on the distant seacoast but on the courtyard below. The poultry lorry was backed up to what by inference was the scullery door, and crates of fowl and other provisions were being discharged. He suddenly realized how ravenous he was for something decent to eat himself.

"I'm ready to hop to it, if you'll show me the kitchen," he said. "How would your Majesty like his chicken tonight?"

"Dead," said the monarch after a moment of thought.

"I'm going round the bend if we don't get out of here," Peter Paltry said. It was three months later. He stood now at the window of their room gazing through detention bars in what he took to be the general direction of London. "Think of it there right this minute," he continued wistfully. "Lady Wobleigh's picked up a rage from the States apparently called the two-party system. You look in on one at nine or so, then shove along to another around midnight. They're all doing it. I'd settle for one good bash right now."

"Bash in the head is all we'll get if those natives don't simmer down," said Miles Butter. "It's those bloody African rhythms he's imported got the beggars all stirred up. Listen." From the surrounding saucer-edge of low hillsides could be heard the implacable throb of "Twelfth Street Rag" as played by the Tigertown Five, dealt at full volume from loud speakers stolen by night in an already portentous raid on Viscount Discount's warehouses. Firelight on dancing limbs could be imagined; the bodies of native women inscribed with graffiti rumored to be plagiarized from some American television entertainment known as *Laugh-In*. "If they ever decide to have themselves a little Bastille Day here, and knock over this ice cream villa, what's to prevent their taking it into their heads we're part of the Establishment? That packet's due back in a few days. When she sails again, I aim to be on her. Any ideas, Paltry? Otherwise cease and desist from barren nostalgias."

"Yes, I've a plan," said Paltry, turning from the window. "You're closest to him. What's to prevent your reading him to sleep and then letting him have it with the nearest blunt object?"

"What would we do with the body? Have you thought of that too?"

"Yes. The Disposalls won't arrive until the packet does, but there's the deep freeze. Properly butchered and dressed . . ."

"It's inventoried every Saturday. What if we haven't got away by then?"

"The beauty of herb cooking is its ability to disguise things. Picks them up, too. Bismuth is by now a full-fledged gourmet and will eat anything. With his appetite a week should be enough. . . . Imagine Vi going in basil and thyme . . . And rosemary. That's for remembrance . . . I mean to be on that boat — enough so that I'd be willing to tuck in my share if need be. How about you?"

Miles Butter awoke the next day to find it was Peter Paltry who had vanished, leaving no trace. Viscount Discount summoned him at the usual evening hour. "Story time," he greeted him with the excruciating smile. It is when our acquaintances behave at their worst that they make their most successful forays on our sympathy, for it is then that we are vouchsafed clearest glimpses of their cross. Discount's was plain: he was an extrovert who hated people. The gregarious misanthrope is, by one of nature's more mischievous convolutions, her commonest variety. Butter had more pressing matters on his mind, however.

"What have you done with Peter Paltry?" he demanded.

"Your quarters were bugged, of course, and all your conversations recorded on those tapes. Would you like to hear a few played back on the Telefunken? No? All right."

Discount strolled to the shelves and ran his finger along a row of titles.

"Last night we finished *Vile Bodies*. Tonight I feel in the mood for *Black Mischief*." He handed the volume to Butter, who carried it to his accustomed chair, beside which at least a long whiskey-and-soda awaited him. "I'm naturally curious about one thing I was pleased to hear you demur in the more dire aspect of Paltry's little plan, or at least not to hear you consent, and hoped it might be loyalty. That you might have come to enjoy these evenings together as much as I. Or is it just that you're a vegetarian now?"

"It's nothing to do with that," said Butter, opening the book. Viscount Discount drew the draperies, lighting a lamp or two as he wandered back to his chair. "You and I are both veterans of the British table; we've both taken many a hard meal in Chelsea and Bloomsbury. But there are some things, my dear Vi, that not even an Englishman will eat "

THE ART
OF SELF-DRAMATIZATION;
OR,
FORWARD
FROM SCHRECKLICHKEIT

IF SELF-PITY is often a justifiable method of meeting reality, its twin, self-dramatization, is even more so, but in an entirely different way. The two are fraternal but not identical twins. "We can be nothing without playing at being," says Sartre, in *Being and Nothingness*. In other words, we cannot *not* be enacting a role. A waiter, Sartre suggests, imagines himself as a waiter as he goes about waiting on tables — and so on. I take this to mean that some measure of private theatrics is not only vindicated but indicated. The problem is one of style: acquitting ourselves like actors, not hams.

I can see now that the whole course of a man's life may be viewed as the pursuit of that ideal. Among my own earliest memories are those of some fairly heady episodes in the bosom of a family unabashedly given to chewing the scenery. One in particular stands out. I am fifteen, and my father is pacing the period parlor, literally smiting his breast. Why? Because I have just been to the theatre, and that is condemned by our church as not just a frivolous pastime but a sin that puts one in danger of eternal hell-fire. Not even the climax of the play I have been to — *Ghosts*, with Nazimova plowing the stage of the Erlanger Theatre, in Chicago, as Mrs. Alving while her son Oswald goes mad with congenital paresis — can hold a candle to the scene being enacted in this humble home where drama is frowned upon. At the scene's peak, I leap to my feet and, stumbling blindly among the Cogswell chairs and beaded lamps myself, beat the sides of my head with my fists and cry, "Abstract me, silent ships!"

This is "starting high," as professional theatre people say of plays that open at a pitch from which there is almost nowhere to go, but our Dutch families were not the only ones in that neighborhood with this tradition of hearthside *Schrecklichkeit*. A few years later, at about the age of eighteen, I became involved with a girl whose folks were also rigidly orthodox, only Jewish, and broth-er! between my being a *goy* and her being a *Philistijn*, the contrapuntal wailing could be heard anywhere in the half block of city street that separated our two houses. I myself, however, had moved away from that brand of histrionics. I was through with all that *Schrecklichkeit*, and beginning to play it cool.

I lay on park grass with my head in the girl's lap, one night after our families had beaten us to emotional pulps, and, flinging an arm carelessly over my brow, again said, "Abstract me, silent ships." But with what a difference! I now murmured Baudelaire's apostrophe quietly, with a kind of rueful worldly wisdom that at the same time carefully focussed the drama on myself. It was I who was suffering — a poetic *misérable* to whom families were so awful that the thought that he should start another of his own was one a girl must not for a moment entertain. She must put it completely out of her head. Yet it was not many years later that I was using the same line, not to mention the same posture, to get a woman to marry me.

We had had supper together on the beach at Lake Michigan, and were lying on the shore, I on my back and she propped, face down, on her elbows. She began to draw figures in the sand with her finger. After a moment, she said, "I've been thinking maybe we should break this off."

I did not cry out. I did not threaten to kill myself. I did not even protest. I simply laid my arm across my eyes and murmured the line from Baudelaire (in the excellent George Dillon translation) that has stood me in such good stead in so many crises in my personal relations, especially with women. The bit of pantomime that regularly accompanies its utterance is by now a perfectly timed and polished piece of fakery in which I only *seem* to be blotting from view a world no sensitive man can endure. In reality, it is a shield from under which to observe the reactions of the person whom I am trying to impress.

The Art of Self-dramatization; or, Forward from Schrecklichkeit

Far trickier than the arts of gaining or keeping an advantage are those aimed at recovering a lost one — say, a fall from domestic grace. Here the utmost in subtlety is required to disguise the manipulations one is up to — to muffle, as it were, the rumble of scenery being changed. One summer evening, for example, when the marriage the suave waterside dramatics had secured for me was eight years old, I "disappeared" at a party with a girl known as Muffins Morrison, and was put so far in the doghouse that I didn't think my wife would ever let me out. I pulled every trick in the book, including the one of standing at the window, looking out, and saying, "I don't exactly like myself, you know." None of it did any good. There was only one thing I could think of. I would go into the hospital for some tests *during my vacation.*

The chief problem of the adroit self-dramatizer — one who plays it down and thereby excites additional admiration — is how to let people know there is something *to* play down. How can you be a bit of all right if the essence of it is not worrying your friends with the fact that there is something to be a bit of all right *about?*

The day before I was to go into the hospital for those tests, we had some friends in for drinks, and I solved the problem that time by leaving a list of dietary and other instructions, which the doctor had given me, lying around where people would be sure to see it. When I was reasonably certain they had — I had left it on the cocktail table in the middle of the room — I suddenly pretended to deplore finding it there, and then pocketed it casually as I took orders for drinks. It all worked beautifully. A few days after I got out of the hospital, I ran into one of the cocktail guests (an English friend who is himself wonderfully adept at this whole business of throwing it all away), and he inquired after my health. "Had you in drydock for a bit, did they? How'd it go, old man?" he asked. The tests had all been negative, but I didn't want to talk about it. I let him know that — not in so many words but by changing the subject and looking up the street in a manner calculated to foster further concern.

Thus one man's progress in the art of self-enactment as son, suitor, friend, and husband. It is the role of parent, however, that is the most important and exacting, as well as the most difficult to sustain over the long haul, as the following incident may serve to show.

Shortly after my son turned fifteen — the same age I was when I was caught going to the theatre in Chicago — the local police telephoned me late one evening to say that he had been picked up with two other boys and three girls on a wild joyride around town in a car owned by the parents of one of the boys. The miscreants had told their elders that they were going to attend some discussion group at the Y.M.C.A. They had then proceeded to the home of that boy, where they had stealthily wheeled the car out of the garage — "while his mother was asleep and his father was in Switzerland," in the words of the official testimony — and set off on their ill-fated spin. The boys, all under age, had taken turns at the wheel.

My jaw was grim as I backed our own Ford Country Squire out of the garage and headed for the police station. I will not describe in detail the scene that took place there. Needless to say, it marked a return to *Schrecklichkeit* — the collapse of all style, all the cool histrionics whose principles had been so carefully cultivated over the years. Not that I was any less conscious of my formal role as parent than the other fathers and mothers I found assembled when I arrived. Far from it! We all paced the station-house waiting room, declaiming, in competitively hysterical accents, our disappointment in our young and flinging our arms into the air for their benefit. Where had we gone wrong? Was it *our* fault — did we give them too much? Didn't they realize that taking the car was a theft, and driving it without a license also a criminal offense? And so on.

I had not even begun to cool off when I got my prize into the station wagon, sometime after midnight, and made for home. "Lying, cheating, stealing, whoring, and hacking around after school! When will you grow up?" I demanded, jerking the lever for the directional lights down with a force that snapped it clean off the steering post, also damaging the mechanism inside so that the blinkers on the bumpers kept going after we had made our turn and could not be shut off. Passing motorists gesticulated obligingly as they went by. "What have I done wrong? I mean, I'd like to know. At Little League, you saluted the American flag with a dirty face. The only cultural thing I've ever got you to was that production of *The Playboy of the Western World,* because you thought it was about hacking around. What have I done to deserve this?"

He did not say. The boy's sangfroid — perfectly discernible beneath the surface protestations of remorse — did little to soothe my temper. The spectacle of his mother waiting at the window stung me to fresh outcries. At their conclusion, I dropped, exhausted, into a chair in the living room, letting my arms dangle over the sides. I sat breathing heavily in this position a minute or two before turning again to the boy, seeking some further expression of how sorry he felt, some healing reassurance. For a moment, I could not locate him. Then I saw him. He was lying prostrate on the couch, one arm flung across his brow, watching me from under the sleeve of his shirt.

THE CHILDREN'S HOUR; OR,
HOPSCOTCH AND SODA

JUST as in a previous generation people were careful not to do or say anything "wicked" in front of the minister, so today one tries to avoid any sign of being "immature" in the presence of psychiatrists, those secular pastors with their gospel of Responsibility, their regular confessionals, and, to lick the metaphorical platter clean, their swelling parishes. Imagine my dismay, therefore, on hearing that a woman in whose earshot I had lost my temper at a recent party was a psychoanalyst, and, to make matters worse, a new neighbor of mine. The incident itself was unimportant: some small petulance of the sort to which we are all prone, in this case climaxing a political argument with a man whom I can't stand and whose wife — to complete the sorry details — had just beaten me at Scrabble. It was with a brackish enough memory of the evening that I asked my wife at breakfast the next morning, a Sunday, "Who was that Valkyrie in the green dress who sat watching everyone with an aloof smile?," and heard her answer, "Frieda Bickerstaffe. I understand she's a psychoanalyst."

"A psychoanalyst!" I said. "Why isn't a man told things like that?"

"You were told," my wife answered, with a punitive little smile. "I told you. It shows again you never listen."

"Bickerstaffe," I went on, pouring myself a fresh cup of black coffee. "That rings a bell."

"I should hope so. I've told you everything about the Bickerstaffes, but I'll run through it again, and this time listen.

240

The Bickerstaffes are the people who just moved into the Martin place," my wife said, pointing toward a house that stands practically across the road from mine. "The man with the meerschaum pipe was Frieda's husband. The woman in the yellow shrug was her sister, Miss Froehlich, who's visiting them. The sisters are Viennese, and bright as dollars, both of them. I have no idea what *Mr.* Bickerstaffe is or does. Anyhow, Harriet Quayle told me Frieda's an analyst. Have you got it all straight now? Because we must have them over soon."

"How about this afternoon?" I said, eager to lose no time recovering face with a woman who was not only a head-shrinker but would have me under year-round scrutiny over the front hedge.

"The Joplins are coming for drinks," my wife reminded me.

"Let's introduce them to the Joplins," I said. "The Bickerstaffes are new in the community. They would like to meet people. Where's your group spirit?"

I went to the phone and called our new neighbors myself. Mrs. Bickerstaffe answered. "Zat would be fine," she said rather dubiously, in reply to my invitation to pop over around five. "But my sister — Miss Froehlich, you know — is staying wiz us —"

"Bring her along," I boomed gregariously into the transmitter.

"How nice of you. But we have zis child —"

"I've got four. Come along all of you. The more the merrier," I said, breathing an air of psychic health and great bonhomie.

"All right," she said at last. "We'll bring Herman."

I was delighted, and hoped that Herman and all my own children would behave abominably, so that I might have as much credit as possible for remaining equable. That was my plan in a nutshell: to keep my shirt on, no matter what.

The early-bird and bibulous Joplins were comfortably installed with Old-Fashioneds when the Bickerstaffes trooped in. Miss Froehlich wasn't with them — she was writing letters and would come along later — but Herman was, and he turned out to be all I could have wished. He disrupted the very introductions by bolting into the dining room to greet my oncoming brood and, in doing so, tracking mud across the parlor floor, it had been raining, and his rubbers, which he had neglected to remove, were luscious.

"Think nothing of it," I said, grinning beside my stony-faced wife. "Good for the rug. Sit you down, all."

That was the keynote of the afternoon. There is no need to relate in detail the successive incidents. The Bickerstaffes had occasion to give Herman what-for several times, as my wife did to one or another of our four. Pressure was finally brought to shoo them all downstairs to the playroom, but I resisted this arrangement as one that would deprive me of my challenge. What apter test of one's mettle is there than his handling of the children's hour? "Now, now, let's not let them get on our nerves so *soon*," I chided good-humoredly.

But in deference to lower thresholds of impatience than mine I did settle the youngsters on the dining-room floor with magazines and scissors, suggesting that they cut out pictures. "Show your things and trade them around," I said, "and play nice in other ways."

I returned to my guests in the living room, where I stood at the mantel packing shag into a briar with that outward poise that comes from inner balance, as the cocktail talk rolled along to this and that. It centered presently on amusing delays people had experienced on railroads. Hal Bickerstaffe told of a trip he had once made to Chicago, in the course of which the train had been marooned in a blizzard for nine hours and he had frozen all night in an upper. Herman left the dining room and nipped in to his mother to inquire what the prospects were for something to eat.

"*Lieber Gott*, Herman!" she said, rolling an eye at her husband.

I beamed down at the scene.

"We were just talking about Chicago, Herman," I said, to demonstrate how the two generations could be integrated into a conversation, given a little tact and understanding on the part of the so-called adults. "Know how to spell 'Chicago,' fellow? Chicken in the car and the car can't go — Chi-ca-go."

My peers were wilting nicely. A harried look passed between the Joplins. I was interested to see that Frieda Bickerstaffe (or Dr. Bickerstaffe, or whatever she called herself) gave evidence of being worn thinnest of all by the *brouhaha*. She had seemed, on arrival, even more statuesquely handsome than I had remembered her from the night before, but now her shoulders drooped with an end-of-the-day fatigue, and the aloof smile I'd recalled as characteristic was gone I wondered whether she was an actual Freudian or a proponent of some other of the schools of psychiatry. Not that it made any difference; I must certainly have redeemed myself in her eyes by now, I thought as I chewed my pipe and was mature, or stood at the fireplace with my feet planted apart in a manner typifying fibre. Still, it seemed to me I could do with some final chance to prove my stability, some particular dramatic incident to cap the impression.

This was vouchsafed me.

"The sun's out — let's all go sit on the terrace," I said, "and I'll fix the kids some lemonade." My own children had begun to propagandize for refreshments, and this offer was greeted with lusty cries of appreciation. We reorganized our-

selves in the pleasant open air, and then I slipped back into
the kitchen to make good my promise to the small fry.

"I wouldn't mind these clammy summers if we only got a
proper spring," I chatted, calling through two open door-
ways from the sink, where I was conjuring the lemonade
from that frozen preparation to which water is added. "The
thermal belts are changing. Oh, well."

The lemonade, with cookies, was soon in young hands,
and fresh cocktails were in old. The elders broke up, conversationally, into pairs. I was sitting next to Frieda Bickerstaffe, and exchanging comments with her about American
educational methods as against European, when there was a
mishap. Two of my kids and Herman, scuffling about nearby
on the lawn, stumbled against the table on which I had set
the pitcher of lemonade and spilled the whole works, ice
cubes and all, into my lap. "The drinks are on me," I said
with a laugh, and rose to mop myself.

It appeared to me that that ought to do it — get me in the
clear. How could you be more mature than this? I rested my
case.

Frieda Bickerstaffe was dressing Herman down in the shrill
tones of one who has cracked. My wife was diplomatically
trying to acknowledge our share in the blame. Hal Bickerstaffe gabbled apology and reprimand in the appropriate directions as he passed me dry handkerchiefs from his own
person and others'. I wiped at my sopping flanks and chaffered, "Now, let's not give the poor creatures Sunday-after-
noon syndrome before they're out of knee pants." And when
the hubbub had abated, I went on, "Wouldn't you say that
the family constellation, as I believe you call it in your pro-
fession, Frieda — wouldn't you say that's the root of most
adult difficulties? I mean, don't you find your patients are
more apt to remember what their families did *to* them than
what they did *for* them?"

"My what?" she asked.

"Your patients."

"You must have me confused wiz my sister," Frieda said. "It's she who's the psychoanalyst. I'm just a housewife wizout enough time to read. Elsa should be along any minute," she added, glancing at her wristwatch.

"I see." I wiped myself a while longer. Then I said, "Excuse me while I put on some dry pants."

In a smoldering rage, I went into the bedroom and changed. When I had finished, I marched into the kitchen, where I found my wife slicing cheese.

"*Well!*" I said. "If *you* don't take the cake!"

"What now?" she asked.

"Telling me she's a psychoanalyst — Mrs. Bindlestiff, or whatever her name is," I snarled in a low voice, jerking my head toward the terrace. "You've got a nerve complaining I never listen or get things right. What the hell kind of information do you call *that?*"

"I only told you what Harriet Quayle said. So she got it twisted. So what? Why make all this of it?"

The sudden realization of the afternoon of wasted quality, sustained with such natural ease and effortless grace, was too much to ask me to take in stride, let alone elucidate. "Give me that knife," I said. "Suppose you try civilizing those brats for a change. Listen to them out there. They ought to have their heads knocked together."

"I simply don't understand you," she said. "One minute you're the soul of —"

"Give me that knife!" I repeated, reaching to take it from her.

Just then, a female voice behind me sang, "Hello, hello!" Pausing in the act of trying to wrest the knife from my wife's upheld hand, I looked over my shoulder and saw the beaming face of Miss Froehlich pressed against the screen door, peering in. "Sorry I couldn't come any sooner zan zis, but it's so nice of you to ask me." She paused herself, to take in the tableau in which my wife and I stood momentarily frozen. "Is there anysink I can do?"

The rest of the afternoon passed without event, except for my overhearing the syllables "essive" cross Miss Froehlich's lips as she sat in murmured conversation with someone, I don't even remember who. I wondered what the word might be of which they formed the suffix. Many possibilities come to mind. She may have been commenting on how oppressive the heat had been lately. Or she may have been using, in some connection or other, the term "regressive" or "aggressive" or "obsessive," or another of the clinical sibilants. I have no idea which of these it could have been, or whether it was something else altogether, and frankly I don't give a damn.

THE IRONY OF IT ALL

THIS WAS a dinner party I faced with more than the usual reluctance. Besides girding my loins for the five or six hours of continuous conversation to which custom maniacally commits us, I had to steel myself to spend them with a man I couldn't abide — the host. (Why our two households had kept exchanging invitations is one of the mysteries of a social system administered by women, and I do not feel equipped to discuss it.) An added hazard in all my meetings with this egg had arisen from his being an author, and one who could buy and sell me and everybody I know. I bristle each time I see, on my way to my office job in the city, a fellow-commuter reading one of his novels.

They are no good, those books. But they sell. They have
the disproportionate quantities of seaminess that gain authors
reputations as realists, and their style is no tax on the brain.
They abound in lines like "Behind him he could hear Dumbrowski's heavy breathing" and "With a bellow of mingled
rage and pain he came at him." There are more descriptive
stencils like "a thickset man with beetling brows" and "a
small birdlike woman" than you can shake a stick at, and the
frequency of "You mean — ?" in his dialogue indicates that
he is no pathfinder there, either. Triter still is the lyric strain
with which the brutal realism is relieved, being marked by
an almost unlimited use of the atmospheric "somewhere":
"Somewhere a bird sang," "Somewhere a woman's laughter
broke the stillness of the night," and so on. Complexity of
characterization is achieved by the sedulous repetition of "part
of him." "Part of him wanted to so-and-so, while another part
of him wanted to such-and-such." It goes without saying that
the "as if in a dream" locution appears on every fourth page.
As befits the work of a fearless realist, the aspect of life most
abundantly dealt with is sex.

It was this particular exaggeration I was reflecting on as
my wife and I drove over to the party at the home of the
man in question, whom I will call Dumbrowski because it's
so typical of the names he gives his characters. I groped for
some thought on which to impale this latter-day obsession
with the frequent and physical depiction of passion — an
ironic phrase for it, which I felt to be teasing the edge of my
mind if not the very tip of my tongue. "Why does he lay
sex on so thick?" I finally asked my wife, who was driving
the car. I thought a little conversation on the subject might
help me snare that elusive conceit. "He and realists of that
ilk? They have people in and out of bed like seals in and out
of water — affairs right and left, sex day and night. Why is
that?"

"Maybe they just don't know the facts of life," she said.

I lapsed into silence, staring ahead through the windshield. We must have gone a mile or more before I turned irritably to her and said, "What the hell are we going there for? You don't like him any better than I do."

She shrugged. "They owed us an invitation."

We slowed and entered the front gate of the house in which we were to spend the evening. I climbed out of the car and made my way unwillingly up the gravel drive to the door.

The house was jammed with guests. Dumbrowski, however, stood out in his pink shirt and black tie, which, in turn, stood out under his light-gray cashmere jacket. He was too tall and too broad-shouldered, I noted, and his hair needed some heavy pruning, like his books. I managed to steer clear of him during the cocktail period and even through dinner, for which the more than thirty guests were distributed among several small tables. After dinner, though, the whole party formed a unified group to which mine host held forth in typical fashion — by which I mean his way of aiming the stem of his pipe at you when making a point, or (another favorite piece of business) swirling his brandy around in a snifter. A man has a perfect right to gaze into a brandy inhaler and swirl the contents around when making an observation, but in that case he ought to get off something better than "I'm sure our ways must seem as odd to them as theirs do to us," and "The burdens of the Presidency are enormous."

I had eaten and drunk heavily, as an alternative to hanging myself from the nearest chandelier, and as a result had the hiccups so badly that for a while I sounded like an outboard motor. Luckily, I found a chair in a remote corner of the living room, and went for the most part unnoticed. At about half past ten, some cretin, a woman who had just moved to Westport and was socially on the make, asked Dumbrowski

to read us a chapter of his work in progress. He modestly re-
fused, and, what with one thing and another, was soon installed with a sheaf of manuscript in his hand and a circle of
prisoners around him.

This was a story, he told us as he stoked his pipe preparatory to the reading, about a burnt-out prizefighter who signs
for one last fight in an attempt to get enough money to marry
a woman he is in love with. He is not only badly beaten but
gravely injured, and is taken to the hospital immediately following the bout.

" 'Stramaglia knew that he lay dying,' " Dumbrowski read,
in a voice that was low and modulated, yet vibrant with respect for the material. " 'Part of him wanted to die.' " See?
" 'Part of him wanted desperately to live. A great weariness
assailed him. Somewhere a cart rattled in the corridor. Then
he was dimly aware that the door of his room had opened
and someone was sitting in the chair beside his bed. He knew
without opening his eyes that it was Constanza.' "

A hush fell across the room as, in a pregnant pause of more
than usual duration, Dumbrowski took a last suck on his pipe
before setting it down in an ashtray at his elbow. There was
no denying the emotion generated among his listeners — a
tension that made even me momentarily leave off tallying the
clichés as they fell from his lips. He continued reading:
" ' "Constanza, I have a request to make that may seem
strange to you," Stramaglia whispered thickly, "but would
you get me my gloves? I'd like to go out with them on." ' "

A snicker escaped me at the same time that a sob caught in
my throat. In addition, I wasn't quite over the hiccups, so the
resulting moment was one of great confusion indeed. Everyone turned to look at me. Dumbrowski himself raised his head
and glanced in my direction, but he resumed reading almost
immediately, in an effort to recover what he could of the
spell he had been weaving. Fortunately, he was near the end

of the chapter, or of the section he had chosen to read, and presently he was putting his manuscript aside, to a ripple of compliments and hand clapping. He acknowledged the applause smilingly, then rose with a brisk "Well so!" and set to work freshening up people's drinks.

I knew that I had got his goat. And I knew, as I'm sure he did, too, that the undercurrent of animosity between us, so long concealed, must break through into open hostility very soon. Dumbrowski, at any rate, took his revenge in short order. A girl of about twenty-five launched a long and detailed account of the trouble she was having finding a job in New York. In the course of it, she asked three or four of the men present, including me, if they couldn't help. I promised to see if there were any openings in my office. "Oh, openings!" she exclaimed, throwing up her hands. "I'm talking about somebody just plain getting me *in*."

Here Dumbrowski slipped in his stiletto. "You mustn't give the poor chap such a time, Nancy," he said. "He doesn't have any of the kind of influence you're talking about — the kind that cuts corners for people. He only just works there himself."

I spent the remainder of the evening spoiling for a fight. I prowled the living room with highball after highball, glaring either at Dumbrowski, who went from strength to strength with one group after another, or at my wife, whom I saw in gay communion with a succession of attentive males. "It's no wonder," I snapped elliptically from behind her as she sat on a sofa waiting for an admirer to trot back with a drink for her. "Next time you go out with me, you'll wear a dress with a top. I mean that." Before she could turn and ask for an exegesis, I was making for a piano, at which I sat for some time picking out chords of an angry and atonal nature. I eased my feelings by reviewing some of my adversary's more blatant shortcomings as an artist, mentally repeating a few of his characteristic effects "Behind him he could hear Dumbrowski's heavy breathing," I reiterated amusedly to myself, and "You mean — ?"

It was toward midnight, when the party was boiling noisily through its climax, that he gave me what I took to be *casus belli*. He was standing nearby with a dapper but gloomy-looking man of about forty, whose name I hadn't caught. As I watched them, it was borne in on me that they were discussing my wife, who was chattering away to several people in the vicinity. The two men nodded and smiled appreciatively. Then Dumbrowski said something that I got only imperfectly but that — under the din, at least — seemed to have something to do with someone's being "picked up without any trouble."

I took a long pull on my drink, rose from the piano bench, and strode over, just as the other man made off. "All right, Dumbrowski," I said. "I heard that."

"Heard what?" he asked.

"Whatever you said Shall we step outside?"

He glanced into my glass. "Don't you think you've had enough, old boy?" he asked.

"More than enough. Just slip out through the terrace, shall we?" I suggested, nodding toward a pair of French doors, closed against the autumn night.

"I'm sure I don't know what the devil you're talking about."

"I think you know what I'm talking about, Dumbrowski," I said, fixing him with narrowed eyes.

He paused and took me in speculatively. "You hate my guts, don't you?" he said at last, in low tones.

"I would if you had any. You get 'em, I'll hate 'em."

"Why, you — !" His fists opened and shut at his sides. "I've got guests to think about, but you come back here any time you wish, and by God —"

"How's tomorrow morning?"

"That's fine with me."

"I'll be here with bells on," I said. "That's a promise."

I awoke the next morning, Sunday, at eleven o'clock. My head felt swollen to twice its size, and as though it had been filled with concrete. When I tried to move it, the room swam in a steady circle from floor to ceiling, like the picture on a television set when it is in need of vertical tuning. The condition cleared up after a bit, and I got up and doused myself with cold water, dressed, and went down to the kitchen, where my wife was sitting over a cup of coffee and the *Times*.

"Good morning," I said, drawing on a tweed jacket, for the day was quite nippy.

"What's morning about it?"

I helped myself to a glass of cold orange juice from a pitcher. I drank it standing up, aware of her watching me. "What in heaven's name happened last night?" she asked. (I had stalked out of the party after my skirmish, pausing only long enough to make sure she had transportation home, and gone straight to bed on getting there myself, so these were our first words since then.) "What was that all about between you and Frank?"

"You'd be surprised," I answered acidly, and marched out of the house, making directly for the car, which I had left parked in the driveway, the keys in it.

I sat inside the car reviewing the hazards of living in a society as complex as ours. The memory of my grievances sent my temper flaring again. Should I keep my date with Dumbrowski? Honor — or at least self-respect — demanded that I do. There seemed no alternative. It was as though we had parted with the understanding "Fists, at dawn."

It was closer to noon when I reached the Dumbrowskis'. Nobody was stirring except the maid, who frowned uncertainly when, standing on the porch with my hands in my coat pockets, I asked for the master. She glanced over her shoulder up the vestibule stairway. "Are you expected?" she asked.

I told her that I was. As we talked, I debated with myself whether to leave a message that I had called, and go. Then a second-story window slid open and Dumbrowski's head appeared between the curtains, his face mangled with sleep, and an ice bag on his tousled hair. "Oh — that," he said, remembering He squinted down through the bright fall sunshine and, with the hand not concerned with steadying the ice bag, gathered the lapels of a bathrobe over his chest.

"I can come back later," I said, squinting back up at him, "if now isn't convenient."

"I'll be down." His head withdrew, and the window slid shut.

I sat on the porch steps to wait, declining the maid's invitation to wait inside. I picked up a handful of gravel from the drive and flicked the stones away one by one with my thumb. After about five minutes, the door behind me opened and Dumbrowski emerged, clad in a black turtleneck sweater and denim slacks. He must have had quite a night (my wife hadn't got home till two o'clock, I learned later), because he looked like something the cat dragged in. I sympathetically murmured something to that effect as I rose to greet him, and repeated my offer to let this go till some other time. "No, let's get it over with," he said doggedly.

"Right," I said, removing my coat as I followed him down the steps to the yard.

We squared away on a width of lawn that was concealed from the house by a group of birches, from which the ground we stood on fell away to a small pond in which the Dumbrowskis had once kept goldfish. We circled one another for a minute or two, our guards up, edging about for the advantage. There was no doubt what that consisted in here; it consisted in remaining above one's opponent.

"This has been brewing for a long time," I observed as we sparred.

"It was bound to come to a head," Dumbrowski agreed. He cocked his forward arm — the right — a bit, and I stiffened my own guard, at the same time thrusting out my chest to give that impression of pectoral strength that is always suggested in photographs of prizefighters.

"We don't cotton to one another, you and I," I went on. "And there you have it."

"You don't like my stuff. I know that."

"It's not my dish of tea."

"I hate that expression," Dumbrowski replied with unexpected violence. "Why don't you come right out and say what you think? Not that I don't know what your dish of tea *is*. That English lot! Twitches and nuances!" Here he reeled off a string of contemporary British novelists who did, with uncanny accuracy, reflect my private reading tastes. "Lint pickers!" he exclaimed in a burst of spirit. "All that eyebrow combing!"

I recognized well enough the animus of the popular artist whom critical approval has bypassed. He was one of those authors read by hundreds of thousands but of whom no one has ever *heard*. They have no *reputation*; they are merely household words. Oh, I knew what was in Dumbrowski's craw all right. But that did not spare me the comparable sting of having my *goût* as a reader under attack. Now I felt the urgent need to strike a blow.

"It's better than that burly realism," I retorted hotly. "And all that sex. Want to know why you chaps slather it on? You don't know the facts of life."

He paused long enough for the exquisite irony of this to sink in — I could sense the shaft going home — then he low-

254

ered his head and came at me with a bellow of mingled rage and pain.

I met his charge by adroitly stepping aside, more or less executing what is known in bullfighting as, I believe, a veronica. He stumbled in his plunge and lost his balance, sprawling headlong among the birches. He got to his feet and came for me again. I lunged forward to meet him, and we came together, our arms going like flails. It was amazing how few blows found their mark — practically none at all. This time, I tripped on a rock and stumbled against him, and, interlocked, we danced down the incline toward the goldfish pond. We fetched up short of it only because, at the conclusion of our career down the grass, we clumsily pulled each other down in a jumble of arms and legs. This had the effect of converting the encounter into a wrestling match, and by an accident of the terrain in my favor I landed on top, but so near the water that any attempt to alter our positions might have meant disaster for both of us. So I sat there on Dumbrowski's chest for a bit.

"This will teach you to speak lightly of a lady's name," I panted.

"Ridiculous." He brought the word out between gasps of his own. "Never understood this — fussing over a — compliment paid a woman."

"Compliment?"

He nodded. "Only told Feversham be — sure go talk to *her* if he wanted picking up."

"You mean — ?" I said.

He nodded again. "Feversham was depressed. So I told him go talk to her. She picks you right up. Always thought so. Great fun. At least appreciate your taste in *that*."

I climbed off of him. I turned away and dropped leadenly to the grass in a sitting position. I knew well enough now what was happening, and I offered no resistance. Behind me

I could hear Dumbrowski's heavy breathing. Somewhere a car backfired, shattering the morning stillness. As if in a dream, I gave my head a shake and said, "It was all a ghastly mistake."

"I'll accept that."

I could hear him getting to his feet now. When he spanked the dirt from his clothes, it was as if the blows stung my cheeks. But when I turned to look up at him over my shoulder, his face was twisted in a grin of forgiving triumph. Dumbrowski knew that he had won, in his eyes there was that quiet knowledge. There is no need to relate the rest in detail: how part of me hated him while more of me hated myself; how I rose, as if in a trance, to dust off my own clothes; and how, at last, Dumbrowski steered me up the lawn to the house and even into it, my arm in his viselike grip. "Wash up in there," he said, not unkindly. When I emerged from the bathroom he had indicated, he said, "Now come into the kitchen for some coffee."

We sat hunched over our cups of strong black coffee, our arms along the table, facing each other in a new understanding that needed no words. Each treasured within him the satisfaction of having stood up to the other, yet respected the other for having done the same. Somewhere a clock struck — one — and I told Dumbrowski that I had to go. I rose and, shaking his hand, took my leave.

As I strode up the walk to my car, I knew a strange peace — the peace of a man who has faced up to what courage and chivalry demanded, and not flinched. I knew it was the same with Dumbrowski. We would never speak of this again, yet we were strangely cleansed. Part of me regretted the incident — always would — but another, deeper part of me would always prize it for the challenge that had come out of it . . . a challenge met. Somewhere a duck quacked. The air was like wine. It was with a high heart that I sprang into my car and drove — home — to the woman I loved.

LAUGHTER IN THE BASEMENT

"She has no mind, merely a mind of her own" is something I recently said in open conversation, with less profit than I had anticipated. When I say anticipated, I mean over a fairly long stretch, for the remark is one of a repertory of retorts I carry about in my head, waiting for the chance to spring them. This is a form of wit I call prepartee — prepared repartee for use in contingencies that may or may not arise. For instance, I have been waiting for years for some woman to dismiss a dress she has on as "just something I slipped into," so that I can say, behind my hand, "Looks more like something she slipped and *fell* into."

There are two types of prepartee: the kind you can wangle an opening for, and the kind you can't. The sally about the woman who had no mind, merely a mind of her own, required no specific straight line but only a general one, in a context I was able to steer the conversation to after bringing the woman into it myself. But my plan to retort dryly when next I hear somebody say that money doesn't matter, "No, provided one has it," is something else again. I can, of course, bring up the *subject* of money any time I choose, but though you can lead a stooge to water, you can't make him drink, and unless somebody says, "Money doesn't matter," in so many words, or virtually that, I will never get to use the riposte.

The chances of my getting a feeder for it are slimmer than you might think. Clichés are like cops, in that you can never find one when you want one. This applies to trite questions as well as trite statements. I have been waiting since 1948 for some poor devil to ask, "What does a woman want most in a man?," so that I can come back, quick as a flash, with "Fiscal attraction." And I have been lying in wait even longer to hear so much as the vaguest reference to current realistic fiction as a reflection of our time, so that I can murmur, "I had thought it rather a reflection *on* it."

I almost murmured that one in Cos Cob. I was at a buffet supper in the home of friends there, and found myself in the library with the hostess and a couple of other guests. It was a week after my quip about the woman with no mind, and I had been trying to analyze just why it had failed. I had finally diagnosed my waggeries as, texturally, the suave and under-played sort, requiring small groups and an intimate, offhand delivery, so I was happy to find myself in the snug library with just a handful of people, well away from the general commotion in the living room, so reminiscent of the previous week's mob. Coffee had been poured and brandy was passed. I began setting up the conversation for my little mot about realistic novels. Having lit my pipe, I squeezed from the packed shelves a volume of fiction suited to my design and casually asked the hostess, "Have you read this?"

She nodded briskly. "Yes, I thought it pretty good of its kind," she said.

"Ah, of its kind. But what good is its kind?" I asked.

By dint of such questions, by tirelessly jockeying the discussion this way and that, by nudging, cuing, and tinkering with her responses, I succeeded in maneuvering her to within striking distance of my aphorism. Prepartee is very much like those games in which, over a course beset with delays, digressions, "penalties," and other pitfalls, one tries to move a disc to a goal marked "Home." After a quarter of an hour, I heard the hostess say, "Well, I mean realistic novels of this

sort, whatever you may think of them artistically, do have
some value for our time."

I sat on the edge of my chair. One more jump and I would
be Home. Very carefully, very deliberately, I said, "How do
you mean?"

At that moment, a hearty character in tweeds boomed into
the room. "Just a minute," I snapped. "Ethel here is talking.
Go on, Ethel. What was it you were saying? What are these
novels in connection with our time?"

"They hold a mirror up to it," she said.

I sat back in my chair. "I see," I said, and reached for my
cold cup of coffee.

With Home so hard to gain in manipulable contexts, the
chances of scoring with rejoinders depending on straight
lines you can't even *begin* to finagle are discouraging indeed.
Thus the odds against my ever being told, by a newcomer to
my community, "We'd like to meet some people who count,"
in order that I may answer, "Well, I can introduce you to a
couple of bank tellers," are really astronomical. And I long
ago decided not to hold my breath till I hear someone refer
to a third party as "my cousin twice removed," so I can
say, "I didn't know he was your cousin, but I knew he was
twice removed — once as treasurer of his firm and later to
the state prison at Ossining."

Recognizing all this, I eventually scaled my ambitions down
to where I bluntly *asked* people to stooge for me, as you do
in putting a riddle. This is a tawdry substitute for the real
thing, but better than nothing when you're bent on making
an impression, as I was recently at a party where I found myself *à deux* with a toothsome girl, a house guest of the host
and hostess. We were sitting together on the floor, through
which the sound of laughter from the basement game room
occasionally seeped. We sat leaning against chairs, with our

elbows hitched up on the seats, having a pleasant chat. I had spotted her from the first as a merry, responsive sort, a kid who could go along with a joke. In no connection, I turned to her and said, "Did I ever tell you about my cousin twice removed?"

She shook her head, tossing a wealth of black hair. "No. What about him?" she asked.

"Well, as I say, he was twice removed — once as treasurer of the bank he was connected with and later to the state prison at Ossining."

She laughed gaily, throwing her head back. "So you've got a banker in jail in your family?" she said. "Well, we've got a congressman at large in ours."

Having failed with large groups, then with small, and finally with a single companion (the less said about that brash chit the better), there seemed nothing left for me to do but talk to myself, a state to which frustration has brought stronger men than I. However, I rallied after making what you might call one more strategic retreat. I thought I would apply the technique I had evolved to the lowest common denominator — the practical joke.

We know a couple, living in one of the suburban towns near Westport, named Moses. They are of impressive Yankee extraction, and moved down from Vermont six years ago. One of the nuisances of living in the country is, of course, power failures, and I got the notion of ringing them up sometime when the electricity was off, and asking, "Where was Moses when the lights went out?" This is admittedly a far cry from my early high ideals for prepartee — so far, indeed, as to be not true prepartee at all. Nevertheless, as some philosopher or other has said, a difference in quantity, if great enough, becomes a difference in quality, and this gag depended on such a number of factors going just right — that is to say, just wrong — that I felt it to be qualitatively unique. It required, to begin with, a meteorological mishap of such extent and duration as to plunge into darkness an area wide enough to embrace Westport, where I live, and the town where the Moseses' place is, a good ten miles inland. It called for the most perfect timing, in that it would have to be pulled when falling limbs had broken the power lines, which are strung along the tops of the poles, but not yet the telephone connections underneath. It would depend on the Moseses and ourselves being brought simultaneously to the same pass. Having met these conditions, it would still require the phone's being answered by Mrs. Moses and not Moses himself. (I couldn't say, "Where were you when the lights went out?") So the sporting odds against my getting Home were actually greater than they had been across more cerebral courses.

It wasn't until the ice storm early last January, or three and a half years after the gag's conception, that the necessary factors coincided. I thought I saw my chance during the big blow of '51, when the winds attained hurricane force, but our power and phone lines were both reduced to spaghetti before I could get my wits about me. However, in this winter's glacéed adventure, our juice went at dusk, taking with it light, heat, and cooking power. The phone still worked, but, of course, it was being monopolized for the time being by housewives on the party line making unnecessary calls.

During dinner, which consisted of shredded wheat crouched over by candlelight, I mentally reviewed the situation. Everything was in order; it remained to be seen only whether the Moseses could be got through to by phone. (That they had no power was a fair certainty, for it had been knocked out or shut off for miles around.) I vibrated like a scientist for whom every long-awaited element is fortuitously aligning itself in his favor, hurrying him toward the exquisite moment of experiment. Dinner over, I slipped into our dark vestibule and sat down at the phone. I found it alive and free, and, what was more, the operator got me the number I wanted after only a few moments' delay Hearing the ring at the other end, I sat erect, realizing I had forgotten there was still a final requisite beyond that of the other phone's working — a woman's voice would have to answer.

I heard the phone picked up "Hello?" a voice said. It was a woman's.

"Where was Moses when the lights went out?" I asked.

"In bed," she said. "He hasn't been at all well."

"Aw, gosh, that's too bad. I'm sorry to hear that," I said. "What seems to be the trouble?"

"Oh, the usual — flu, grippe, or whatever you want to call it," Mrs. Moses said. "Who is this?"

I told her. Then I added, "I've had a cold myself, which is probably why you didn't recognize my voice. Well, we were just wondering how you two were making out over there. Is there anything we can . . ."

Thus prepartee, in either its pure or debased form, is no indolent hobby, no pastime for the weak-nerved. The life of a parlor desperado, with its long hours in ambush, is a hard and often wearing one. It has its midnight post-mortems just like its more familiar counterpart, departee — which is, I think, the proper term for remarks thought up on the way home. I don't know which is the more frustrating, moments to which one has proved unequal or stunners for which no occasion arose, but I have found both abrasive. My little tit-tup about Moses and the lights came to an end when I hung up to find my wife behind me with a flashlight, a child clinging to either leg. "Who was that?" she asked, playing the beam on me. I told her. I also told her why I had phoned, and said that I wondered why Mrs. Moses hadn't been more on the ball. I asked my wife whether *she* didn't think the line was funny. "*Funny!*" she said. "Don't make me laugh."

PART OF THE FAMILY PICTURE

AT FORTY-EIGHT, Vogelsang had a profitable dry-cleaning plant, a house in Armonk, a wife his own age, and a son named Kermit who was attending a boys' college in Massachusetts. The son was not fat, but a prevailing rotundity made him seem so. He had a round face in which two pink cheeks misrepresented him as cherubic, and he wore glasses, which he kept on when he went in swimming.

One Sunday when he was down from school, the family spent some time discussing what next to do about the mother, who had a stomach complaint which had baffled two doctors. Vogelsang became aware of a repressed eagerness in the boy, who caught Vogelsang's eye at length and beckoned him upstairs to his room with a jerk of his head.

"I want to talk to you," Kermit said in his room, shutting the door. "Sit down."

"Thanks," Vogelsang said ironically, taking the chair that Kermit waved to.

"It's about Moth," Kermit said, using an abbreviation which set well with nobody. "These doctors can't find anything and probably won't. It's something functional." Vogelsang hesitated. "Psychological."

"You mean upstairs?" Vogelsang said, entertained. He tapped his temple with two fingers.

Kermit shook his head. "There's no upstairs. The body and the mind are one."

Information such as this was borne regularly southward

from Massachusetts. The boy knew that the origins of monogamy were economic, that religions are deflections of the sexual nature, that symmetrical living had perished with the ancient Greeks. Now he knew this.

"There's no upstairs?" Vogelsang said softly, in mock reverence. He was really waiting it out. Muffing words like "functional" had bred in him a wariness — the last time it had applied to architecture. He had once gone halfway through a bitter argument with Kermit under the impression that erogenous zones were vice districts.

"I don't want to see you throw good money after bad," Kermit went on, as Vogelsang, who had been looking forward to a fresh cigar and a still unopened copy of *Esquire*, glanced unhappily at the closed door. "You're speaking of a clinic. Well, ninety percent of the cases that get to clinics are psychic. And ninety percent of those are stomach cases. What's at the bottom of Moth's condition is most likely an emotional disturbance. Believe me. The thing to do is to get her to an analyst."

Kermit had drifted over behind a small writing desk which was tumbled high with reading matter, so that he offered the illusion of standing waist-deep in books. It was a kind of tableau which Vogelsang worked up in his mind, then resisted. Kermit continued his explanations for five or six minutes, then he said: "Well? What do you think?"

Vogelsang had been thinking that Jake Vandermeer, a friend of his who owned a chain of dry-cleaning stores and a country place near Darien with sixty acres, had given more money to the school Kermit went to than Kermit would probably make in his lifetime, and had not finished eighth grade. The reflection was a siding from which to watch the streamlined verbiage go by. "Malingering," "psychic," "neurasthenic" streaked past like the names of coaches of which Vogelsang had not even got the spelling. With a small gold penknife he pruned a panatela, dropping the hull into an ashtray, or rather missing, so that it fell to the rug. He checked the draft of the cigar with an experimental suck, but delayed lighting up till he should be at peace. "Like what kind of emotional disturbance?" he asked.

"Who knows?" Kermit shrugged. "Some, oh, lack — frustration — boiling up in Moth's time of life," he said. "It would have to be dug into, probably in relation to the family picture. That's what those troubles are part of — the family picture."

Vogelsang surveyed his son from beneath heavy lids. "For instance," he commanded.

Kermit went over and picked up the cigar hull and dropped it in the ashtray, like a bug. "Oh, one approach might be that Moth is a sort of business widow. For years you've been buried in either your work or a magazine. You're a good guy and all, but you couldn't exactly say you wore your heart on your sleeve."

Vogelsang folded the knife shut and pocketed it. "Hasn't my heart always been in the right place?" he said with resentment.

"It's not that. You know how women are."

Vogelsang fidgeted forward in his chair. The virgin cigar grew tattered in his clutch. "No," he said derisively, "I don't. How are they?"

"They live for affection, and if it's denied them — well, any part of the body can become an attention-getting mechanism. That, in a nutshell, is psychosomatic medicine."

Vogelsang felt an angry rapture at the promenade of learning for which he footed the monthly bills. He turned and smiled one-sidedly, as though to a third party in the room. "Why spend another buck when we got a psychiatrist right here in the house?" he said. He immediately regretted "buck," which had been vaguely retaliatory.

Kermit made a gesture of defeat. "That bourgeois superstition over the very word 'psychiatrist,' " he said.

Vogelsang rose.

"Maybe there is this new kind of medicine that's going around. And maybe I'm anyhow seeing signs of what you think you'd like to be," he said. "Well, when you've made out in life half as good as some of the people you lump in that class, bourgeois, why, we'll decide how good your advice is." He walked to the door. "And I'll tell you this. There's two words I'm damn sick of — bourgeois and psychosemantic!" Wounded in spirit, he withdrew to his room, where instead of picking up the *Esquire,* and with his tongue repairing the lesions in his cigar, he sat thinking of Jake Vandermeer, whose house had twenty-seven rooms and who also had a swimming pool with an island in the middle of it on which guests could eat, and with a catwalk for the servants to bring the food on. It was a thought from which he frequently drew encouragement.

Putting his wife in the hands of a top stomach man, as Vogelsang instantly did, was an act of self-defense. It was as though his honor, having somehow been indicted, was now on trial Since the conversation with Kermit, Vogelsang had had a plummet of misgiving. A bookkeeper in his own office, now that he came to think of it, had told of an aunt who had been troubled with headaches, dizziness, and repeated nausea, all inexplicable — until a mother-in-law had been removed from the house. Then it had cleared up. Vogelsang wondered how anybody could survive such farcical injury. The new specialist phoned Vogelsang a report on the first X-ray, and it was negative.

"We'll take others," Vogelsang said. "There's lots of them — a series. We'll spare no expense." He sat watching his wife narrowly "Haven't I always been that way — spare no expense? Car of your own, the best in kitchen equipment, a maid the minute I could afford it?"

His wife nodded mechanically, finding these protestations elliptical, but grateful for the growing solicitude. He poked a thermometer in her mouth with a tender tyranny and went to the kitchen to make some tea, with his own hands, though the maid was in her room. The thermometer read ninety-nine and eight-tenths. Kermit, home for the next weekend, told them not to worry too much about it — "Low-grade fevers can be functional." Vogelsang, whose exasperation with this nettle of a boy was exceeded only by his anxiety for his wife, told himself that when this was all over he was going to take him out to the garage, as to a woodshed. He would literally do this, carrying a hairbrush or strap.

News came of what was presumably the last of the X-rays. It was negative.

Vogelsang wet his lips and gave his belt a hitch, sensing Kermit beckon him into the living room. He saw his wife at the analyst's, unwinding the cerements of secrecy from the chronicle of their marriage bed. "Psst," Kermit called. Vogelsang went over.

"Fortescu, this chap at school I think I've mentioned, knows a good psychiatrist. They had him for his aunt," Kermit said. "Now let's simply go ahead and make a date for Moth."

Something in the sequence of syllables, the juxtaposition of "chap" and "Moth," rallied Vogelsang's resistance. He answered in the tone of a sentenced prisoner declaring that he will fight his case to the highest court. "We'll take it to Mayo Brothers," he said.

"Mayo Brothers!" Kermit said, with a frown. "The Mecca of neurotics."

"Be careful what you call the mother who bore you!" Vogelsang said in a loud voice, glancing out the door to see if his wife was anywhere near and had heard. She had, and came in. Seeing a chance to convert retreat into an offensive, Vogelsang quickly pointed at Kermit and said, "He claims it's all in your head."

Protesting that this phrasing put them back a hundred years, Kermit insisted on stating the matter himself. His mother heard him out, and agreed with unexpected compliance, if with a shrug, that they might as well try that next.

"The doctor's name," Kermit said, with a glance at his father, "is Strogonoff."

Strogonoff, a lean, weary man with exquisite haberdashery, sorted patients instinctively into two categories — those who had read Freud and company and those who hadn't — not that he was sure in his mind which was better. Mrs. Vogelsang at any rate fell smoothly into hers as, thickset, short, and fair, and clutching an armful of bundles from a round of shopping, she entered the office looking around for the couch made familiar by stage and screen. Strogonoff had bought one because it was expected. He was oppressed by a sense of vogue, of too many people aspiring to be patients. Mrs. Vogelsang made her way with smiling interest toward the couch, on which had previously lain a sculptress whose husband tortured their infant son with ice cubes, and before that a young meteorologist who wondered whether he should buy a house in the country because there he continually picked up twigs and broke them in half, then into quarters, then into eighths.

"Shall I take my shoes off?" Mrs. Vogelsang asked, having dropped her parcels on a chair.

"Go right ahead," Strogonoff said. He had already abandoned the case.

Her shoes shucked off and nudged out of sight, she lay down with a grateful sigh. "When I was a little girl I used to like to —"

"Over the phone something was said about your having pains," Strogonoff said. "What is the matter with you?"

She commenced a recital of her difficulties. Strogonoff cued her to trace them backwards through the years, interrupting only enough to keep her, as with the deft pressure of a snaffle, on the subject of her symptoms. A half hour passed, three quarters. Strogonoff's ear picked up something, and he straightened in his chair.

"This pain you say you had 'more on the right side,' the night your husband took you to the bowling match," he said. "Was it sharp, and up here perhaps?" He laid a hand on his trunk, well away from the stomach. She raised herself up to see, and nodded, doubtfully at first, trying to remember.

"A little baking soda seemed to help, at least it went away," she said, nuzzling a stockinged arch over an instep.

"Have you ever had your gall bladder checked?" Strogonoff asked.

"No."

"Do so."

With this dug up out of the patient's past to go on, the family doctor got in touch with a gall bladder specialist, who explored exhaustively, in his fashion, thought about it all, and suddenly decided to operate. Vogelsang stepped into a Western Union office and dispatched a wire to Kermit running: "Trouble gall bladder stop specialist set operate Wednesday stop expect you here." He pressed the pencil so hard that when he left the place, the indented message was legible on the next sheet of the pad.

Kermit, who arrived too late Tuesday night to talk to the specialist, sought him out at the hospital the next morning a few minutes prior to surgery. Vogelsang trailed a step behind him, going down the hospital corridor, performing the introductions when he drew up.

269

"May I ask what the X-ray showed?" Kermit asked the doctor, an urbane, elderly man named Smollett.

"Nothing," Dr. Smollett replied agreeably. He had a chart cradled on one arm. "Stones," he went on, as though he were a lapidary rather than a medical man, "are sometimes translucent, and thus escape detection. Second, they migrate." He paused and jotted something on the chart with no impairment of his courtesy.

"Then how do you know they're there?"

Dr. Smollett looked up and explained, "Diseases often travel incognito. I'll grant you the bulk of the symptoms here are dyspepsia, but that's one of the guises assumed by the disorder it's my job to find. You don't always grease the wheel where it squeaks, don't always grease the wheel where it squeaks," he went on, as though he had obtained his education from a cracked phonograph record, but he was only being elementary, and thus repetitious. "I'll stake my sixty-two years on this case." Vogelsang stood by as though witnessing a thrashing he had authorized. It was like the end of the thrashing when Doctor Smollett said "digestive constellation," words which reached Vogelsang heroically, like band music. He allied himself with the aplomb, though Smollett might as well have been talking Choctaw. "The stomach," Dr. Smollett finished, in modulations Vogelsang could only worship from afar, like an island in a swimming pool, "has been called the greatest liar in the anatomy."

Kermit glanced from the doctor to Vogelsang and back again to the doctor, like young men Vogelsang had seen in motion pictures, then shouldered his way off between them.

That was ten o'clock in the morning, the hour scheduled, and by twelve Dr. Smollett had not yet come down to the lobby where Vogelsang and Kermit were waiting. They would get up out of a chair and pace, or get out of one chair and into another. Kermit had a book with him, from force of habit, which he didn't open. Vogelsang drifted over and glanced at the title — twice, because he had forgotten what he'd read the first time, or even that he had looked. Something about semantics. Suddenly Vogelsang broke through the swinging doors at the end of the lobby and went out to a bar across the street.

"Rye and soda," he ordered. He had an urge to release his anxiety in talk, any kind of talk, and did. To a bartender inured to obscure circuits of association, he related something of the affairs of Jake Vandermeer. "There's a terrace on this place," he said, by way of concluding a lengthy description of it, "with a statue of Venus that's got a radio in her stomach. Like those clocks, you know?" The bartender continued impassive, as though something more were needed "Paul Newman was there," Vogelsang said.

He saw that twenty minutes had gone, gulped his drink, and galloped back to the lobby.

Still no Dr. Smollett, it was plain from Kermit's posture — his feet spread out and his head back on the chair — as well as from his expression as he rolled an eye at Vogelsang without moving his head. An apprehension clawed Vogelsang: Smollett had found nothing and was afraid to come down. Vogelsang could see him, put to rout in his sixty-third year, an effigy of self-possession. Then the elevator doors slid open, and there he was.

"Everything is okay," he said. He pinched his eyeballs in toward the bridge of his nose in that gesture which is one of the ciphers of fatigue. "I found about what I expected — not much, but enough to have caused the trouble. We've got the culprit at last."

When Vogelsang drove home, late that night, Kermit sat beside him, looking out of the car window and saying nothing. Vogelsang steered onto the drive, at last, and across the gravel which gave forth its welcome scrunch and into the open garage. He slid the fenders carefully to rest alongside a protruding row of firewood which was stacked against one wall. Kermit opened his door and got out.

"Just a minute," Vogelsang said. Kermit, who had started away, turned back. "You forgot your book." Vogelsang picked it up off the seat and handed it to him. Kermit took it and went in the house.

The maid fixed them a bite of supper — their first food since a sketchy breakfast, though it was nearly midnight. They sat in the living room waiting for it, Vogelsang with his coat off and his tie loosened. Kermit put his legs straight out ahead of him on an ottoman, his feet side by side, the flat of the soles toward Vogelsang. Vogelsang looked at him, then looked away. He thought of how the boy went in the water with his glasses on.

"That book," he said, pointing at a table where Kermit had set it when he entered. "It's about this new stuff, semantics, I see." He hooked a chair toward him with his toe and slung a foot on it. He fished a cigar from a nearby humidor and dressed it. "What the devil is that all about, semantics? Explain it to me." He raised his head and laughed. "But take it slow. The first time I saw the word I thought it was all about pottery."

YOU KNOW ME ALICE

(Some correspondence we might have
if Ring Lardner were alive today)

DEAR ALICE.

Well hon here I am managing a Little League team in
Westport. The job at the Bridgeport Brass is all set and we
can get personaly welded as soon as your mother's hip mends
and you can get out here. Meanwhile I'm living in a rooming
house near the Penn Central R.R. tracks here riding the train
to work so I'm what you could call a commuter only going
the other way, not one them Madison Ave. birds carrying one
them lether reticules into the Big Town and back every day.
So hence the postmark which must of gave you quite a turn.

Managing a ball team ain't what it use to be in the old days
and may still be out there in Keokuk. Time was when all
you had to know about your material was wether they could
do something with a bat besides supply a little extra ventilation on hot days or pull down a fast clothesliner off second.
Now you have to worry about tension spans and what they
call stribling rivalry and one thing another — in other words
why they might not be performing up to snuff on the above.
The last mentioned is when you have two brothers on the
same team as I happen to of drew. Their mother told me
they have these feelings of mutual hostlity due to a family
situation which she will go into with me in more detail later
if they is any danger of our not copping the penant and that
it was her experience that the best way out of a jam was
substitute situations. So I says how would it be if I always

273

had one them warming the bench to go in for the other if
needs be and she siezed my hand and kissed it and then went
and hid in the car she had brung them in, a blue Jag convertible which the family have been driving with the top up
I understand because they are in mourning.

Well kid they being the first arrivals for the opening prac-
tise I got a bat and started hitting them some fungos. The
mother sat shivering in the Jag watching the proseedings
through the windshield. This is what she seen.

The one kid whose name is Martin had this idea that somebody had ast him to impersonate a croquet wicket in creative
play because every time I hit him a grounder he would have
his feet planted the exact distance apart at just the right time
for the ball to pass through without no hindranse. After
about five or six of these flawless imitations the mother came
over to shed some light on it. He has this will to fail she said
and went back to shiver in the Jag some more. I thanked her
for this piece of info to help me in forming my first team
and turned to look for the brother.

This kid is a compulsory eater they call them. He was
nowheres to be seen at first then I made out a speck against
the refreshment stand which at this field is about 500 yards
from our diamond, one of 3, no doubt telling the woman on
hot dogs there to keep 'em coming. The mother started up
the Jag and drove over to get him hollering out the window
at me He fears competition and seeks ecscape in food as she
went by. When the car was gone I yelled to the other kid
What's your brother's name? and he yelled back Stringfellow
and I had the case diagnozed.

By now the mothers were arriving in droves with their
hopefuls by auto (nobody walks in Westport unless an ump
gives them a base on balls) most of the mothers and an occasional father staying to have a word with me and there

being enough kids to keep theirselves busy for a while on their own I went over to the bleachers where I set up a small office to hear out the parents lining up with dossiers on the prospective athaletes.

I'll give you my starting lineup next time preferring to use the rest of this sheet to remind you that letter writing ain't my fort and that I wisht you was here in person holding it with me. You know me Alice.

Yours sincerely,
ED.

Bridgeport, Conn., May 18.

Dear Alice:

Well hon I'm writing this in the shop where I got a little lunch time left over on top of a crate.

Well Alice my starting lineup on the first game was as follows. In left, center and right I got three oral types which is fine for talking it up around the outfield. On first a kid who has a thing about sliding. I let him bat just before my two best hitters so in case he gets on third he'll have the highest possible chance to coalchute it home looking dramatic and important like his mother says he needs to while he spanks the dust off hisself to gain confidence. Martin is on second. I can't do nothing with his brother while he is on the pickalily and if he muffed one might head strait for the refreshment stand to seek consolation there and never be seen again. I can't take the responsibility. Shortstop and third I have very little to go on as they are underpriviledged kids from the r.r. tracks nobody ever gives no thought to, just good ball players in the hot spots though I am told one of them might be out stealing something more serious than second if they wasn't second to steal with the girls looking on. The catcher is a swell natured kid whose as broad as he's long and can stop any reasonable pitch because of the sheer bulk there is to get past. You can always use an obeesity case behind the plate.

Now on this level hon which is the beginners from 8 on up your everperennial problem is pitching. Few have the experience or control at that age. In making up my notes on my squad a woman named Mrs. Niswonger said to me in a interview I granted her conserning her son Artie who wanted to pitch Nicknames are very revealing don't you know and they call Artie the Strike Out King. Well I learned through some side investigation that they call him that when he is at bat, when he is on the mound he is known as the Sultan of Swat due to how good he can make even a kronic whiffer look. I ast her didn't she think in that case we had ought to start somebody else in the box and she says What and deel him a blow to his eggo from which he might never recover? In this part the country where they know more about those things you put players in where they're weak so as to bolster their confidense and make athaletes out of them. The only other pitcher I had was no better than Niswonger anyway so I started Niswonger.

So that was the opening roster for our first game. It was with the Bluejays We're the Robins so you can see we have a bird moteef this yr. The plate ump was the guidance counselor for one of the schools so hence he knew most of the kids' potenshul already and how to sound off the calls wether loud or easy on their nerves and etc. A local dentist umped bases for us.

Niswonger wasn't no worse than the Bluejays' pitcher. He walked the first eight of our batters giving us five runs and three men on base with none away. The suspense was unbearable — when would he put one over? In the consulting room (formerly known as the bleachers) the mothers were yacking it up amongst theirselves, trading slants on their sons and occasionally shouting That's looking 'em over! and It

only takes one¹ and so on from lists that they carried with
suitable things to holler. At this point the kid with the thing
about sliding was on third and with ball four called on the
batter he came home — another forced run. As he strolls
home his mother jumps to her feet in the stands and yells
Slide¹ He does. He takes a running start and then dropping
down on one side just as pretty as you'd want shoots across
the plate like a torpedo nearly spiking the guidance counselor
who got his feet out of the way just in time.

Suddenly the pitcher got his range and retired three of
us in a row and in the bottom of the inning Niswonger
promply oblidged the opposition by starting up the Big
Parade around the bags again. He walked seven in a row and
then finally got one over that the Bluejay at bat sent into
left field for a homer and a two run lead for the enemy.

At this junkture I debated yanking Niswonger. But sensing what was in the wind Mrs. Niswonger hightailed it
over to our dugout hauling the plate ump with her — this
guidance counselor. He sketched in the basic factors in the
bind we were in. The kid's father couldn't get past the Biltmore Men's Bar unless hogtied and dragged past and then
only with the reminder that they was still the bar car to sit
in and overshoot his station by a couple stops landing him
closer to Wallingford than Westport and this together with
the threat of iminent divorce it led to give the kid such a
feeling of uncertainty that if I pulled him at this crisis I and
I alone would have to answer for the consequences. He
wouldn't — the ump that is. He seemed to know what he was
talking about. He got his P.H.D. at the U. of Pennsylvania
with a thesis on sulking which he is the leading authority on
so I let things ride. All this while the base ump was handing
out spice drops to the infield from a good sapply he had
on him. As a town dentist he can't see why all the to do
about a few cavities.

Suffise it to say Niswonger worked his way out of the hole and we tied the score and then they was a sudden shower which the way they performed I says they should ought to all go take anyways includeing the mothers. One woman listening to me dish it out in that vain said You must get a grate deal of compensation out of bossing a bunch of kids around and I says to her Lady nobody offered me a nickle to do this and I would not except it if they did. I couldn't button my lip but went on to say that I liked working with boys if only I could get rid of the full cooperation of the parents espesially the women. Then the kid with the will to fail's mother got into the act to my surprise. She was eavesdropping on the rhubarb from the Jag where she suddenly must of got her courage up because she says Evadently you are equally good at pushing ladies around and do we deserve to sirvive as a race and I says If you weren't all ladies I would give you my opinion of you in two words, blather skites. Then she says My husband will wish to see you tomorrow or so and I says Send him around, haveing visions of being strode up to by this guy in one them gaberdeen suits Alice and being slapped across the chops with one them lether handbags that they carry. Which would at least bring the rhubarb up to the man to man level where it belongs. All this while we were getting no dryer accept for the woman snug in the Jag. I was between her and the first woman with two out in the top of the third and the score tied eight all and a man on second. Then the first woman says You certainly seem to have a lot of hidden hostilities and I says What's hidden about them? and she didn't have no comeback. I may of been a little sharp but my job is hard enough without a lot of bystanders going off ½ cocked about how it should ought to be done.

Well with the rain showing no signs of letting up they was nothing to do but call the game a tie to be played off later though who picked up the marbles on the rhubarb I will leave you to be the judge. You know me Alice. I don't want nobody sticking their $0.02 into my affairs though I am perfectly willing to listen to any reasonable offer of advice even in this matriarky I think they call this type of culture.

I agree with you about the amount of furniture we should start off with though why it should all be bird's eye maple I fail to see. I have always kind of had this feeling of mutual hostility toward bird's eye maple. More of this later.

Yours,

E_D_.

Westport, Conn , July 2.

Dear Alice.

It's grate news your mother's hip is better and well enough for you to practically garantee you'll be here in a week. All as I can say is I'll be glad when we can get settled. But I wisht you could of been here with me last night. As you know we finally had this playoff of that tie game with the Bluejays which was also a game breaking a tie with them for fourth place and brother! I never see such exitement. It was the most satisfying evening of my life sports-wise.

To begin with they was no mothers around. They all went to the Mental Health Ball which is more important this year than ever before they tell me because of the whopping amount that has to be raised. Malajustments are on the increase in all these communities where they take such an interest in their children's minds and organize their play and all for some strange reason another. The guidance counselor was chairman of the affair so he wasn't on hand neither. The dentist umped both plate and bases, doing so from the pitcher's box.

While he may be a firstrate dentist he could use a good eye doctor hisself judging from some them calls Alice. The

kid with the thing about sliding has got another thing about
ducking pitches. It's the same thing really the way they
explain it. He has the same chance to drop beautifully putting on the same kind of show stirring up dust which he
spanks off his uniform like one who has just ecscaped sudden
death to bolster his eggo. They was a fast ball heading straight
for his coco but even as he made for terra firma the ump
yelled Steerike! pointing a thumb over his shoulder in the
general direction of Cos Cob to say he was out. Well Alice
it is the first time I ever see a man called out on two strikes
but the ump's memory was as stubborn as it was wobbly and
he stood on his right not to have to reverse a decision if he
didn't feel like it. I for my part told the kids to show some
sportsmanship and stow the repertee such as Get a tin cup
with some pencils in it! and etc. But that ain't how we made
Little League history that night. I'm coming to that now.

Emotions by this junkture were raw. Both sides had suffered equally from the ½ baked umping so never mind that
but by the last inning as a result and with no mothers to
guide them they were playing like fiends. Since we were the
home team this time we had last licks. Not that we ever got
them — and thereby hangs the tale.

Midway through their licks the Bluejays put in a pinch
hitter with two on and two away and the score tied five all.
Here the Bluejay runner on first started yelling to the batter
Put one through second where you like to Jack! He couldn't
catch a cold in an icebox in Alaska! Meaning rightly enough
Martin our croquet wicket. But by now Martin had had it.
His dandruff was up like nothing I ever see. Thank God his
mother wasn't around to badger me with no substitute situations, just let him stay there and take it. When our catcher
threw a bad return to Niswonger who was pitching it went
over Niswonger's head toward Martin and this time he managed to get hold of it. Well taunts the wit on first what

happened? This says Martin and threw the ball at him like
a rock. He caught it making sure to keep his foot on the
bag so as not to be called out and shot it right back just as
hard as *he* could. This time it went as usual through Martin's
legs and the other kid says You'd make a grate football
player — a center. That did it. Martin ran over and let him
have it with both fists.

Well hon don't ask me to describe in detail what happened
because I couldn't. In a second the whole infield was a malay
I couldn't begin to give a blow by blow account of and blow
by blow it would have to be because this wasn't just no ordinary rhubarb. This was It. Neither I or the other manager
interfered. It did our hearts too good to see it. It thrilled us.
Something went up my spine like band music good and loud
at the sight of those boys out there mixing it up. Being boys
at last. I never see a group so integrated. You couldn't tell
whose arms and legs belonged to who they was such a solid
tangle of them whaling the tar out of one another. The ump
didn't interfere neither having even less objection to loose
teeth than to cavities. He stood smiling by along with us
managers.

I'd say we beat the Bluejays that night though I'd have no
way of proving it accept by a count of shiners and bloody
noses. By the time we did pull the last ones apart figuring
we had had our hearts done enough good and got our charges
tidied up a little it was too dark to resoom. The other manager and I chipped in to buy them all pop at the refreshment
stand where they all rushed pellmell like one happy family
now.

Well so ends one Little League season for one manager.
Probably his last judging from what the mothers said when
they heard what happened. But it's just as well they bad me
fond ado before the official farewell because the boys chipped
in and bought me a beautiful silver money clip with my

inishles on it whereas if the mothers had of still had a hand in the proseedings you and I might now be libel to own one them pieces of dead wood that looks so charming on tables that ain't got no shape neither and how would you fit that in with bird's eye maple Alice? But it has been a mighty educational experience for this gink. I picked up some pretty good pointers on raising kids so come on out here and let's get started on that family. Boys that is. We'll add the girls later for you if needs be. Financially speaking-wise I know what a full house means these days but I'm game. You know me Alice.

Love,
ED.

A WALK IN THE COUNTRY; OR, HOW TO KEEP FIT TO BE TIED

WALKING has always been a favorite pastime of mine as well as my chief physical exercise, and it was natural, therefore, that when I moved from New York City to the outskirts of Westport, the prospect of pleasant rambles about the Connecticut countryside ranked high on my list of expectations. My first act of leisure, once the strain of getting organized had relaxed and my family was settled in the new house, was to don an old tweed coat and set off briskly down the road.

I had gone about a hundred paces, swinging my arms and breathing deep lungfuls of the crisp air, when a car approaching from behind slowed to a stop and a face in a brown beret peered anxiously from the tonneau of an open sports convertible to inquire, "Anything wrong?"

"No," I said, "nothing wrong. Thanks just the same."

The man nodded, slipping the car into gear, but turned and glanced doubtfully back before peeling out of sight around a bend.

I resumed my hike. I walked well over on the shoulder of what was a very winding, as well as sparsely populated, road. Cars outnumbered the houses there by a considerable margin. Four or five came by, from both directions, before I sensed another slowing to a stop at my back. It was a blue sedan with a middle-aged couple in the front seat. The woman cranked a window down and thrust her head out.

"Is there anything — ?" she began.

"No," I said rather peevishly. "Nothing at all. Everything is O.K. Thank you."

"Because we thought you might have . . ." Her voice trailed off on some vaguely articulated species of human difficulty — mechanical in nature, to be sure, because it was by now clear to me that anybody seen walking in these parts was presumed to be making his way from, or to, a stalled vehicle.

I stood a moment in the road, after the latest Samaritans had gone, debating whether to strike out across the fields. But that wasn't what I had come out for. I didn't want to pick my way through meadow grass and wood lots; I just wanted to go for a walk. I had done so to my heart's content on the sidewalks of New York. Why not out here in the open?

I gave it up for now, making a mental note to try, next time, a narrow thoroughfare that intersected this road at a corner a few thousand feet on the other side of my house. It was called a lane, rather than a road or street, and looked very rustic. I took off down it the following Sunday morning.

It was a nice little lane indeed, and, I noted with relief, much less heavily traveled than the road. Practically deserted.

A Walk in the Country; or, How to Keep Fit to Be Tied

For that reason, however, anyone seen afoot on it must seem doubly an object for solicitous inquiry. I swung a hastily cut elm stick, hoping thus to advertise my ambulatory intent, but it did no good. There was presently the squeal of slowing wheels at my back, and a black Jaguar sedan rolled to a stop. The front window came down and a voice with a weary Harvard accent said, "Give you a lift?"

"Right," I said, feeling that resistance was useless, and also that a brief tour of a road unfamiliar to me might yield a byway or two more suited to my needs. I climbed into the back seat, in which a youth with a cigarette burning in his fingers sat comfortably slumped. At the wheel, beside the man who had hailed me, was a very personable young woman with her hair bound in a silk scarf. She asked sociably how far I was going, and I said, "Oh, just up the road a bit I'll tell you where."

As we started away, I appraised my companions. They appeared to be a family, of which the man in front, with the Harvard accent, would be the father. They were all attractive, and all desperately well-bred. The youth beside me was in his twenties. He produced a silver case and offered me a cigarette, which I declined. He wore a blue flannel blazer with white piping, gray slacks, and white socks with violet clocks. I imagined him to be a ne'er-do-well of the amiable Wodehousean sort.

Once I was settled and we were on our way, the father resumed a conversation that I had apparently interrupted. "No, the whole thing about Lettie is that she's nostalgic for a Paris that simply never was," he said.

"And that she hasn't seen in any case," said the young woman at the wheel.

"That's the kind of nostalgia it's hardest to cure," the youth put in, from the back seat. "For places you've never been."

284

"And as for the old Germany!" the young woman said.

"You can see that in Milwaukee," said her brother.

It was not enough that they pick me up and spirit me away. They had to encircle me with brittle conversation into the bargain. The father, shaking his head, made some deploring allusion to a housewarming party this Lettie friend of theirs had recently given. "The natives in New Canaan are still talking about it," he said. "Climbed the hill for miles around to watch. I mean if you want to live in something designed by Marcel Breuer, the least you can do is draw the draperies at night."

"People who live in glass houses shouldn't throw parties," I said, glancing out the window.

So we bandied pleasantries for ten minutes or more — until I woke to the realization that we had gone three miles. "Good God!" I said. "Let me out. Isn't that the Post Road up there? I've gone way past my place."

When I had got out, I saw that I should have let them take me clear up to the Post Road, because it was the shortest way home now. I made for it, and struck back toward Westport on foot once more.

Well, this was a different story. Here there was no danger of one's walk being interrupted. The cars simply shot past in a glittering stream. Yes, this was something else again. When I had tramped a mile or so, I felt that I had fulfilled my calisthenic purpose, and I began to turn and cast receptive glances at the rushing traffic. Nobody even slowed. At last, reluctantly, I lifted an arm and pointed a thumb over my shoulder. With no result. I did so a second time, then a third.

There was something wrong here. This was all mixed up. What I saw was a grave confusion in public thinking, if not a split in the national psyche. Why, when so eager to stop on idyllic back roads to the annoyance of pedestrians wishing simply to ramble there, must these same people, on a highway that patently none but a maniac would choose for a constitutional, flash past at speeds up to sixty and seventy miles an hour without giving a man so much as a glance?

"You're sick," I called to the whizzing phantoms. "Sick, do you hear!" I had left my stick in the Jaguar, to my keen regret; I could have used one now — if not to flourish, then to lean on. There was no question of cutting myself another; the terrain was barren of verdure. The midmorning sun blazed in the sky, growing steadily hotter. I squinted into it every time I turned to solicit an approaching car. I finally gave up trying to excite interest in myself. I took off my coat and mopped my brow. I had walked a mile and a half at least, with only half the distance home, or maybe less, traversed. Though I was physically rather bushed, my mind was extraordinarily alert.

The figure I cut out there must, I imagined to myself, have an element of objective loneliness, like that of the solitary Man on the Road that illustrated the dust jackets of so many novels of social protest in the thirties. To pass the time, I experimented with symbolic variations of this. By trudging doggedly along, I typified the bindle stiffs who in the early works of John Steinbeck roamed the countryside in search of employment. By grinning witlessly, I evoked the grotesquely doomed Southerners of Erskine Caldwell. Pausing before a billboard emblazoned with some token of a materialist culture, I struck an ironic attitude that suggested the perceptive underdog as celebrated by William Saroyan. Hooking my coat over my shoulder on two fingers, I executed a nervous, almost dancelike step that characterized a punch-drunk boxer out of Hemingway. A tilt of the head as in the appraisal of fields in which one could take pride recalled a whole school of Iowa regionalists — eulogists of the Breadbasket of a Nation.

By now I was famished as well as footsore, and I was glad

to see a diner ahead. I entered it with a hobble aimed at favoring a blister on one heel. I sat down on a stool and ordered a hamburger and coffee. I was aware of the counterman's hesitating. The favorite old tweed coat I again had on was out at the elbows, giving the sleeves the effect of shot-off firecrackers, and I realized that I was dusty and unshaven, and might very well be taken for a Steinbeckian vagrant. He seemed, at any rate, to prefer to see the color of my money before filling the order, so I laid a handful of loose change on the counter. It was enough for the food, and for a quarter tip for him. As I chewed, I read backward on the window the legend "O.K. Diner," for which I mentally substituted the words "Hamburger Hell."

When I had eaten, I wiped my mouth with such fragments of paper napkin as I could coax from a dispenser and said, "Do you have a phone I could use?"

"No," he said. He had continued to take me in thoughtfully. "Is it — urgent?"

"I wanted to call a cab."

"Cab?"

"My dogs are gone." I stooped to loosen my shoelaces in a way that eased the pain in my boiled feet somewhat.

"Oh." He pointed out the window. "There's a public booth right over there, by the bus stop."

"*Bus* stop," I said, enraged at having overlooked that whole possibility, out there on the blasted pike. "You mean local buses?"

"From Bridgeport. They run every half hour. There'll be one along in" — he consulted a wall clock — "ten minutes."

While waiting for the bus, I rang up my wife. I figured she might have begun to worry, my absence from home being as prolonged as it was, though I was not above extracting some perverse relish from her anxious "Where are you?"

"I'm on the Post Road," I said.

"The Post Road!" she said. "What on earth are you doing out on that?"

I couldn't very well tell her I was recapitulating recent American literary history in terms of a series of gaits, or stances, so I said, "Oh, I just went out for a walk and landed over here. I'll mosey on home."

The bus was coming, so I hung up.

"How much is it?" I asked the driver when I had climbed on. "The fare."

He scrutinized me with an interest similar to that of the diner attendant. "Where to? Which stop?"

"Maple Avenue."

"Fifteen cents."

"I'm sorry," I said, "but this is all I've got."

I was glad to be able to annoy the poor devil with a twenty-dollar bill.

THE LAST OF THE BLUENOSES

I HAVE RECENTLY HEARD several people complain of insomnia who are under no discernible stress. This being precisely my own current state of affairs, I set my brains to work trying to unravel the mystery. The solution came to me in one of those pre-dawn stretches of rumination that are the result, of course, of the condition herein under scrutiny.

I had just awakened, not screaming by any manner of means, but merely yawning, from a dream so boring as to send me gratefully back into the psychically more rewarding world of wakeful woolgathering. I dreamt, so help me, I dwelt in marble halls. To a more platitudinous level no slumberer can sink, short of Jeanie with the light brown hair, or some unimaginably unimaginative equivalent. Dreaming you dwelt in marble halls wakes you up in bed the way it puts you to sleep at the opera. Thus it isn't that we low-key insomniacs — apparently a vast international club of which you yourself may well be a member — it isn't that we can't sleep as much as that we don't want to. We'd really rather not: there is more percentage in fantasy.

Dreams are fifty years behind the times, like opera, and in need of the same drastic overhaul. To use another comparison, dreams are in somewhat the same critical position as fiction today, lamented by publishers everywhere as not selling simply because it can't hope to compete with the infinitely more exciting world of fact. Pursuing this line of analysis one final step further, we reach the heart of our problem and the solution to the mystery.

Dreams have become Dullsville because we have failed to do in that branch of entertainment what we've managed to do in all the others get rid of the censor, or at least haul the schnook up to date. There's a sexual revolution going on, for God's sake — in fact the junta has succeeded and the regime has been recognized — but the monitor running the subconscious is still schlepping along on the same Victorian standards that obtained when Freud first spotted him pounding the night beat. Thus there is this ever-widening gulf between our waking world and that of beddy-bye, ruled by an unreconstructed Viennese schmaltz-pot.

What do we see eighteen hours a day? Miniskirts, see-through dresses, topless waitresses, and movies in which the sexual principals thresh about in the raw as a matter of course. And as for the remainder, intended not only for rest but also for some kind of psychic refreshment? It's all this turn-of-the-century flatfoot can do to give us a prettily turned ankle, and that in the form of a baseball bat or a Coca-Cola bottle. No wonder people are schizoid. And they will remain

schizoid as long as Nocturne Boulevard goes on being pa-
trolled by a Keystone Cop. It may be that he fancies himself
a last holdout, digging in the more doggedly because all the
other censors have capitulated — but ankles! Can't he get his
mind on higher things? He still thinks it's a big deal letting
us walk half-naked down the street a couple of times a year,
but what kind of hacks is that these days when in point of
fact the public is half-naked to begin with? Why go to
sleep to see a little skin?

Nor do the old staples in the standard repertory — dreams
of falling or flying, or trying to run with your feet stuck in
cheese fondue — seem to offer anything in the way of dramatic punch anymore.

The result was predictable. The added burden thus thrown
on waking fantasy as a consequence has people woolgathering, not just when they should be sleeping, but when they
should be living. My erotic fantasies, for instance, sometimes
continue uninterruptedly even when I'm making love to my
wife — these often being erotic fantasies about *her*, mind you,
in which the matters in hand are given marked imaginary
escalation and enhancement. Such a one-man band knows
that his dreams have let him down, thanks, as I say, to this
proctor who must be impeached or brought abruptly up to
date. "How?" you might ask.

I employ a number of devices in at least making the attempt. I'll reshuffle the night scene by swapping beds with
my wife — a ploy that probably nets little more than my
getting her censor, scarcely an improvement. More radical
measures consist in going into the city from the suburbs and
checking in at some shady fleabag, disguised in dark glasses
and a soft hat pulled over one eye in hopes of shaking the
censor, so he won't know where I'm holed up for the night.
Also the generally laxer moral atmosphere may get through
to him and shake him up, as it were, if I fail to shake him.

The results are not swift and rarely dramatic, but occasionally an improvement can be detected in the dream content, a sense that concessions are being exacted.

In one fleabag, I dreamt that I was living in a cave in Crete with a young dropout from a well-known women's college. What could be more Now, more with it, than that? True, what we were doing in the cave was some kind of committee work, but it's a start. My immediate association with "committee work" reminds me to add how the whole psychoanalytical principle of sublimation has been reversed as a result of the sex revolution. Instead of sublimating the libido into art and philanthropy, as they used to, people are pouring into sex the energies that ought to go into worthy causes. In real life I had been, just prior to the Crete breakthrough, to a committee meeting for our local symphony. There were seven of us. The other six paired off and wandered away into the night, and I spent the evening with some pornography I found behind the host's set of Balzac.

One more point. I have never, frankly, understood why we have to dream in code anyway. If we are perfectly willing to admit to ourselves consciously that we covet our neighbor's wife — may even casually mention the fact to our own — then why must we express this wish in terms of mixing bowls and locked potting sheds? Of course, breaking the code can be part of the marital sport, at first. Once at breakfast, early on in our domestic life, my wife related a dream she had had the night before about going to the aquarium. "It was the oddest thing," she said. "The eels were cut into slices, pickled in aspic, and were lying in jars at the bottom of the tank."

"Thank you," I said coldly, putting down my napkin and leaving the room. "I'm glad to know what you think of me after only eight months of marriage."

When, all these years later, I told her about the Crete cave, she immediately wanted to speculate with me who the girl was — that is, might have been meant to represent, for in the dream she was nobody I knew. We sorted through a list of local candidates, and I finally hit on a girl up the road from our place, a secret yen for whom might have been embodied in the dream. The permissive standards of today were here again reflected in the mild reaction of my wife, who took exception only to my taste. "Isn't she kind of dumb?" she said.

"Not from the neck down," said I.

And so it goes in a swiftly changing modern world for which the censor as we've known him has become absolutely and utterly unsuited. What can one man do about it? Nothing, except add his voice to a swelling chorus of protest that, if strong enough, can ultimately alter the collective psyche, and make the hope of unseating this last of the bluenoses something more than just an empty dream.

SCONES AND STONES

(After reading "Parents and Children," "Men and Wives,"
"Daughters and Sons," and so on, by Ivy Compton-Burnett)

"ALL THAT ECTOPLASM," the father said.

"We won't have to hear that joke much longer," his six-year-old daughter said to her three-year-old brother. "Everyone will soon have color."

"Not in their cheeks. Huddled indoors at their sets, all parents, all children. The upshot of everyone's having color," the father went on, testing the tensile strength of the aphorism on which he had stumbled, "is that no one will have it." He flapped out his luncheon napkin like a white flag.

"They must have our antenna nearly up," the mother said, hearing overhead a succession of dull thuds.

"But not so dull as the end product will be," the father said, assuming this common circuit of associations. Ellipsis was the hallmark here.

Cook punted open the swinging door and dealt them plates of haddock from a tray, simultaneously removing soup in quantities almost as large as she had set before them.

"I don't know what's eating this family," she said, such being her way of commenting on what it did not eat.

"R.C.A. Victim," the boy murmured, licking clean a jellied scone.

"You are clever with your tongue," the father observed sardonically, of this act.

The mother made a sign of pleasure.

"He will be elliptical," she said, evaluating rather what had been said. "He is referring to R.C.A.'s losing to C.B.S. on the color thing."

"The child does not speak distinctly," the father differed.

"But I heard distinctly. The boy has made a *mot* of sorts, and you should not let your natural resentment stand in the way of your recognizing the fact."

"Must you raise your voice?"

"I do so in the cause of harmony. You love your children so much," the mother went on for the latter's benefit, "you will not have their cleverness come between you."

"The child mouths his words."

"What else is there to do with them?" the boy said.

"The truth is growing clearer every day," the mother said. "He will be more elliptical than all of us."

The girl swiveled a fist in a dry eye.

"There, there, *you* are elliptical *too*. Is she not?" the mother prompted her husband.

Pledged to understress, he shrugged one shoulder and

smiled in the girl's direction. This, though lacking the texture of praise, restored the girl's normal indifference. The family ran as smoothly as most, their years of intimacy having quite anesthetized them to emotion. Nevertheless the mother turned to the children and blessed them with individual glances.

"Precious," she said.

"That is not the same as elliptical," the father said.

"There!" the mother said, making him the beneficiary of this new remonstrance. "Your father's subtlety should be obvious."

"It is, but whether it should be is another question," the boy said.

"It looks as if he will be oblique as well!" the mother exclaimed, veering freshly in these loyalties.

The father glared into his plate, momentarily, as though he were an osprey and the fish alive. Now pride even more than the rules of the game forbade him to discharge his pique with his young in any other fashion than tangentially. He therefore turned from the haddock to his wife, and in the expectation of stinging her blurted, "I cannot bear children."

"It is a function to which nature has perhaps better suited the woman," she answered fairly.

Two workmen carried into the house something in a cabinet of fumed oak, but the father averted his face as though they were rather bearing from it the corpse of literate dialogue.

"And so the coup de grâce to what remains of conversation in our time," he said.

They spoke of this and that. Because of the door that was soon to close on civilized communion, and wishing to leave no residue of prior heat in their adjourning mood, the father strove to close the luncheon on a note of persiflage.

"Your mother does not understand me," he chaffered with that levity which may be after all the soul of wit.

"Then suppose you do not talk with your mouth full," the boy gave answer.

"Are you the father here?"

"No, sir."

"Then stop chittering like a ninny."

The father rose and led the way into the living room, where, disposed in their accustomed chairs, they witnessed the installation of the set. One workman had remained to effect it. Lengths of wire lay about like some degree of briar.

"So another trap is about to shut," the father said.

"I thought we might not use the word in that sense," the daughter said.

"Your father meant in the sense of snare," the mother said, looking at her.

"Which is everywhere," the father said, looking at the son as well.

The workman bolted on his knees about the polished floor. "By fall you will have an attachment for color," he said.

"I shall feel none whatever for it," the father interjected swiftly, as if mere moments remained for nuance.

"What *does* he feel?" the girl whispered

"Nothing," the boy said. "When I can talk, I shall call him Ice Cold Pop."

"And when he is old, Epigrampa."

"Now, now, your father is sound," their mother said. "Sound as a nut."

"You can say that again," the girl retorted.

The father made a truncheon of his *Harper's*. "There will be no needless repetition," he said.

"It will distract you," the workman said, in defense of the instrument it was his to install.

"No more than the prospect already has," the father said.

"A living must be made," the workman said.

"And a life unmade."

"A way of life. And a new way born," the workman said.

"By some not able to bear it."

"We talk again of bearing." the mother interposed, prising from her daughter's grasp a cutting tool not meant for play.

"It is merely more surrender to material progress," the father said. "We worship the Golden Calf."

"It is not the calf that is worshipped on television," the workman said. "Though that too is visible."

The color drained from the father's face leaving a pallor, which in turn gave the illusion of draining from it; as though they had already heard a fragment from the instrument.

"And for children? This imagery and this plane of reference?" he demanded.

"They must be torn away from the continuities which thrive at evening, and which magnetize them until then," the workman said. He inserted an extremity of wire into the machine and secured it there. "Whether the innovation is therefore a blessing or a bane is moot in many households," he said with a smile. Then he paused and rummaged in his hair. "Since setting foot in this house I speak increasingly in this way."

"It is nothing but understatement," the mother said.

"Restraint run wild, if I may say so, ma'am." The workman rapped a knuckle on the cabinet. "But not here. In this medium, overstress."

"And in the humor?"

"Muscularity. In a diversion last evening one comedian said, 'My dog is sick, I should have given him asafetida.' And another better known replied, 'Asafetida made any difference.'"

The father nudged an ashtray a quarter of an inch to the

left, illustrating the anguish of cerebral types. But there was a sense of swift recovery. He had been evaluating what the workman had said about the household young, which had seemed to lay bare implications he had not realized in his own strictures. Credits and debits had been toted up, a balance struck.

"You say the children must indeed be torn from the sets?" he said, bowing his head and joining together the fat of his thumbs.

"You don't even know they're in the house." The workman plied a knob. "Ah, there we are. Puppets."

As his wife went about drawing the shades, the father seemed to see the house in a new light. The children's faces were already transfigured. The resulting glow of warmth in him was so great as to move him momentarily to hypocrisy.

"You were so good as to speak of the level of intercourse of all beneath this roof. Surely it's nothing new, understatement," he said modestly to the workman.

"Oh, no," the other answered, refining a nebulous image. "But not everyone can lay it on with a trowel."

FOREVER PANTING

STILL, I have a certain ramshackle charm. So that when I took her young hands in mine across the restaurant table she did not immediately withdraw from my grasp, nor from the larger, bolder plan of action, which I now proceeded to sketch out for her benefit.

"What I'm going to do is, I'm going to declare moral bankruptcy," I said. "I mean, we keep using the term in that sense, why not follow it through? When a man can no longer discharge his financial obligations, we let him off the hook. Why not when he can no longer meet his ethical ones? I have too many emotional creditors hounding me, I tell you! That's all there is to it. A man simply cannot meet all the demands made on his resources, simply cannot be expected to keep his books balanced. It's too much. Everybody keeps talking about moral bankruptcy but nobody does anything about it. Well, I'm going to. I'm going to declare it. I'm going into receivership. I'm going to pay everybody so much on the dollar."

"In other words, Duxbury," she said, calling me by my last name as people affectionately do, "you want to tell your wife about us."

"I do," I said, "and I've spoken those words only once before in my life."

She gazed thoughtfully into her post-luncheon mint, stirring the icy sludge around a bit with her straw.

"How will you go about it?" she asked, at length. "I mean, how much will you pay everybody on the dollar, as you put it?"

I frowned into my third brandy as I mentally reviewed the scale of figures I had already more or less worked out. Proclaiming to the world that one is materially insolvent is a serious enough step, posting notice that one is no longer ethically liquid is an even graver one, especially if, as appeared to be true here, one is the first man in history to be doing so in a formal sense. The case would be precedent-setting. It might even become a *cause célèbre*, with all the attendant widespread publicity that I must be prepared to shoulder and to shoulder alone. I therefore weighed my words carefully.

"I figure I can pay fifty cents on the dollar," I said at last. "That will be all told and across the board. It will be divided up as fairly as I know how among the claimants. That is to say, half of what is expected of this man on all fronts is really all there is of him to go around. That's all there is, there ain't no more." Here I paused to ask, "You understand that I am talking about the *moral equivalent* of money, in the mart of human relationships." She nodded, sucking up the bright-green cordial with lips pursed into a scarlet bud. "All right, then," I went on. "I shall continue to make my disbursements — of loyalty, cooperation, et cetera — at that level; I mean, I intend to stay in business as a human being. There will never be any question about that, nor that my wife and family will come first, my friends next, and then such things as obligation to community and whatnot, in the ever-widening circles of responsibilities as one sees them — and prorated as I say."

"What about your parents, Duxbury?" she asked, looking up. "You admitted you haven't been back home to see them in over a year. I don't like that in a man. A man should be thoughtful and considerate about things like that."

"All right, I'll throw in another nickel for them, so to speak. I mean, I'll stretch a point in what I'll give, so the others concerned won't get less of my time and devotion. But that's my top figure. More than that can simply not be squeezed out of the orange."

"What about me? What do I get?"

"You get me. A man out from under at last, ready to make a fresh start free and clear. How's that? Ah, macushla . . ."

There was a silence, broken only by the hydraulic sounds of the last of the mint going up the translucent straw, which was finally put by with a dainty crimson stain on its tip. "Well, all right," she said. "I expect you'll want to get home early tonight and have it out I'm glad I won't have to be there," she added with a little shudder. "I just hope it won't be like the sordid blowups you can hear through the walls of apartments. The couple next door to mine actually throw crockery at each other."

"Love is a many-splintered thing. Heh-heh-heh. Ah, baby, the fun we'll —"

"So why don't you call for the check?"

I flagged the waiter, still brooding over the various aspects of this thorny problem, which I am sure vexes every man from time to time — just how much of him there is to go around. "As for one's country," I said, "that's all well and good, but I doubt whether in peacetime a man owes it any more than is extorted from him in taxes to maintain God knows what proliferating bureaus and agencies going to make up what is still essentially an eleemosynary goddam government."

"You don't have to swear to show how limited your vocabulary is," she said, reaching for her gloves and bag with a hauteur well supported by the patrician profile that had from the very first struck me to the heart. She is a tawny girl with long legs and hair like poured honey. In her brown eyes is a vacancy as divine as that left in the last motel available to the desperate wayfarer. My knees turned to rubber as I read the check and produced the forty clams necessary to discharge my immediate obligations. "Keep the change," I told the waiter in a voice hoarse with passion.

"If you do have it out at home, then you'll be able to make it for dinner tomorrow instead of lunch, I expect?" she said, rising as the waiter swung the table aside for her exit.

"Name the place," I said, trailing in her wake.

"The Four Seasons is nice."

When I got home, after the usual grimy and spasmodic ride on that awful railroad, my family were already at meat. My wife looked up from a gardening magazine she was reading as she ate, and waved cheerfully. Our sixteen-year-old son was paging through a motorcycle pamphlet over his own heaped plate, while his ten-year-old brother pored, fork in hand, over a comic book. The latter wore a switchman's cap with the visor behind. Dented beer cans were clamped to the heels of his shoes, and his bubble gum was on his wrist. It seemed as good a time as any to make my declaration. My eighteen-year-old daughter, a free spirit now apparently touring Europe or something, would, I knew, heartily applaud my action, if I could only locate her.

I helped myself to some food from a casserole keeping warm in the oven and joined them at the table. But I could not eat. Finally, I shoved my plate aside and said, "I have an announcement to make."

There was a rustle of turned pages and a nod or two.

"You have all no doubt read Ibsen's *The Wild Duck*," I said "That anti-morality play, perhaps his best, in which he makes the point that we cannot always be pressed with the claims of the ideal. That we should not be forever dunned," I went on, consulting a frayed cuff on which I had jotted what I could remember of Relling's crucial speeches in that drama, "forever dunned for debts we cannot pay. Isn't that fine? Doesn't that make reasonable sense? All right, then. I take this to mean, therefore, that a person who has reached a certain point in the general drain on his resources may with impunity say, 'I herewith formally declare myself bankrupt. I am going into moral receivership. Creditors, take note — you will henceforth get so much on the dollar,' said creditors to include all those reasonably embraced by that corporate term 'society,' on whose Accounts Receivable we are all permanently enrolled: family, friends, community, and so on. Now then for the figure I am prepared to give you. The absolute maximum disbursement I can manage is, roughly, fifty cents on the dollar. Put in plain English, this means that in future I shall be half the husband I was, half the father, half the friend, and so on down the line. Well, there it is. What have you to say?"

My wife dropped her magazine and passed a plate of home-made rolls around the table.

"Why, if she's what you want, go to her," she said. "Go away with her even, for a while, if it will help get her out of your system."

I rose and shoved my chair back with a force that sent it clattering to the floor behind me.

"I wish you'd stop treating me as an individual in my own right," I exclaimed. "All of you! Nothing is more irritating than that, or more demoralizing. As though a man has to be humored like some damn kid!" With that I flung out of the room, slamming the door after me.

My resolve to leave was by now quite firm. I marched to my bedroom and, pausing only long enough to stand modestly before a wall glass and say, "You ain't nuttin' but a hound-dog," I packed three bags, which I carried, forever panting, along the corridor and down the stairs to the vestibule. There I momentarily dropped my luggage to recover my wind.

As I stood there, I sensed a footfall in the passage along which I had just come. Looking up the stairs, I saw my mother-in-law approaching, in velvet slippers and with the aid of her stout cane. Slightly indisposed, she had had a tray in her room, the door of which she had left open, as is her wont, so as not to isolate herself entirely from the life of the house. She paused at the head of the stairs and from under her white lace mobcap fixed me with a bright eye.

"I could not help overhearing," she said, "and with all due apologies, I should like to remind you of one person you have overlooked in your list of creditors, as you put it. Someone to whom you also owe something."

"Who might that be, Mother Bunshaft?" I asked.

"Yourself," she answered, smiling.

"Ah, Mother Bunshaft," I said, "the longer you live with us the more your wisdom —"

"Correction — I think you mean the longer you live with me." The house is in her name for legal reasons (she owns it). "The longer you live with me, the more I find I have to tell you, it seems. Now I suggest you owe it to yourself to pause a moment and count the cost. Of a second establishment, which I assume is in your mind — especially if we increase the cost of this one by starting to ask for rent again. The upkeep of two cars, the many other possessions bought on time. I expect we're quite the ticket out there in the big city" — here she humorously cocked the tip of her stick at me and sighted along its length as along the barrel of a rifle, at the same time making that chucking noise out of the side of her mouth that once was used to make horses giddyap but now conveys the idea of hot stuff — "but it might just pay us to take a good hard look at our bank balance, if any, our arrears with the loan company — Just a minute. I'm not finished," she called as I hurried out the front door without the bags.

Well, that's how the cookie crumbles. It took very little probing to make clear the scale of living the other woman had in mind — a single phone call from a public booth, in fact. Her response to my suggestion that we meet at some convenient Schrafft's or Stouffer's, instead of the Four Seasons, with all that nonsense about flaming skewers and telephones brought to the tables, alone did the trick.

So that seems to be the point of this whole incident in a nutshell, its moral, you might say, which I pass along to any man contemplating the same course of action I was. Before you start declaring moral bankruptcy, make damn sure you're in good shape financially.

JAMES THURBER:
THE COMIC PRUFROCK

IT WAS on an evening in the late spring of 1938, at a banquet at the University of Chicago, while crawling around on my hands and knees under the speakers' table looking for Ford Madox Ford's glasses, that I first knew I was going to write an article on Thurber. It was a moment of murk and strain: I remember the women just standing there, and getting in my hair, most of which hung over one eye. I suppose there have been occasions when I looked even more like a Thurber drawing, but there has been none when I felt more like one. I have had this queer feeling of looking like a Thurber drawing on four distinct occasions in my life, counting the evening I failed to find Ford Madox Ford's glasses — or "glosses" as he said when he promptly singled me out from among the group of intellectuals as probably the ideal man to whom to report the loss of spectacles. The other times were: once when turning around to glare at a woman talking behind me at a concert; once while crawling around on the floor of a cold garage looking for a cotter pin while the neighbor lady whose car I was presumably going to fix, when I found it, hung around, and once reciting "No, no, go not to Lethe, neither twist wolf'sbane" in a drug store to a girl who I found had turned to the menu.

I am not sure what poetic sensibility is, but I am practically certain Thurber has got it. Though artists work in different forms there is a contemporary tissue which connects them, and the things they have in common spiritually are greater than the differences among them technically. Thurber has

304

more in common with modern poets than, for instance, he has with any other present-day humorist you might mention.

I do not know whether the critical landlords of Axel's Castle — our customary symbol for Symbolism — list him among the occupants or not, or whether they are aware he is on the premises. It is that house (to call a partial roll) through whose silences can be heard the interminable scratching of the pen of Proust, and the sad sound of his cough. Here Prufrock, lost in the fumes of introspection, lay damned in the late afternoon From its window Yeats saw the centaur stamp in the black wood, and Joyce labored mightily in its towers. If fancy and the imagination and "subjective" as opposed to "objective" reality is the emphasis we are talking about, then Thurber can certainly be included. The filaments of individual sensibility are seldom more sharply wrought, or more constantly manifest, than in his work. The psychological nuance is rarely more intricately drawn, even in those tidy sketches in which he is reducing it to absurdity. His inner states and private convolutions are, if not as profound, as skillfully projected as any. He may be least of the family — indeed perhaps just a quizzical lodger cutting up in some remote corner of the premises — but this is the address all right.

It is hard to think of anyone who more closely resembles the Prufrock of Eliot than the middle-aged man on the flying trapeze. This preoccupied figure is Prufrock's comic counterpart, not in intensity of course, but in detail. There is, for instance, the same dominating sense of Predicament. The same painful and fastidious self-inventory, the same detailed anxiety; the same immersion in weary minutiae, the same self-disparagement, the same wariness of the evening's company. And the same fear, in summary, that someone — in Thurber's case a brash halfback or maybe even a woman — will "drop a question on his plate." Prufrock, taking stock of himself, concludes that he is no Prince Hamlet, "nor was meant to be"; is merely one who will do

> *To swell a progress, start a scene or two.*
>
> .   .   .   .
>
> *At times, indeed, almost ridiculous —*
> *Almost, at times, the Fool.*

Thurber tells us that he is no Lord Jim, nor any character whatever out of Conrad. Among the southern seas none guessed his minor doom, though he sat in tropical cafes twitching his jaw muscles, in the attempt to look inscrutable. Prufrock in his lush fantasies "heard the mermaids singing, each to each." And concludes, "I do not think that they will sing to me." Among the seductive islands Thurber found no Tondelaya, or any facsimile thereof, offering to go to pieces with him. Of the women he is terse:

> *They tried to sell me baskets.*

If Eliot symbolizes his spiritual intricacies in terms of mythological beings, so that we get the Eumenides lurking, at last, behind a curtain in an English drawing room, Thurber can personify his own modest nemeses in figures as concrete, always afraid he is "being softly followed by little men padding along in single file, about a foot and a half high, large-eyed and whiskered." This ability to project the fanciful enables him to get pretty much the effect of poetry itself. The banquet I mentioned stands out in my memory for one other thing. It is a phrase in Carl Sandburg's talk: "Those who write the poetry of an age, whether in verse or prose . . ." Enough. If poetry is an essence produced by the discharge of the contents of the Leyden jar of the nervous system (and it most certainly is not but at this point we want one of those

definitions which serve chiefly to prove that poetry can't be
defined) then Thurber has produced poetry in at least a few
cases Poetry is where you find it, and I find it in *The Black
Magic of Barney Haller*, one of the best of those exquisite
little sketches which see more drafts than many poems. You
will remember it as the account of the caretaker whom storms
follow home, whom Thurber suspects of trafficking with the
devil and exorcises by incantations of Frost and Lewis Carroll.

The title of Eliot's poem is ironic — it is a "love song." It
is certain that Prufrock never got around to asking his lady
the question: the masculinity of this parched sophisticate
seems specifically inoperative. In that other landmark of
Eliot's early period, *The Portrait of a Lady*, the female is
roundly satirized, but the narrator is singularly unable to cope
with her, there is a "sensation of being ill at ease." Is there a
sensation of which Thurber has given more repeated illustra-
tion? The oppressed narrator of Eliot's poem has the feeling,
after climbing the stairs, of having "mounted on my hands
and knees." One can imagine what Thurber would have done
with *that*, had he included it in his series in which he illustrated famous poems. It will be observed that in all of the
instances in which I felt like a Thurber drawing there were
women around — behind me, in front of me, and, most of all,
above me. What contemporary disquiet has he caught here?
The woman satirized in *The Portrait of a Lady* was trite, but
she was alive and certainly operating conversationally, and
the women lampooned in Thurber are alive and operating
too, at their worst when they are a little too much like the preoccupied men (like the woman who came up and announced
to the man shrinking in the chair: "I have a neurosis"), at their
best possessing a certain virility lacking in the male. They
perch confidently on the arms of sofas, drag their men to
bridge parties, drive cars well, are in the embalming game.
The male is on the wane, corroded with introspection, de-

flated by all his own inefficient efficiency, without "strength to force the moment to its crisis," his love lyric in desuetude. There is a sketch in which Thurber does not want to go some place — out some place, perhaps a bridge party or something like that — and he says he would rather stay home. "That's the place for a man to be anyhow — home." It is not a long step from there to: "A man's place is in the home," a generalization the feminists of the hour might like to adopt as a battle cry.

Anybody who would rather not throw a javelin because Babe Didrikson could probably throw it farther, which is one of Thurber's reasons, is in a bad way. In *The Case Against Women* Thurber lists the reasons why he hates them, not, of course, that we don't, by this time, know. The boneless batter of the famous drawings is of course a caricature; but a caricature of a sharp contemporary sensation. Maybe it is only the first bug-eyed bewilderment of man startled and dazed by the little helpmate's first brisk emergence into the wide world. It is to be hoped that such is the case and that the notorious Thurber male, subsiding, in bed and chair and at last on the rug, in various postures of anthropoid humiliation, is not a preview of the shape of things to come.

There is another possible construction on the matter, intimated by Thurber himself, which, though not rich in consolation, is a little more palatable to the male. Thurber qualifies the often echoed forecast that we are going to pot, with the specification that man will go first. The cities in which he has so long conducted his business, contrived his morals and debauched his politics, and in which he has now grown futilely introspective, are to be taken over by the praying mantis and the steppe cat. But before that there will be an interlude in which the women will be in there pitching. That dwindling masculine first person singular who has not written a single amorous poem nearly as good as the famous "love

song" in which Prufrock never got anywhere, will be in circumstances over which it were perhaps better not to speculate in too great detail. But woman's emergence, now dramatic, can be expected to go on apace. She is already everywhere in industry; she is in Congress, on the pulpit and, as has
been noted, in the embalming game — standing ready to com-
mit us to the earth. Women live longer, too. Studying the
newspaper accounts of forty-three people who got to be
more than a hundred, Thurber notes that thirty-seven are
women and six men, and four of them were written about
because they died. And the women were reported as having
celebrated the day by chinning themselves, riding in airplanes
and performing other feats too depressing to mention. The
female's retention of vigor, straight-forwardness and the positive values is, perhaps, quite logical, for is she not more
directly and intimately the custodian of life? It is Molly Bloom
who closes the incredibly elaborate *Ulysses*, pulling the whole
business back down to earth.

"The poet of *The Waste Land*," writes Edmund Wilson,
"is living half the time in the real world of contemporary
London and half the time in the haunted wilderness of medi-
eval legend." Thurber too is half the time God knows where.
"One's head may be stored with literature but the heroic
prelude of the Elizabethans has ironic echoes in modern London streets and modern London drawing rooms." Reality in
Thurber undergoes filterings and transmutations as curious
and as abrupt. He deflates famous poems with cruelly literal
illustrations, achieving bathos as jolting as Eliot's:

> *When lovely woman stoops to folly and*
> *Paces about her room again, alone,*
> *She smoothes her hair with automatic hand,*
> *And puts a record on the gramophone.*

Confronted by details, moments, of that dull environment with which he is long weary of coping, he contrives his own little substitutions, and his transformer is always at work altering, to suit his fancy, the currents of experience. With characteristic self-deploration he admits to the inanity of many of the oddments that "slip by the guardian at the portal of his thoughts," but vouches for their tenacity. Thus

> *A message for Captain Bligh*
> *And a greeting to Franchot Tone!*

sung to a certain part of *For He's a Jolly Good Fellow*, occupied him for some time. A connoisseur of mispronunciation, he was happy when a malapropping domestic called the icebox "doom shaped," thus investing it with a quality which fascinated him for days, and by a similar alchemy exercised by Barney Haller, the caretaker already mentioned, there are warbs in the garrick, grotches in the wood and fletchers on the lawn — all details possessing a charm with which their real-life counterparts cannot compete. To make the transformation complete, the maid has only to step on his glasses. Then do the flags of South American republics fly over the roofs of Manhattan banks, cats cross the street in striped barrels, old women with parasols walk through the sides of trucks, bridges rise "lazily into the air like balloons." "The kingdom of the partly blind," he assures us, jesting of his affliction, "is a little like Oz, a little like Wonderland, a little like Poictesme." He never drives alone at night "out of fear that I might turn up at the portals of some mystical monastery and never return." He has but to do that, and the parallel with Eliot is complete.

Now all these qualities in Thurber serve to illustrate again this fact that attitudes, details, elements, are intimated in poetry before they are widely apparent in the general contemporary consciousness, or in popular literature. The truly original poet is often prescient. Swinging the classics, as our jazz bands now do, the fluid technique of shuttling arbitrarily between the past and the present without transition, of which novelists and playwrights now freely avail themselves, our pleasure in mimicry, all these and so many less tangible elements in the climate of our time were contained and foreshadowed in a single poem which was called senseless when it first came out. Poetry is sometimes an antenna by which the race detects actualities at which it has not quite arrived.

The contempt of the man with both feet on the ground for the artist with one of them in fantasy is familiar. Such a condition is regarded as a schizoid separation from reality. The answer is of course, simply, what do you mean by reality; and the point is an important one. I referred, with rather loose whimsicality I suppose, to Thurber as jester in Axel's Castle, and his work may be a rivulet running "individual sensibility" off into a kind of *reductio ad absurdum* — not that some of the serious exponents of Symbolism haven't already done so But whatever the excesses of Symbolism may have been, it has not only made a notable contribution to modern literature but by its emphasis on subjective experience has helped us to a richer idea of what "reality" is. Just as poetry and profit are where you find them, reality is what you make it. The angle of refraction according to the perceiving psyche is *always* there, and the individual's extracting from the world around him constitutes an experience that is itself a reality; a point which modern artists have been trying to make for over a generation. It is to be admitted that Symbolism, falling prey to another of our many false dualisms in its reaction to Naturalism, has sometimes gone to excesses, but we may hope, as Edmund Wilson suggests, that something of a healthier balance will be derived from a synthesis of the two.

To get back a moment, before closing, to Thurber, whom we have left peering into the abyss, on all fours no doubt: We do not know that art and life will continue in the direction which he, in his peculiar way, has brought to such sharp emphasis. We do not know how events and literature, in their endless and intricate interaction, will condition the man of tomorrow, whether to more evaporating introversions or to new expansions. We know that the large pendulum which enables us to tick our little ticks keeps swinging. Prophecy is an easy and a dangerous thing, for thou knowest not which shall prosper, whether this or that, or whether they both shall be alike good. And as to women, if the Curtain is one day coming down, well, Thurber's own prediction that they will outlast men only bears out once more the fact that men, more sensitive organisms, are pioneers in everything, even decline. And we need not vex ourselves with the illusion that the sexes were ever anything but opposed (the literature Thurber might illustrate going back to Genesis — "The woman whom thou gavest to be with me, she gave me of the tree, and I did eat"), nor face our future oppressed by the extraneous consideration that it will be survived by gnats.

EXPLORING INNER SPACE
(*The University of Michigan Hopwood Lecture, 1969*)

THERE IS MORE than a faint element of imposture in my standing before you in the role of lecturer, since to discharge that function creditably is to play the critic, which is not at all my speed — or bag, as one should perhaps say today. I suppose it's hard to know what to say about my books. Some think of them as caricatures of the white race. Others assign them to their classes as suggested or required reading, and even approve them as subjects for dissertations. All of which I think vindicates me by bearing out what I've been saying in those books all along — that everything is going to hell in a hand-bucket.

At least some of you out there are scholars, full-blown or in embryo, and I'm sure you're thinking to yourselves, possibly even murmuring to one another, "This character will talk for half an hour about the creative process, or some such, without telling us a damned thing." I shall not disappoint you. You may return to your classrooms and studies confirmed in the knowledge that what goes on in an artist's head is something about which he hasn't the slightest personal comprehension, but is the proper concern of scholars, and after I have returned home you can write crisp notes to the Hopwood Committee saying, "Why do you invite cows to analyze milk?"

Nevertheless, I can ask intelligent questions, furnishing answers of whatever calibre. Simply as readers we periodically wonder, by way of taking inventory, what the literature of the hour is up to. We know what our scientists are up to: one mechanistic triumph after another. By contrast, our artists grow more determinedly humanistic, private and, as the cries of lay protest occasionally have it, obscure. That the twain will never meet, that the gulf grows ever wider, is a concern of course formally expressed by C. P. Snow, articulating for all of us with his idea of the two cultures, the scientific and the intellectual running full-speed away from each other, or at best in irreconcilable parallels. Still, it's important to remember that over the long haul men do work together whether they work together or apart, as Robert Frost reminds us in the poem *The Tuft of Flowers*. In the distant future, or even now in some larger perspective, there may be somewhere an ultimate fusion of the two seemingly hopelessly divergent elements. For the time being, I have at least mentioned Frost and Snow in the same breath, which will have to suffice us as a token unity.

The rickety spirits and demoted egos whose inner space our best novelists navigate in the name of characterization are very good counterparts of our own, and whether we shall be vicariously enlarged by our astronauts' exploration of outer space, or merely shrunk into punier earthlings by contrast, depends on our individual makeup. There will certainly, in any case, be further feats to leave us magnified or dwindled, for make no mistake about it: our arrival on the moon and our departure for points more distant will without a doubt be counted among the scientific miracles of this century of the common cold. The humanistic scruple remains, "Should we spend all that money on trips to other astral bodies when there's such a heap still to be done on this one?" Should man go to the moon? The romantic instinctively replies, "Yes. He must have been put on this earth for a purpose."

In any event — to get this so-called lecture in orbit — it's fair to say that literature has found the exploration of private consciousness and even unconsciousness, which I am calling inner space, enough of a challenge. It is perhaps just as well that our poets and novelists — and you can name them for yourselves — concern themselves principally with the microscopic half of the full human reality, leaving the telescopic to science. It would take a combined Homer, Milton, and Shakespeare to dream our cosmological dream in an epic commensurate with the commonplaces of the front page. But to think of the "two cultures" as absolutely polarized is too neat, too slipshod, as I tried to say a moment ago. That men do work together whether they work together or apart, that there are points of similarity between such seemingly irreconcilable endeavors as the artistic and the scientific, is suggested by our very attempts to understand the one in terms of the other. Some of you may remember how, in the first blush of Virginia Woolf's vogue, terms like "rain of atoms" and "atomic dance" were applied to the minute and seemingly random thoughts, associations, and particles of memory out of which she constructed, particular by particular, the evocations of individual consciousness that in turn collectively made up, for her, a novel. Rereading her now, as I recently did, one would be lured a step farther into the metaphor and say that she was bent on a kind of psychic fission, which releases the energy of the association.

Edmund Wilson first elucidated Proust to us as the literary counterpart of Einsteinian relativity, with time so clearly a fourth dimension as to make *Swann's Way* end: ". . . remembrance of a particular form is but regret for a particular moment; and houses, roads, avenues are fugitive, alas, as the year." If Joyce's stream of consciousness is no stream at all but precisely the sequence of disconnected droplets it appears on paper, it may suggest to us that psychic energy flows as quantum physics tells us physical energy does, not continuously but in individual packets. A Joycian association — a Planckian erg-second? Why not? And as though this were not enough, even as a humble humorist scurrying back to his proper depth, I might define the self-disparagement in which modern humor almost exclusively consists as the human counterpart of what is known in atomic physics as the loss of unstable carbon isotopes — and if *that* doesn't hold the boys on the academic quarterlies, I don't know what will. If from here on in I talk about myself a lot, you will understand that I do so out of insecurity. There goes an unstable carbon isotope already!

I thought that in the remaining minutes I might perform a
kind of public exercise aimed at showing how the writer can
only explore the inner space of his characters by perceptively
navigating his own, and that this, and this alone, results in
anything worth calling characterization. To say that literature illuminates life is platitudinous enough, and I haven't
come nine hundred miles to sock that apocalypse to you, but
it may be instructive to suggest how the sheer *practice* of
fiction as such can sometimes help the practitioner understand
what he is writing about, that is to say living with, and to
conduct the experiment by recalling an incident that recently
befell me — or rather, to focus the point down to where I
want it, a character I ran foul of, and he me, and whom I
misjudged completely at first and did not comprehend until I
had spent some time trying to put him down on paper, though
he may have had my number from the beginning on a somewhat more primitive level.

The purpose of fiction is still, as it was to Joseph Conrad,
to make the reader see. That is our quarrel with television, is
it not? That it is not visual enough? It cannot make us *see*
Jeeves, the butler, entering the room, "a procession of one."
It cannot make us see the woman in *Dorian Gray* whose
dresses always looked as though they had been designed in a
rage and put on in a tempest. It cannot make us see the
character in Ring Lardner who served what he thought was
good Scotch though he may have been deceived by some
flavor lurking in his beard. Least of all can it ever hope to begin to make us see anything like the young girl in Elizabeth
Bowen's *The Death of the Heart*, who "walked about with
the rather fated expression you see in photographs of girls
who have subsequently been murdered, but nothing so far
had happened to her. . . ." Such wild rich subtleties require
transmission from one mind to another via the written word

upon the printed page, and remain beyond the power of the boob-tube to convey.

The task I recently set myself was to make the reader see — and now for the next few minutes to make you see — a character who was nothing if not flamboyantly vivid on the merely visual plane in real life. I was prepared for him by my wife, whom I saw, as I came home one evening, waiting for me at the front door, not with a smile of greeting but somewhat grimly, her arms folded on her chest, holding in one hand a magazine that she had rolled into a club.

"Wait till you see this one," was her first remark after my bestowal of the greeting kiss, and something in her tone made me know exactly what she meant, and made me hurry on past her into the house and head straight upstairs for my pre-dinner bath. Scars left by hospitalities recently extended to my fourteen-year-old son's friends were an aid to the instinctive understanding that this elliptical opening referred to the latest specimen he had brought home, in the way of an overnight guest. "Remember the last one?" my wife pressed on, close at my heels.

I did indeed. This was a thirteen-year-old character who excoriated the false values my generation had given his, and who expressed his disapproval of bourgeois criteria by keeping his chewing gum in his navel. He believed in the abolition of money. Not that he conclusively infected my son with any of those iconoclastic notions. I still keep missing dollar bills and an occasional fin from my wallet just the same. "So cheer up," I said to my wife, summarizing the episode briefly in those terms as I hurried down the passage to the bedroom. "Things aren't always as bad as they seem."

"And the one before that?"

Him I remembered too, him indeed. Lad who brought a gerbil. Lad who also believed in the primacy of instincts, and who pursuant thereto got up some time during the night and ate all the breakfast Danish, and who in his freedom from the tyranny of material possessions inadvertently walked off with one of my derby hats.

"Well, when you get a load of *this* one," said my wife, "you'll wish you had either of *them* back, *if not both.*"

"I love the way you talk in italics," I said, throwing a fond smile over my shoulder as we sped down the passage toward the bedroom.

There I had a moment to catch my breath and get my bearings, the dinner my wife was preparing requiring, presently, her attention in the kitchen. But it was only a moment. I was pulling off my clothes and flinging them in every direction in my haste to get into the tub before hearing anything else that might qualify the peace in which I planned to luxuriate there, for a bit, when the door I had shut behind me opened and she reappeared, again nursing the cudgel. She tapped it mysteriously in a palm as she sat down on the bed to resume the interrupted dossier. (What such a cylindrical elongation might mean to a housewife I have no idea, having lost my taste for symbolism with the two steel balls the crazy captain in *The Caine Mutiny* kept rolling in his palm.)

"We're used to kids who live with one or the other of their parents, right? Well, *this* one doesn't live with *either* of *his.* Oh, he's with the mother technically, because she has custody of him, but he only goes there to sleep because he can't *stand* her, while his *father* can't stand *him.* So he likes to farm himself out to *other* people."

"Abrogation-of-the-family-pattern bit, eh? And must you speak in italics all the time, dear? It gives a man such a sense of stress."

"The father," she continued, crossing her legs, "says the mother lost the toss, so let her see to him. That's how he puts the custody decision. Apparently this one likes to sleep with the phonograph going — he's brought along an album of some group called The Burning Bananas that'll make you hanker after the gerbil days — and is said to make passes at his school teachers." I cleared my throat, kicked my shoes about, and in general made as much noise as possible in order to hear as little of this information as I could before gaining the safe haven of the bathroom. "Now, as to the father, *he's* currently shacked up with some cookie half his age in a cottage by the beach. She's about twenty, and models for —"

I sprang into the bathroom, clapped the door shut and turned the tub faucets up full-blast, instantly cutting off all further data. I lolled as best I could in the promised warmth, for five minutes, perhaps ten. She was waiting for me when I emerged.

"— and models for these."

She opened the magazine and exhibited a picture of the baggage the father was knit up with. I pored over it as she held it out for my inspection, nodding as I dried my shoulders with the towel. It showed a girl of the age specified, posing at the water's edge in a polka-dot diaper and nothing more — half a bikini. I set her up in a small waffle shop in the east Fifties, read aloud to her evenings from my favorite authors, and in general exposed her to something better than was intimated by the evidence in hand.

"A face that could launch a thousand ships, all right," I murmured, dropping the towel on a chair. "To say nothing of the topless towers of Ilium."

"You don't ask how I got this magazine. Aren't you curious? Well, Mike — that's your guest's name, Mike Hackett — carries it around with him to show people. *As though it's something about his father to be proud of.*"

"*Stop talking in italics.*"

A knack for dramatic construction will have been discerned in my narrator. Nothing more displayed this gift than the manner in which she now inserted the keystone in her

319

expository arch Setting the magazine down on a table, she waited until I had finished extracting a clean pair of shorts from my bureau drawer, then yet a moment while I drew them on. Then she said:

"So that is what the father is lollygagging around with, leaving it to other people to raise — *that*." She pulled aside a corner of the curtain and pointed down into the yard. I stepped to the window to look out.

I saw an Old Testament prophet dressed in loose-fitting vestments of muslin, or perhaps hopsacking, haranguing my attentive son. A lighted cigarette hung in one corner of his mouth, flapping briskly as he spoke. He talked with apparent authority, judging from the rapt, nodding concentration he received. He seemed to be denouncing something, possibly the garage against which he slouched, because once or twice he poked a thumb at it over his shoulder, as though he opposed it on some ground or other, possibly as symbolic of something he must deny his personal approval — such as the two cars it normally houses. Presently, and rather abruptly, the diatribe ceased, and the two gazed about them at the waning day. The prophet drummed the side of the garage with the palms of his hands. Then he took a last drag on the cigarette and snapped it into the shrubbery.

"Well," I said, turning from the window, "we can't judge all our young people by the behavior of most of them. But what's with the long hair? I thought that was on the way out."

"Huh!"

I swam into a pullover shirt of bleeding Madras, paused at the glass to brush my displaced hair, and then from the closet selected a pair of mulberry slacks. Leaning against a wall with folded arms, much in the manner of the prophet against the side of the garage, my wife coldly watched these sartorial preparations. My feet I slipped into a pair of white calfskin Belgian casuals.

"So you say his father won't have him around. It's probably his way of atoning for his adultery. Denying himself the pleasure of his children."

"Oh, will you stop being perfect!" my wife snapped with unaccustomed zest. "Nothing is more irritating than that. And all that I-would-never-sit-in-judgment cool is really a form of holier-than-thou, you know." Then she began slowly to pace the room. "But how to handle the boy is the problem now. The thing is, he doesn't let on his old man won't have any part of him. His story is that he's there with him all the time, that they're real pals, go for rides together in the father's Porsche roadster and what not. Skippy told me the real dope on the side — that the old man hauls off on him whenever he shows up. So we play dumb about that."

"All in all then, what the boy seems to need is some good normal family life. Let's give him a little of that, shall we?" I said, signalling that I was ready to go down.

"All right, but one thing. Don't go being incomparable at table. Nothing confuses children more than that. It upsets them. They don't understand it, and so they resent it. So lay off the savoir faire for tonight, shall we? — the style?"

Hardly. Standards must be upheld, a tone set at all costs, that setting, in turn, an example. That was especially important for those hailing from environments so lamentably lacking in it as that of which I had just been vouchsafed a glimpse. One must put one's best foot forward at all times.

Proof of how the grossest origins may be transcended lay allegorically in wait for us in the very soup to which we sat down — four cups of that vichyssoise whose genesis in the lowly potato of peasant France may be forgotten in the elegant restaurants (and fine homes) in which we sip it. I opened the table talk on just that point, in a properly oblique and subtle fashion of course. We were disposed round a circle of gleaming marble set with snowy napery and hereditary plate, the prophet on my right, Skippy on my left, and my wife visible across from me above a floral centerpiece. Her lips delicately puckered to a spoonful of her soup, she watched the boys drink theirs, not to say listened to them, for they made hydraulic noises as they fed. "You may pick up your cups if you wish," she said, addressing to both boys an assurance aimed principally at the prophet, whose hair was hanging in his soup.

"You like this?" Skippy asked him.

"Yar's like groovy. But whasssat like bee-bees?"

"We like to float a few grains of caviar in it," I said. "Gives it a certain zing, don't you think? Tell me," I continued in a pleasantly rambling fashion, "has anybody here been to that new diner on the Post Road yet? Teddy's. I dropped in there for a hamburger the other day and noticed something on the menu that struck me as funny Among the desserts was listed a Jello du Jour. I thought that rather amusing."

"Kina flavor's that, man?"

I opened my mouth to explain, but a terse headshake from my wife persuaded me to shove along to other matters. The subject of mothers somehow came up, and I noticed a play of pained grimaces cross the prophet's face. A reference to his father, however, brought a broad smile to it. "He's got this cool place on the water," he related. "Man, you get up mornings and jump right in. Then he takes me for rides in his Porsche. He's got a Porsche that's like really where it's at."

No one taking as sacred the obligation to evolve — the progressive refinement of sensibility of which Henry James was so exquisitely a stage, now restated as Pierre Teilhard de Chardin's principle of "complexification" — will ever unrealistically blind himself to the impediments everywhere await-

ing this long and uphill climb. The struggle to elevate our
guest's temper was beset at every turn by a commensurate
threat: I mean the decline of our host's. For the next quarter-
hour we heard little but paeans of praise to the prophet's
father, deluded as we know. He told of waterside sport (with
or without Miss Twin Peaks was never said), of camaraderie
in the open Porsche and convivial hands of rummy. Throughout the encomium, the prophet sat hunched over his plate
with his hands around it, as though it were itself the steering-
wheel of a motor car in which he and, indeed, we all were
traveling at high speed, his hair streaming behind him like a
witch's instead of depending like a beagle's ears into his food.

The conversation at some point turned to hippies, and their
ironical migration to Boston.

"You think they're like the early Christians, Pop?" Skippy
asked. "You buy that?"

"I do indeed," I said. "And I would like to see the parallel
completed by having them thrown to the lions. If not the
Kiwanians. Fix both sides."

"The idea is to live as though every day is Christmas,
right?"

"Right. And dress as though every day is Hallowe'en.
Where did you get that chiropracter's tunic and those bare
feet?" He had been given dispensation to come to the evening board unshod, in deference to his guest's state.

"Timothy Leary's got charisma," said the prophet con-
tentiously.

"Aw, I'm sorry to hear that," says I. "He certainly doesn't
look well. I hope he's taking something for it."

The prophet shot a look into the kitchen over his shoulder.
"Like I have some beer? My father lets me have it."

"Mine doesn't let me. But there are plenty of soft drinks
out there," I said, seeing he hadn't touched his milk. "Coke,
Seven-Up, Like. Ever had Like? You might like like Like."

323

My wife was noting that he had also, in all this time, scarcely touched his food, since the soup. "Don't you like lamb chops?"

"Well, no. I don't seem to care much for chops of any kind."

"Maybe he'd like a karate chop," I said, looking into my wine glass.

There was no doubt I was being worn thin. The odds seemed too great, at least so far. We had by midnight not discernibly evolved. Indeed, the backslidden state apprehended above increasingly marked the scene. The hour found me hammering my pillow and hissing the name of the Nazarene into it at the sound, issuing faintly but remorselessly from the boys' bedroom, of the Burning Bananas. The struggle for men's minds was not going at all well. Perhaps a battle must be granted as lost while bearing the war in mind. I tossed onto my back with a fresh oath as the vocalist, apparently pursuing a technique of singing the "words" of a song other than that being performed by the instrumentalists, belted out: "Atsa mah wah dig muh baby, lemme rock ya frunks!" or some such.

I sprang out of bed and thudded down the passage to the other bedroom. I snapped off the light, switched off the machine, and barked, "O.K., that's it. That wraps it up, know what I mean? No more playing, talking, nothing. Good night!"

This night's sleep was a sequence of snoozes from the next of which I awoke to the murmur of voices below my chamber window. Leaning out of which I saw them sitting on the doorstep leading to the flagstone terrace. They were both smoking cigarettes, and the prophet was sucking on a bottle of Löwenbräu.

I suppose my manner, as I thundered down the stairs again in the Belgian casuals, resembled that of the movie actor

Franklin Pangborn, whose thirty years of apoplectic fits still checker the Late Late Show. No later than this one, this was the Late Late Show too. They parted to let me storm down the stoop between them. I marched out to the terrace and wheeled to face them.

"Now then. You will go back in there — right in that house," I said pointing to it so there would be no mistake about which house was meant, "you will go back in there and get to bed. And if I hear one more peep out of either of you it'll be the razor strap. Now git!"

My kid skedaddled. The prophet, however, hung back a moment, gesturing with his free hand. "But like we couldn't sleep, so we just —"

I snatched the bottle from his grasp and flung it into the bushes, dealing a generous spray of foam about, and flecking us both with it. "Goddamn you, get in there!" With that, I drew my right foot back and let fly with all my might.

We use the term "good swift kick" with an everyday familiarity, as though delivering one were a regular occurrence, whereas in fact most of us go to our graves without experiencing the solid satisfaction of doing so. This one was well planted. But in planting it, I lost my balance and sat down on the terrace with an impact at least equal to that felt in the prophet's case. Also, in finding its target my foot lost its slipper, one of the white Belgian casuals, which sailed an inch past his head, through the open doorway, and straight at my wife, who had by now been awakened by the ruckus and come down herself to see what was going on. She ducked just in time, the slipper spinning end over end into the room giving onto the terrace, which is the library, where it struck a far row of bookshelves with a flat *splat* and dropped to the floor behind an easy chair. "Son of a *bitch!*" I said, closing the generation gap.

That did it. That turned the trick. The prophet from then

on was nice as pie. I set to work the very next day on a story about the incident, about how young people really do want a firm hand (if that's the mot juste); discipline, a sense of authority. But when I reached the turning point of the narrative, the crisis I've just described, something about it didn't ring right Some sneaking doubt about my grasp of the prophet's motivation nagged me. It was his grin as he bade me goodbye, thanking me for my hospitality, that hung me up. Each time I reread my interpretation of the prophet's sudden shift of attitude, as exhibiting the masculine adolescent's need for the authority principle, it rang hollow. The grin became a laugh, remote but unnerving. The principle was true enough, but not in this case. Something told me it was not relevant to this story. The author himself did not quite dig what he was illuminating.

I put it aside, and, as one often does, let the unconscious get in its licks. The badgering question on which the conscious agenda remained stuck was: why had my central character become nice as pie if not for the reason so far stated? Why had he come to like like me? The firm-hand theory didn't seem right in the exposition, any more than the best-foot-forward hypothesis.

The key to his sudden change lay, of course, in his relationship with his own father, so obviously that it is still a matter of embarrassment to me that light didn't break over me sooner. It broke, at any rate, in the form of an incident involving my own son and me, of no significance in itself; a minor traffic altercation between me and another motorist, in which he got decidedly the best of me. He had made what I thought a dumb move, for which I undertook to rebuke him with what I regarded as a rather neat thrust while we were both waiting for a green light. His riposte still makes me think of the cartoon of the prize-fight manager saying to his battered boxer between rounds, "The next time

you think you see an opening, duck." Having sent his repartee home, he shot away through the intersection and disappeared — leaving my son, who was sitting in the front seat
beside me, blushing a brick-red. I was startled to find how
my humiliation stung him, until I remembered from my own
boyhood how keenly a father's shame can become the son's.
In the twinkling of a split second I had orbited all those
memory-miles of inner space, and in that splinter of time my
literary problem was illuminated. I understood what had
made the prophet so happy.

His boasts of companionship with his father were only a
cover-up, a shell carefully concealing an inner hurt, a wound
that throbbed anew with every fresh evidence of parental
decency and familial integrity elsewhere, stilled only by any
proof, again at last, that his own old man wasn't so bad after
all, relatively speaking. The last thing he needed was the
civilized domestic environment I had egotistically striven to
supply. Confronted with such another hazard to his self-
esteem, he had spent that whole damned evening. and then
half the night as well, reducing it to the shambles his own
private life had become; in particular, reducing me to a clod
at least as bad as his old man, if not worse. He had proved —
or I had proved — the truth of Mark Twain's remark, that
there are few things in life harder to bear than the irritation
of a good example. That example liquidated, he could get on
with the business of behaving toward me with comparative
decency.

He still does, though it is now I who find the example
hard to bear. I catch glimpses of him about town, always
nodding politely to me and with a grin behind which lurks
the gleam of cunning, the secret knowledge that I know
what he knows.

That is the story of how I restored one boy's faith in his
father. Little wonder it remains unwritten! I had sat down

to write it without the faintest idea that was what it was about. I had surmised it to be about something else altogether. Thus it was the practice of my craft that, ultimately, enabled me to understand the reality the craft was intended to illuminate. Light did not break as I sat at the typewriter. That's not what I mean. I simply mean that my struggle with the literary problem kept my mind and spirit open to the revelation when it came, in the shape of real persons, places, and things.

To say that the story remains unwritten is to ignore its unexpected culmination in lecture form. It is in that form that I may now analytically equate my loss of heart for the narrative with the loss of my role in it as the hero. For the flash of illumination entailed, of course, my sudden switch to that of villain In real life, the story with its transferred functions remains unresolved, since I keep seeing the putative villain, now its martyr. Indeed, I saw him only last week when he was once more an overnight guest, and this time I had to steel myself for the confrontation in quite another manner than in the original instance when my wife's exposition had set up the drama to follow. Perhaps it is thus not a story after all, much less a novel, or a play, but the subject of a poem, and that, indeed, already written, put down not by a latter-day exponent of the suburban mores, or an interpreter of corroded metropolitan egos, but by the white-clad recluse of Amherst, Emily Dickinson, who a hundred years ago said:

> *What fortitude the soul contains,*
> *That it can so endure*
> *The accent of a coming foot,*
> *The opening of a door.*